BERTRUMS

A GREAT PLACE TO STAY

A BERTRUMS PUBLICATION
PENRITH, CUMBRIA,
ENGLAND

Published by: Bertrums Ltd, Alaska Building, Ullswater Road, Penrith, Cumbria, CA11 7EH, England

ACKNOWLEDGMENTS

Edited by Ken Plant

Design and layout by Jennie Prior & David Beesley

Administration by Joanne Cullen

Editorials by Pam Wilson

Illustrations by Jenny Walter

Picture stories by Jenny Walter

Cover Picture
"Summer Flowers" by Stephen Darbishire

ISBN Number 1-902890-04-3

Distributed by: Windsor Books International
The Boundary, Wheatley Road, Garsington, Oxford OX44 9EJ

A GREAT PLACE TO STAY
Alaska Building
Ullswater Road
Penrith
Cumbria
CA11 7EH
England

Sponsored by www.tuckedup.com

"Let's get away this weekend darling" Bertie said to Belle, "I know some great places to stay"

BELLE & BERTIE IN WALES

CONTENTS

"Belle?", said Bertie, "How about a few days in Wales? Looking at castles, maybe. Just to celebrate the new car"
BELLE & BERTIE IN WALES

FOREWORD

A Great Place to Stay features some of the best bed and breakfast accommodation throughout Great Britain. Proprietors who are able to offer an individual service, of a quality envied by many of the top hotels...comfort and cossetting in surroundings quite impossible to match by larger and as consequence more impersonal establishments.

The range of properties in **A Great Place to Stay** is as diverse as the area it covers. There are thatched cottages and Georgian town houses, converted stables and former vicarages and castles. Whether you're visiting a historic city, heading for the gentle countryside of a southern county or seeking solitude in a remote part of Scotland or Wales, you'll find a property offering good accommodation and good food at a good price. And you'll discover much more than a bed to rest in. There are properties with a history, others with literary connections and many with beautiful gardens. One of the great advantages in staying at an establishment which is proprietor run is the warmth of the welcome you receive. Another benefit is the wealth of knowledge that your hosts will have about the area.

What our hosts offer varies considerably, so if you have particular preferences it is advisable to check on booking...some offer vegetarian dishes...some, particularly in Scotland, offer high-tea instead of dinner. Some welcome dogs, some decidedly don't, some allow smoking only in designated rooms, some are licensed and others not...and it is well to ascertain if cheques or credit cards are acceptable.

Whether you are a visitor to Britain or one of the ever increasing number of people discovering the joys of the "short-break", our aim is to give you all the information you need to choose the establishment that is right for you. Details of properties have been supplied by the owners themselves so you can rely on their accuracy.

There is simply no doubt about it, **A Great Place to Stay** aims to be excellent value for money, and if you haven't tried it yet - we think you'll enjoy it.

"Bertie! It's tiny!", exclaimed Belle, "How shall we fit all the luggage in?"
"Don't worry - Lot's of space" said Bertie
BELLE & BERTIE IN WALES

LONDON

One of the world's finest cities and certainly the largest in Europe in terms of size, population and per-capita wealth, London is a premier capital in every sense of the word. Steeped in history and home to a wealth of iconic landmarks such as Big Ben, St Paul's Cathedral and Buckingham Palace, London's abundance of art galleries, museums, grand public buildings and stately homes is sure to satisfy even the most voracious of cultural appetites.

Famous home to the Crown Jewels, The Tower Of London is situated on the River Thames at Tower Bridge and makes as good a place as any to start a tour of the capital. Built by William the Conqueror in 1078, the Tower's more sinister highlights include Traitor's Gate and the White Tower where prisoners were held before execution. Nearby St Paul's Cathedral, famously and somewhat controversially built by Christopher Wren between 1675 and 1710, still dominates the city skyline and wows the visitor with quite breathtaking interior proportions – the soaring dome being one of the largest in the world.

For visitors as much interested in domestic interiors as ecclesiastical, the Geffrye Museum, situated slightly north on Kingsland Road, provides an interesting find. Via a series of period rooms this fascinating exhibition presents the changing styles of English interiors from 1600 to the present day. On a slightly quirkier note – and to experience a period home in an altogether more 'sensual' manner – Dennis Sever's House in Spitalfields is sure to intrigue. Using the imagination as a canvas, the house harbours 'spells' within its ten rooms to engage the senses and transport the visitor as far back in time as 1724.

Back on the South Bank of the Thames and directly opposite St Paul's, Thespian lovers can absorb the wonderful atmosphere of Shakespeare's Globe. A fascinating exhibition brings the city in the days of The Bard to life and shows how the theatre was painstakingly rebuilt using hand tools and Elizabethan materials and techniques.

Situated between South Bank and Covent Garden, the newly-restored Somerset House is a joy to behold and offers a particularly fine example of Palladian architecture. Two fascinating museums, the Courtauld Gallery and the Gilbert Collection, are housed within. Further upriver, the charming Chelsea Physic Garden nestles quietly in its fashionable surroundings. Established in 1673, this is the second oldest botanic garden in England and features many fine plants and pleasant walks. While in the Chelsea area, a fine example of a Queen Anne villa can be found in Carlyle's House, residence of Thomas Carlyle the Sage of Chelsea until his death in 1881.

Westminster – the hub of the Britain's political scene – is home to The Palace of Westminster, incorporating The Houses of Parliament and The House of Lords; Whitehall and the exquisite Banqueting House (the only remaining part of the Tudor Whitehall Palace where Charles I was executed in 1649 and which burned down in 1698); and spectacular Westminster Abbey, the finest remaining example of early English Gothic (1180-1280) and where sovereigns have been crowned since William the Conqueror in 1066. Westminster Cathedral and Tate Britain – which houses the national collection of British painting – are also nearby.

It is within the prestigious borough of Kensington that some of London's finest cultural, scientific and academic institutions can be found, thanks mainly to Prince Albert and the hugely successful Great Exhibition of 1851. The Natural History Museum, Science Museum and the vast Victoria and Albert Museum are all situated along Cromwell Road and make for an interesting day's exploration. The Royal Colleges of Music and Art are also nearby, as is the stunning Royal Albert Hall. This unique Italian Renaissance building, built to an elliptical Roman design by Messrs Fowke and Scott, enjoys world stature and is as much celebrated for its exterior architecture as its amazing acoustics within.

Kensington Palace, former home to Diana, Princess of Wales, dates from 1689 and features magnificent State Apartments, including the lavish Cupola Room where Queen Victoria was baptised. The nearby Sunken Gardens and Orangery – with carvings by Dutch carver Grinling Gibbons – provide an oasis of peace from the hustle and bustle of the city.

Overlooking Green Park is Spencer House – London's finest surviving 18th century town house, now returned to full splendour after a decade of restoration. The stunning neo-classical interiors, which include John Vardy's Palm Room and James 'Althenian' Stuart's Painted Room, were among the first of their kind in Europe and should not be missed. On Hyde Park Corner stands Apsley House, former London palace to the Duke of Wellington and once boasting the prestigious address 'No. 1, London'. Originally designed by Robert Adam, this grand home features heady interiors and some of the Duke's fine personal collections.

Also of world renown but lying somewhat tucked away behind the department store Selfridges, the celebrated Wallace Collection features thousands of works of art – the majority dating between the 16th and 19th century. Fine furniture, porcelain and sculpture abound alongside world famous paintings by Rubens, Rembrandt and Frans Hals – all housed within the grandiose setting of one of London's most aesthetically pleasing 19th century homes, Hertford House.

LONDON

LONDON Home from Homes

Home 01,	*Map Ref 1*	Tel/Fax: 020 8566 7976	*see page 11*
Home 05,	*Map Ref 2*	Tel/Fax: 020 8566 7976	*see page 11*
Home 10,	*Map Ref 3*	Tel/Fax: 020 8566 7976	*see page 11*
Home 12,	*Map Ref 4*	Tel/Fax: 020 8566 7976	*see page 12*
Home 14,	*Map Ref 5*	Tel/Fax: 020 8566 7976	*see page 12*
Home 15,	*Map Ref 6*	Tel/Fax: 020 8566 7976	*see page 12*
Home 201,	*Map Ref 7*	Tel/Fax: 020 8566 7976	*see page 13*
Home 202,	*Map Ref 8*	Tel/Fax: 020 8566 7976	*see page 13*
Home 203,	*Map Ref 9*	Tel/Fax: 020 8566 7976	*see page 13*
Home 206,	*Map Ref 10*	Tel/Fax: 020 8566 7976	*see page 14*
Home 207,	*Map Ref 11*	Tel/Fax: 020 8566 7976	*see page 14*
Home 208,	*Map Ref 12*	Tel/Fax: 020 8566 7976	*see page 14*
Home 402,	*Map Ref 13*	Tel/Fax: 020 8566 7976	*see page15*
Home 405,	*Map Ref 14*	Tel/Fax: 020 8566 7976	*see page 15*
Home 406,	*Map Ref 15*	Tel/Fax: 020 8566 7976	*see page 15*
Home 407,	*Map Ref 16*	Tel/Fax: 020 8566 7976	*see page 16*
Home 411,	*Map Ref 17*	Tel/Fax: 020 8566 7976	*see page 16*
Home 412,	*Map Ref 18*	Tel/Fax: 020 8566 7976	*see page 16*
Home 602,	*Map Ref 19*	Tel/Fax: 020 8566 7976	*see page 17*
Home 605,		Tel/Fax: 020 8566 7976	*see page 17*
Home 606,	*Map Ref 20*	Tel/Fax: 020 8566 7976	*see page 17*
Home 608,	*Map Ref 21*	Tel/Fax: 020 8566 7976	*see page 18*
Home 610,	*Map Ref 22*	Tel/Fax: 020 8566 7976	*see page 18*
Home 611,	*Map Ref 23*	Tel/Fax: 020 8566 7976	*see page 18*
Home 613,	*Map Ref 24*	Tel/Fax: 020 8566 7976	*see page 19*
Home 614,	*Map Ref 25*	Tel/Fax: 020 8566 7976	*see page 19*
Home 618,	*Map Ref 26*	Tel/Fax: 020 8566 7976	*see page 19*

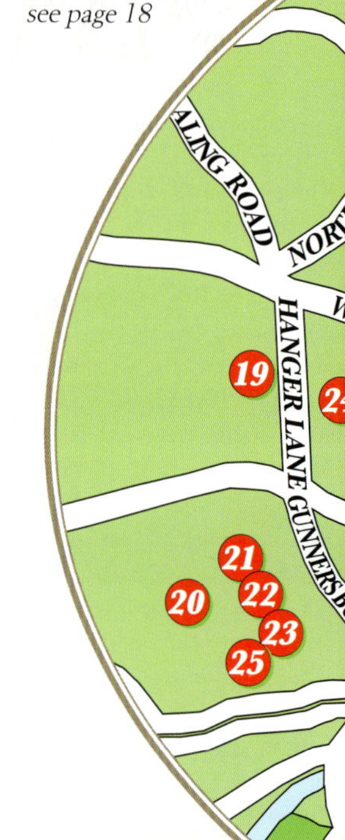

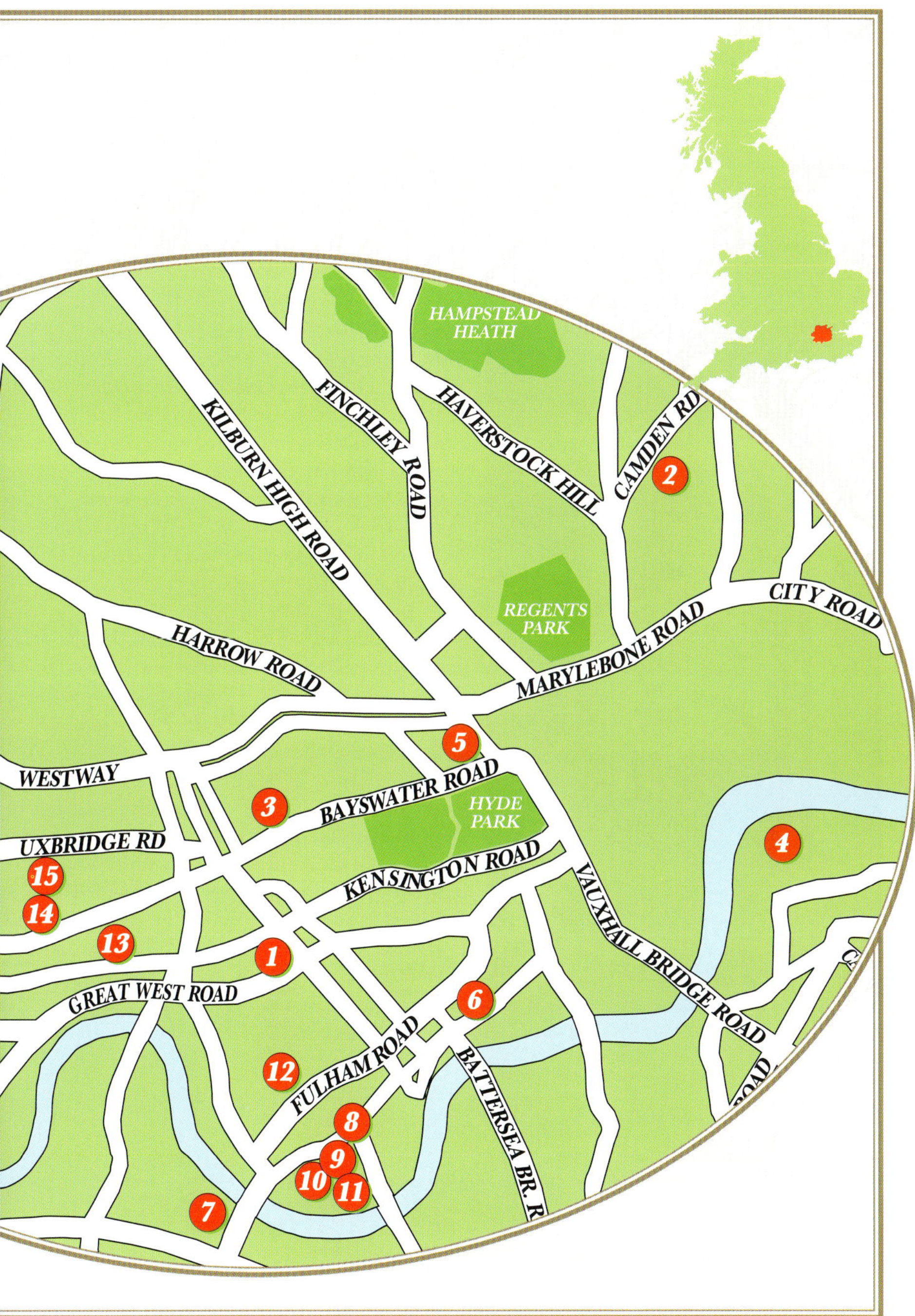
HAMPSTEAD HEATH
FINCHLEY ROAD
HAVERSTOCK HILL
CAMDEN RD
KILBURN HIGH ROAD
REGENTS PARK
CITY ROAD
HARROW ROAD
MARYLEBONE ROAD
WESTWAY
BAYSWATER ROAD
HYDE PARK
UXBRIDGE RD
KENSINGTON ROAD
VAUXHALL BRIDGE ROAD
GREAT WEST ROAD
FULHAM ROAD
BATTERSEA BR. R
1
2
3
4
5
6
7
8
9
10
11
12
13
14
15

Beautiful Bed & Breakfast in London

Anita Harrison and Rosemary Richardson specialise in arranging good quality Bed and Breakfast accommodation in London homes. All have their individual style and charm and offer exceptional value for money. A very affordable alternative to hotels! London Home-to-Home is one of the original bed-and-breakfast organisations in London and is proud to have kept itself small enough to retain a personal interest in both guests and hosts.

Most of the accommodation is located in the leafy West London areas of Parsons Green, Putney and Fulham, Hammersmith, Chiswick and Ealing, convenient to shops and restaurants. It is reached easily by Underground from Heathrow Airport, or London-Victoria, the terminal for the Gatwick Airport Express. We also represent homes in the central areas of Marble Arch, Waterloo, Chelsea, Notting Hill, Kensington, Swiss Cottage, Camden and Islington.

The accommodation has been chosen with great care, with hosts who take pleasure in welcoming guests to their homes. Whilst making you most welcome, they will respect your privacy and provide a quiet haven at the end of the day.

Each home is unique. The guest rooms are comfortable and attractively decorated, with the emphasis on cleanliness and warmth. TV and tea and coffee-making facilities are provided and a generous breakfast is included in the tariff. The minimum booking period is 2 consecutive nights. Following is a selection of B&B homes. Others are available on our website.

LONDON HOME-TO-HOME
19 Mount Park Crescent
London W5 2RN
Tel/Fax: +44 (0) 20 8566 7976
email: stay@londonhometohome.com
web: http://www.londonhometohome.com

HOME 01, Kensington (Central London)
Nanette & Steli
Email stay@londonhometohome.com

Map Ref 1
Nearest Underground: Kensington High Street, Earls Court

Situated just off Kensington High Street, this beautiful, preserved Victorian town-house, which is tastefully decorated, incorporates all modern facilities for guests' comfort, whilst retaining the authentic features of the period. TVs, hairdryers and hospitality trays are available in all the rooms. Vivacious hosts offer high-quality accommodation, serving breakfast in the elegant family dining-room. They offer a welcoming atmosphere and ensure a friendly service.

London Home to Home
Tel/Fax: 020 8566 7976

B&B from £99-£104 per room (Single occupancy £80), Rooms 2 twins, 1 double, all en-suite, Non smoking, Parking by arrangement.

HOME 05, Camden Town (Central London)
Sue & Rodger
Email stay@londonhometohome.com

Map Ref 2
Nearest Underground: Camden Town

Guests are made most welcome in the modern home of an architect and his wife. The house was designed in the 1980's, with much use of glass. Two guest rooms available: an unusual double-bedded room where the bed is sunk into a low platform, and a single room, with guest bathroom. Continental breakfast is served in the open plan dining area, which overlooks a courtyard garden or in summer, it is served in the courtyard itself. Peckham the macaw is the family pet.

London Home to Home
Tel/Fax: 020 8566 7976

B&B from £80 per room, (Single occupancy £60), Rooms 1 double, 1 single, private bathroom, Non smoking.

HOME 10, Notting Hill (Central London)
Mrs Juliette W.
Email stay@londonhometohome.com

Map Ref 3
Nearest Underground: Notting Hill

In trendy Notting Hill, hosts offer six spacious guest rooms in a beautiful home, a five-minute walk from the Portobello Road street market. Two to four guests can be accommodated in each room with a choice of king-size doubles or twin beds. One room also has a double sofa bed, and a single futon is available to add to a room. All rooms have an en suite shower bathroom. A generous Continental breakfast is served at the dining table in each room. Hot drinks can be made in the guests' kitchenette.

London Home to Home
Tel/Fax: 020 8566 7976

B&B from £80-£100 per room, (Single occupancy £65), Rooms 4 trirple/doubles, private bathrooms.

HOME 12, Waterloo (Central London)
Victoria F.
Email stay@londonhometohome.com

Map Ref 4
Nearest Underground: Waterloo

12

Stylish accommodation in a Victorian terraced house, situated in an olde-worlde street which is used for film and television dramas. Victoria offers two guest rooms: one with a king-size double bed and the other with a standard double bed for a single guest. The bathroom, shared just with the hostess, has a bath and a separate shower. Breakfast is served overlooking a miniature town garden. A home of utmost charm. In the street is a traditional English pub and a fine patisserie. Less than a five-minute walk to Waterloo station for the underground and Eurostar terminal. Also within walking distance of The London Eye, the Tate Modern, Covent Garden and the National Theatre.

London Home to Home
Tel/Fax: 020 8566 7976

B&B from £70-£90 per room, Rooms 1 double, 1 single.

HOME 14, Marble Arch (Central London)
Roberta & Robert
Email stay@londonhometohome.com

Map Ref 5
Nearest Underground: Marble Arch, Edgware Road

14

A modern townhouse offering three large guest rooms of very high quality, situated on the Hyde Park Estate, just ten minutes from Marble Arch. The rooms, all with en suite bathrooms, are spacious and able to accommodate up to four people. King-size, double or twin beds. Each room has an additional double sofa-bed. A generous Continental breakfast is served in the beautiful dining room. An interesting, dynamic hostess.

London Home to Home
Tel/Fax: 020 8566 7976

B&B from £80-£100 per room, (Single occupancy £65), Rooms 3 en-suite double/triple.

HOME 15, Chesea (Central London)
Maggie & Peter
Email stay@londonhometohome.com

Map Ref 6
Nearest Underground: Gloucester Road

15

It is a very pleasant surprise to find such peaceful accommodation in the heart of Chelsea, just two minutes' walk from the King's Road and the Fulham Road. In their family home - a large apartment in the heart of Chelsea - Peter and Maggie offer a stylish and airy double room with queen-size bed and a marble-finished en suite bathroom (with bath and walk-in shower). The guest room looks out onto the private garden. The breakfast menu is Continental, and egg dishes are also on offer. Maggie is South African; Peter was born and brought up in the area and knows London well.

London Home to Home
Tel/Fax: 020 8566 7976

B&B from £84 per room, Rooms 1 large double en-suite, Non smoking.

HOME 201, Putney
Julianna & Harry
Email stay@londonhometohome.com

Map Ref 7
Nearest Underground: Putney Bridge

Artist hosts offer a comfortable room in their beautifully restored Victorian home, which has some unusual architectural features. The double-bedded room has an adjacent private bathroom. A generous continental breakfast is served in the family kitchen/diner which overlooks the garden and the River Thames. Putney High Street shops and restaurants are nearby.

London Home to Home
Tel/Fax: 020 8566 7976

B&B from £64 per room, (Single occupancy £52), Rooms 1 double with private bathroom, Non smoking.

HOME 202, Parsons Green
Anne & James
Email stay@londonhometohome.com

Map Ref 8
Nearest Underground: Fulham Broadway

Three beautiful rooms available in this elegant home of the highest standard. Twin room on first floor, and large triple room (double and single beds) on second floor, both with full private bathrooms. On the lower ground floor, a triple room with a king-size and a single bed with marble shower bathroom. Fashionable area, where antique shops and restaurants abound.

London Home to Home
Tel/Fax: 020 8566 7976

B&B from £70-£95 per room, (Single occupancy £60), Rooms 2 triples, 1 twin, private bathrooms.

HOME 203, Parsons Green
Jennie & Clive
Email stay@londonhometohome.com

Map Ref 9
Nearest Underground: Fulham Broadway

In fashionable Parsons Green, Jenny offers three beautifully decorated guest rooms in her turn-of-the-century townhouse: a double and a twin, each with private bathroom, and a single which shares a bathroom. This accommodation is of an excellent standard, designed with guests' comfort very much in mind. Breakfast is served in the formal dining-room.

London Home to Home
Tel/Fax: 020 8566 7976

B&B from £68 per room, (Single occupancy £48-£60), Rooms 2 double/twin with private bathroom, 1 single, Restricted smoking.

HOME 206, Parsons Green
Frank & Moira
Email stay@londonhometohome.com

Map Ref 10
Nearest Underground: Parsons Green

Beautiful self-contained apartment for two-to-four guests on the first floor of a charming family home. Comprises a twin bedroom with en suite bathroom, large dining/living room, with TV and comfortable double sofa-bed, additional bathroom, and fully equipped kitchen. Lounge overlooks a pretty park. Frank and Moira are gracious and welcoming hosts, who live on the ground floor. This apartment is self-catering, but the hosts provide breakfast foods and linen. Children over 12 accommodated. Unusually for this area, free parking is available.

London Home to Home
Tel/Fax: 020 8566 7976

Apartments from £65-£123, 2-4 guests apartments, Non smoking.

HOME 207, Parsons Green
Felicity & Hugh
Email stay@londonhometohome.com

Map Ref 11
Nearest Underground: Parsons Green

Ideally situated within a short walk of the tube station, excellent restaurants and antique shops, this charming home offers three twin-bedded rooms, two of them with en-suite shower/bathrooms. One twin can be zipped to make a king-size double. The third twin room has a private bathroom, which can be booked in conjunction with a single room. TV and hot drinks in all rooms. Good quality accommodation in a smart area. An example of the continental breakfast provided: cereals, yoghurt, choice of fruit juices and teas, coffee, hot crumpets, toast and preserves.

London Home to Home
Tel/Fax: 020 8566 7976

B&B from £68 per room, (Single occupancy £42-£54), Rooms 2 en-suite twin, 1 twin, 1 single, Non smoking.

HOME 208, Fulham Broadway
Dulce & Manuel
Email stay@londonhometohome.com

Map Ref 12
Nearest Underground: Fulham Broadway

A charming Portuguese couple offer a specially warm welcome. In their recently refurbished Victorian home, they provide two delightful double guest rooms, both with en-suite bathrooms. Manuel, who is a chef, serves a Portuguese or traditional breakfast in the spacious, open-plan kitchen. Many restaurants and shops in the area.

London Home to Home
Tel/Fax: 020 8566 7976

B&B from £70 per room, (Single occupancy £60), Rooms 2 en-suite double, Non smoking.

HOME 402, Hammersmith/Stamford Brook
Dominie & Kenneth
Email stay@londonhometohome.com

Map Ref 13
Nearest Underground: Stamford Brook

A superb double or triple room with king-size and single beds with en suite bathroom is available in this comfortable family home, very conveniently situated for the underground. The guest room has TV and video recorder, also a trouser press. Breakfast is served in the conservatory overlooking a pretty town garden. A typical breakfast menu consists of juice, ham and cheese, brioche and croissants. Be assured of a warm welcome in a lovely area of London.

London Home to Home
Tel/Fax: 020 8566 7976

B&B from £66-£86 per room, (Single occupancy £54), Rooms 1 en-suite double/triple.

HOME 405, Chiswick/Turnham Green
Peter & Valerie
Email stay@londonhometohome.com

Map Ref 14
Nearest Underground: Turnham Green

Stay in the unspoiled village of Chiswick where many writers and actors live. On the Bedford Park Garden Conservation Estate, this 1880s Norman Shaw-designed home is just a short walk from the Tube station, interesting boutiques and eating places. Valerie and Peter offer three guest rooms: a double and a twin with guest bathroom, plus a comfortable double with queen-sized bed and shared bathroom. Sitting/TV/breakfast room for guests. The attractive home of a retired architect and his wife.

London Home to Home
Tel/Fax: 020 8566 7976

B&B from £54 per room, (Single occupancy £40), Rooms 2 double, 1 twin, sharing bathrooms, Non smoking.

HOME 406, Chiswick/Acton
Charo & Antonio
Email stay@londonhometohome.com

Map Ref 15
Nearest Underground: Turnham Green

A beautiful airy loft room in the home of Spanish hosts who have lived in England for many years. King size or twin beds, TV, hot drinks tray and a spacious sitting area. Shower bathroom en-suite. High standard of cleanliness and a very warm welcome. Well worth the long walk from the underground. Not available in August.

London Home to Home
Tel/Fax: 020 8566 7976

B&B from £62 per room, (Single occupancy £50), Rooms 1 en-suite double/twin.

HOME 407, Chiswick
Biljana & Michael
Email stay@londonhometohome.com

Map Ref 16
Nearest Underground: Stamford Brook

Self-catering apartment of a very high standard on the second floor of a modernised, terraced home. Comprises a twin bedroom, a lounge with additional single sofa bed, dining area and TV, galley kitchen and private bathroom. Hosts provide all linen and breakfast foods for guests to prepare themselves. Riverside walks along the Thames. Excellent restaurants and shopping close by. A similar apartment is available next door with Biljana's parents.

London Home to Home
Tel/Fax: 020 8566 7976

Apartments from £65-£103, Sleeps 2-3, Non smoking.

HOME 411, Chiswick
Bridget & Jerry
Email stay@londonhometohome.com

Map Ref 17
Nearest Underground: Chiswick Park

411

Five comfortable guest rooms are offered in this well-maintained family home. Both of the modern bathrooms have showers. A private bathroom is occasionally an option. A suite of a double and a twin room can be booked by families. Excellent tube connections to Heathrow and Central London. This home is recommended for its warm welcome.

London Home to Home
Tel/Fax: 020 8566 7976

B&B from £50 per room, (Single occupancy £36), Rooms 3 double, 2 twin, shared bathrooms, Non smoking.

HOME 412, Chiswick
Mary & Alan
Email stay@londonhometohome.com

Map Ref 18
Nearest Underground: Chiswick Park

Generous hospitality is offered by these hosts in their family home, which is situated within a very short walk of Chiswick Park station. They have one twin room and two other large rooms which can be double or triple; one can even sleep a family of four! En-suite showers and washbasins, guest bathroom with bath and toilet, and additional toilets are available for guests.

London Home to Home
Tel/Fax: 020 8566 7976

B&B from £54-£70 per room, (Single occupancy £40), Rooms 2 triples, 1 twin, en-suite showers/sharing bathroooms, Non smoking.

HOME 602, Ealing
Anita & David
Email stay@londonhometohome.com

Map Ref 19
Nearest Underground: Ealing Broadway

In a spacious Victorian home, these warm and welcoming hosts offer two attractive twin/double rooms, each with wash basin.

London Home to Home
Tel/Fax: 020 8566 7976

B&B from £54 per room, (single occupancy - £40), Rooms 2 double/twin, sharing bathroom, Non smoking.

HOME 605, Ealing Broadway
Jane & John
Email stay@londonhometohome.com

Nearest Underground: Ealing Broadway

A lovely family home of great character offering one twin room and private bathroom adjacent, overlooking landscaped patio and gardens. The home, built in the mid-1880s, has been tastefully furnished. Breakfast is served in the family kitchen/breakfast room, which leads onto the garden. Hosts take every care to ensure their guests' comfort. Five minutes' walk to a modern shopping mall and several first class restaurants. Open parkland nearby.

London Home to Home
Tel/Fax: 020 8566 7976

B&B from £52 per room (Single occupancy - £50), Rooms 1 twin with private bathroom, Non smoking.

HOME 606, South Ealing
Ann & Richard
Email stay@londonhometohome.com

Map Ref 20
Nearest Underground: South Ealing

A spacious studio apartment in a family home, situated in a cul-de-sac of Tudor-style houses with cottage gardens. A lovely location. The apartment has a king-size double and a single bed, en suite shower-bathroom, a living/dining area with TV and a kitchenette with microwave. Ann, who is an actress, offers a warm welcome.

London Home to Home
Tel/Fax: 020 8566 7976

Apartments from £50-£80, Sleeps 2 or 3, Non smoking.

HOME 608, Ealing Common
Rosemary & Ian
Email stay@londonhometohome.com

Map Ref 21
Nearest Underground: South Ealing

Australian hosts offer attractive self-contained accommodation in their spacious upstairs studio flat. Overlooks gardens and a pond. Double bed, en-suite shower bathroom, kitchenette with microwave, dining/sitting area with TV. Linen and breakfast food provided. A warm and friendly welcome in a lovely home.

London Home to Home
Tel/Fax: 020 8566 7976

B&B from £62 per room, (Single occupancy £50), 2 studio apartments, Non smoking.

HOME 610, Ealing Common
Maria & Damien
Email stay@londonhometohome.com

Map Ref 22
Nearest Underground: Ealing Common

Warm and friendly hosts offer a large triple loft room (three beds) and another triple room (double and single bed), both with en suite shower bathrooms. Breakfast is served in the conservatory overlooking the garden. Situated in a quiet, tree-lined street, a short stroll from shops, restaurants and two stations. Maria is a French teacher.

London Home to Home
Tel/Fax: 020 8566 7976

B&B from £62-£80 per room, (Single occupancy £50), Rooms 2 en-suite double/triple, Non smoking.

HOME 611, Ealing Common
Rita & Geoff
Email stay@londonhometohome.com

Map Ref 23
Nearest Underground: Ealing Common

These welcoming, well-travelled hosts offer a self-contained studio room on the top floor of their spacious Victorian home. There is a double bed and a sitting/dining area with all facilities for self-catering and fully equipped kitchenette. A private bathroom is adjacent. An additional single room is sometimes available for a group booking. Available for bookings for two weeks minimum. Long-term rates apply.

London Home to Home
Tel/Fax: 020 8566 7976

Prices on application, 2 studio apartments, Non smoking

HOME 613, West Acton
Diana & Louis
Email stay@londonhometohome.com

Map Ref 24
Nearest Underground: West Acton, North Ealing

Relaxed, friendly hosts offer a loft conversion comprising a spacious and airy twin/triple room, with shower bathroom en-suite. TV and hospitality tray. A modern three-storey home, conveniently situated for two underground lines.

London Home to Home
Tel/Fax: 020 8566 7976

B&B from £62-£78 per room, (Single occupancy £50), Rooms 1 en-suite twin/triple.

HOME 614, South Ealing
Gill & Mark
Email stay@londonhometohome.com

Map Ref 25
Nearest Underground: South Ealing

Comfortable and spacious twin room accommodation in a family home, located in a quiet residential street, just a couple of minutes walk from shops, restaurants and the Underground. Gill is a professional gardener.

London Home to Home
Tel/Fax: 020 8566 7976

B&B from £54 per room, (Single occupancy £40), Rooms 1 twin with shared bathroom, Non smoking.

HOME 618, Ealing
Ursula & Jim
Email stay@londonhometohome.com

Map Ref 26
Nearest Underground: Ealing Common

Attentive hosts offer flexible accommodation in their comfortable home in a quiet and leafy residential street. Two spacious triple rooms, each with a large double bed and a single bed and en suite shower bathroom. Also a twin room and a double/single sharing an impressive Art Deco shower bathroom. Ursula teaches English as a foreign language and speaks fluent German.

London Home to Home
Tel/Fax: 020 8566 7976

B&B from £66-£83 per room, (Single occupancy £37-£50), Rooms 2 en-suite triples, 1 twin, 1 single, sharing bathroom, Non smoking.

BATH, BRISTOL & NORTH EAST SOMERSET

Until around the end of the 18th century Bristol enjoyed a prosperous reputation as one of England's key trading ports, accruing its wealth by means of the 'triangular sale' of slaves, sugar, tobacco and cocoa between Africa and the New World. Indeed it was from the very docks of this major south western city that John Cabot set sail in 1497 to discover Newfoundland. Good living and grand homes abounded in Bristol as a result of trading wealth and, although much of the city was destroyed during World War II, the northern suburb of Clifton displays some impeccable examples of grand Georgian architecture. The spectacular Clifton Suspension Bridge can also be admired nearby, designed by Bristol's celebrated son and engineering genius Isambard Kingdom Brunel (1806-59).

Purveyors of the most exquisite architecture in the south west region, however, will certainly have to leave Bristol behind – although perhaps dallying in the quaint and historic towns of Axbridge, Wells and Frome in North East Somerset en route – and journey to that most grand of cities: Bath. Said to rival Florence in its grandeur, the ancient Roman spa town of Bath dates back over 2000 years and contains some of the best Georgian architecture in the country. For over 300 years Bath has attracted aristocracy and royalty – including Queen Elizabeth I in 1574 and Queen Anne in 1692 – and in the 18th century English society flocked here to build the magnificent terraces, crescents and squares that shape the city today.

A particularly grand town house of this period can be viewed at No 1 Royal Crescent – the first home to be built in this impressive crescent and now fully restored and authentically furnished thanks to the Bath Preservation Trust. Another jewel in Bath's crown – and one that attracted the highest of glittering society in its day – is the former Georgian Sydney Hotel on Great Pulteney Street, now the Holburne Museum of Art. Home to many of the treasures collected by Sir William Holburne, including porcelain, silver, majolica, Renaissance bronzes and works by Turner, this was also a favourite observation point for author Jane Austen, who fortuitously lived in the house opposite. For magnificent views of Bath and to escape the sometimes madding crowds, Prior Park Landscape Garden cannot fail to impress. Its serene and intimate ambience was lovingly created by local entrepreneur Ralph Allen in the 18th century, with a little helpful advice from Lancelot 'Capability' Brown and poet Alexander Pope. Set in a sweeping valley, the garden features extensive woodland, three lakes and a quite remarkable Palladian bridge.

BATH, BRISTOL & NORTH EAST SOMERSET

George Hall, Holly Lodge
Tel: 01225 424042
Map Ref 1 *see page 24*
David & Jenny King, Oakleigh House
Tel: 01225 315698
Map Ref 1 *see page 24*
Roy & Lois Thwaites , Villa Magdala Hotel
Tel: 01225 466329
Map Ref 1 *see page 24*
Tony & Jan Poole, Cranleigh
Tel: 01225 310197
Map Ref 1 *see page 26*
Ken & Angela Pritchard, Pickford House
Tel: 01373 830329
Map Ref 1 *see page 26*
Daphne Mackay, Bridge Cottage
Tel: 01225 852399
Map Ref 2 *see page 26*
Wendy Wheeldon, Dundas Lock Cottage
Tel: 01225 723890
Map Ref 3 *see page 27*
Marilyn & Bob Downes, Box Hedge Farm
Tel: 01454 250786
Map Ref 4 *see page 27*
Philippa Tasker, Downs Edge
Tel: 0117 9683264
Map Ref 5 *see page 27*

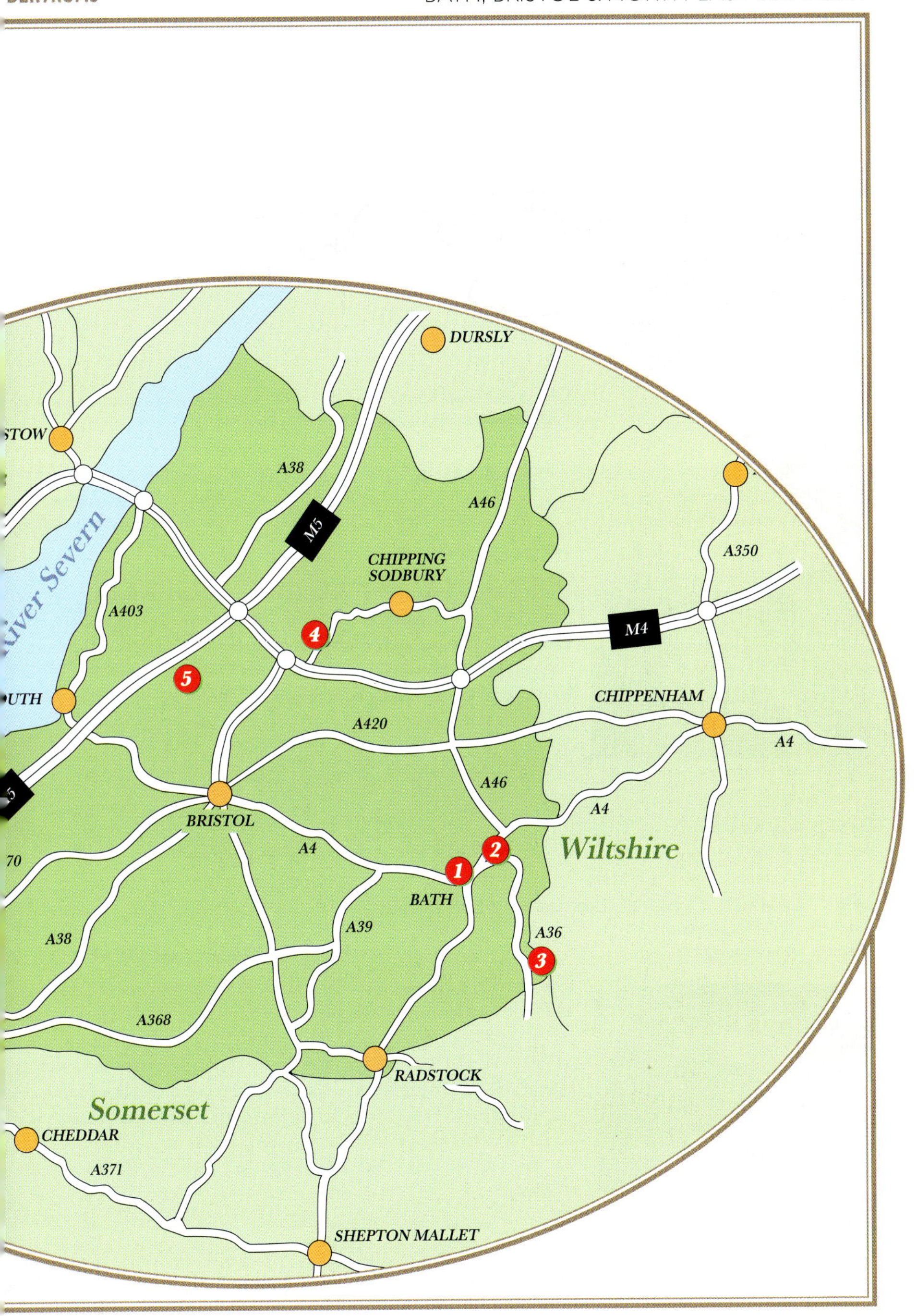
DURSLY
STOW
A38
A46
M5
River Severn
CHIPPING
SODBURY
A350
A403
M4
UTH
CHIPPENHAM
A420
A4
A46
BRISTOL
A4
Wiltshire
70
A4
BATH
A39
A36
A38
A368
RADSTOCK
Somerset
CHEDDAR
A371
SHEPTON MALLET

HOLLY LODGE, 8 Upper Oldfield Park, Bath BA2 3JZ
Email stay@hollylodge.co.uk
Website www.hollylodge.co.uk

Map Ref 1
Nearest Road A367

This charming Victorian town house commands panoramic views of the city and is delightfully furnished with individually designed bedrooms, some with 4 posters and superb bathrooms. Elegant and stylish, it is owned and operated with meticulous attention to details by George Hall. Superb breakfasts are enjoyed in the appealing breakfast room with the yellow and green decor and white wicker chairs. Furnished with antiques, this immaculate establishment, winner of an 'England for Excellence' award makes a pleasant base for touring Bath and the Cotswolds.

George Hall
Tel: 01225 424042
Fax: 01225 481138

B&B from £40pp, Rooms 1 single, 2 twin, 4 double, all en-suite, No smoking, Children welcome, No pets, Open all year.

OAKLEIGH HOUSE, 19 Upper Oldfield Park, Bath BA2 3JX
Email oakleigh@which.net
Website www.oakleigh-house.co.uk

Map Ref 1
Nearest Road A367

Oakleigh House is situated in a peaceful location 10 minutes from the centre of Bath. Victorian elegance is combined with present day comforts and all bedrooms are en-suite and benefit from tea/coffee making facilities, colour TV, clock radio, hair dryer and tasteful furnishings. There is a car park for guests. A good base for touring Glastonbury, Stonehenge, Bristol, Wells, Salisbury and the Cotswolds.

David & Jenny King
Tel: 01225 315698

B&B from £35pp, Rooms 2 double, 1 twin, all en-suite.

THE VILLA MAGDALA HOTEL, Henrietta Road, Bath BA2 6LX
Email office@villamagdala.co.uk
Website www.villamagdala.co.uk

Map Ref 1
Nearest Road A36, A4, M4 Jnt 18

Built in 1868, a charming Victorian town house hotel with its own car park, is ideally situated for those wishing to explore this famous city. It enjoys a unique and tranquil location overlooking the beautiful Henrietta Park, but is only a 5 minute walk to the city centre and Roman Baths. Bedrooms are spacious, comfortable and have private bathrooms, TV, direct-dial telephone, hairdryers and tea/coffee etc. Enjoy our speciality - the Magdala full English breakfast - in our sunny dining room with views of the park. You do not need your car when you stay with us - enjoy Bath as it should be enjoyed on foot. Credit cards accepted.

Roy & Lois Thwaites
Tel: 01225 466329
Fax: 01225 483207

B&B from £40-£60pp, Rooms 2 single, 8 double, 4 twin, 4 family, all en-suite, No smoking or pets, Children over 7, Open all year except Christmas.

Full page photo opposite

ILLA MAGDALA

CRANLEIGH, 159 Newbridge Hill, Bath BA1 3PX
Email cranleigh@btinternet.com
Website www.cranleighguesthouse.com

Map Ref 1
Nearest Road M4, A4, A431

Away from the traffic and noise but just minutes from the heart of Bath. Cranleigh has lovely view, private parking and secluded sunny gardens. Guest bedrooms are all en-suite and exceptionally spacious. Ground floor rooms available. A non-smoking house. AA 4 Diamonds. Recommended by "Which" Good B&B. Member of "Real Bath Breakfast Scheme". Free golf for all guests.

Tony & Jan Poole
Tel: 01225 310197
Fax: 01225 423143

B&B from £33-£48pp, Rooms 4 double, 2 twin, 2 family, No smoking, Children over 5, No dogs except guide dogs, Open all year except Christmas.

BRIDGE COTTAGE, Ashley Road, Bathford, Bath BA1 7TT
Email Daphne@bridge-cottages.co.uk
Website www.bridge-cottages.co.uk

Map Ref 2
Nearest Road M4, A4, A46

Located in east of Bath in rural setting. Ideal location for Bath and surrounding attractions. Accommodation - 2 en-suite double rooms and linked cottage with fitted kitchen, bathroom, twin bedded room, lounge (2nd bedroom) and private courtyard garden. Also en-suite chalet set in award winning gardens. Several good eating places within walking distance. 15 minutes bus service to Bath centre. Special rates for single occupancy.

Daphne Mackay
Tel: 01225 852399

B&B from £40-£65pr, Rooms 3 double, 1 twin, all en-suite, No smoking or pets, Children welcome, Open April to October.

PICKFORD HOUSE, Bath Road, Beckington, Bath BA11 6SJ
Email AmPritchar@aol.com
Website www.pickfordhouse.com

Map Ref 1
Nearest Road A36, A361

Pickford House is an elegant Regency style house built in honey coloured Bath stone. It stands on top of the hill overlooking the village of Beckington and surrounding countryside. Some bedrooms are en-suite and all have tea/coffee making facilities and TV; all are very comfortable and tastefully decorated. Angela is a talented and enthusiastic cook and offers an excellent 'pot luck' meal, or on request an extensive menu for celebrations. The house is licensed with a large and varied wine list. In summer, visitors may be offered an "off-the-beaten-track" pre dinner drive.

Ken & Angela Pritchard
Tel/Fax: 01373 830329

B&B from £18pp, Dinner from £15, Rooms 1 twin, 2 double, family, some en-suite, Restricted smoking, Children welcome, Pets by prior arrangement, Open all year.

DUNDAS LOCK COTTAGE, Monkton Combe, Bath BA2 7BN
Email dundaslockcottage@freenet.co.uk

Map Ref 3
Nearest Road A36, B3108

Built in 1801 with additions in 1947 and 1987 this pretty Bath stone cottage has views from the bedrooms of both the Kennet and Avon and Somerset Coal canal that runs through the lovely garden, which is full of camellias and hellebores in Spring and roses and clematis in Summer. Brightly coloured boats pass through from their moorings. There are boats and bikes to hire. 400 yards down the towpath. Set in the beautiful Limpley Stoke valley, close to Bath, Bradford on Avon and many places of interest.

Wendy Wheeldon
Tel/Fax: 01225 723890

B&B from £25-£27.50pp, Rooms 1 single, 1 double with private bathroom, 1 twin/double with private bathroom, No smoking or pets, Children welcome, Open all year except Christmas & New Year.

BOX HEDGE FARM, Coalpit Heath, Bristol BS36 2UW
Email marilyn@boxhedgefarmbandb.co.uk
Website www.boxhedgefarmbandb.co.uk

Map Ref 4

Box Hedge Farm is set in 200 acres of beautiful rural countryside. Local to M4/M5, central for Bristol and Bath. An ideal stopping point for the south west and Wales. We offer a warm family atmosphere with traditional farmhouse cooking. All bedrooms have colour TV and tea/coffee making facilities.

Marilyn & Bob Downes
Tel: 01454 250786

B&B from £25 single, £30 single en-suite, £40 double, £46 double en-suite, Rooms 8 single, 8 double, 2 family, Restricted smoking, Open all year.

DOWNS EDGE, Saville Road, Stoke Bishop, Bristol BS9 1JA
Email welcome@downsedge.com
Website www.tuckedup.com/downsedge.html

Map Ref 5
Nearest Road A4018, B4054

Set in magnificent gardens opening onto the Bristol Downs, an open park of some 450 acres, Downs Edge enjoys sweeping views across the Downs. "Truly a countryside location in the heart of the city". Surrounded by fine antiques the comfortable en-suite bedrooms are well appointed with particular attention to detail. Downs Edge is ideally situated for the city centre, Clifton, the universities and the motorway network. It is served by an excellent public transport system. Off street parking in grounds. Choice of delicious gourmet breakfasts. Credit cards accepted.

Philippa Tasker
Tel/Fax: 0117 9683264

B&B from £45-£48pr (single), £65-£68pr (double), Rooms 2 single, 4 double, 1 twin, all en-suite, No smoking or pets, Children over 6, Open all year except Christmas & New Year.

BEDFORDSHIRE, BERKSHIRE, BUCKINGHAMSHIRE & HERTFORDSHIRE

Often referred to as the home counties, Bedfordshire, Berkshire, Buckinghamshire and Hertfordshire lie close to London and provide rural homes for a significant number of the capital's workforce. Predominantly agricultural, peaceful and quintessentially English, each county holds its own geographic and historic attractions.

Compact Bedfordshire is a flat, agricultural county featuring the Great Ouse river to the north, slowly winding its way to Bedford – main town of the county and famous birthplace of Non-conformist preacher John Bunyan. Born the son of a tinker in 1628, John Bunyan is celebrated for his allegorical work Pilgrim's Progress – and indeed many visitors make their own special pilgrimage to Bedford to pay homage to the great man. Also of particular note in the Bedford area is the vast Woburn Abbey – home to the Duke of Bedford for nearly 400 years and housing one of the important private art collections in the world.

Berkshire features stunning countryside, including the popular Berkshire Downs to the north of the county, and some very agreeable towns and villages, most famously the ancient college town of Eton and, of course, Royal Windsor. Home to the British Royal Family for over 900 years, Windsor Castle is a must for any visitor to this county, enjoying world-renown as one of the greatest surviving medieval castles. Also blessed with a global reputation is nearby Savill Garden in Windsor Great Park, a stunning 35-acre garden providing a wealth of colour and beauty throughout the year. Daffodils, rhododendrons, camellias, magnolias and roses abound here amid dappled woodland and welcome tranquillity.

The county of Buckinghamshire is a mixture of both urban and rural landscape, featuring the chalk ridge of the Chiltern Hills to the south and the Great Union Canal to the north-east. Particularly famous for its poets, Buckinghamshire was home to John Milton, TS Eliot and PB Shelley among others – and towards the end of the 19th century, the county town of Aylesbury and its environs attracted the influential Rothschild family to construct some stunning country homes, most notably Waddeson Manor. Completed in 1889 in French Renaissance style for Baron Ferdinand de Rothschild, this stunning home contains superb collections of art, Sevres porcelain and furniture – and connoisseurs can even view the family's extensive wine cellar. Just 13 miles from Aylesbury, Claydon House is also well worth a visit, not merely because of its historic links with one time resident Florence Nightingale, but also for its fine interior decoration – thought to be England's finest example of decorative rococo style.

Within the small, neighbouring county of Hertfordshire, the visitor can enjoy idyllic rural vistas to the north, and to the south, St Albans, one of England's most charming Georgian towns. Dating back to Roman times, St Albans has a magnificent cathedral featuring spectacular murals – whitewashed during the Reformation and not discovered again until 1862 – and the magnificent St Alban's Shrine, guarded by a stunning carved oak Watching Chamber. Just a few miles from St Albans is situated another of the county's fine historic treasures – Hatfield House. Built in red brick and sandstone between 1607 and 1611 for Robert Cecil, this is one of England's most impressive Jacobean manors, housing impressive portraits of Elizabeth I and a particularly grand staircase decorated with oak figures (including that of botanist John Tradescant who designed Hatfield's extensive gardens). Also near St Albans, and a must for those who enjoy the quirky, is Shaw's Corner. The Victorian villa was home to George Bernard Shaw until his death in 1950 and within the pleasant gardens can be found the revolving summerhouse where he is thought to have written several notable works, including Pygmalion.

BEDFORDSHIRE, BERKSHIRE, BUCKINGHAMSHIRE & HERTFORDSHIRE

Rachael Hodge, Bellows Mill
Tel: 01525 220548
Map Ref 1 *see page 32*

Mrs Chapman, Lyndrick Guest House
Tel: 01344 883520
Map Ref 2 *see page 32*

Carole Ticehurst, Marshgate Cottage Hotel
Tel: 01488 682307
Map Ref 3 *see page 32*

Mr & Mrs M.Power, Woodpecker Cottage
Tel: 01628 822772
Map Ref 5 *see page 34*

Mrs Maureen Marsh, Whitewebbs
Tel: 01753 884105
Map Ref 7 *see page 34*

Mrs Christina Payne, Spinney Lodge Farm
Tel: 01908 510267
Map Ref 8 *see page 34*

Sarah Hood, The Congregational Church
Tel/Fax: 01296 715717
Map Ref 9 *see page 35*

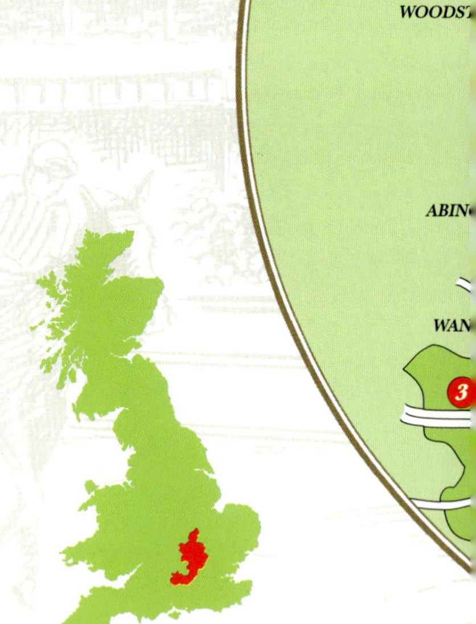

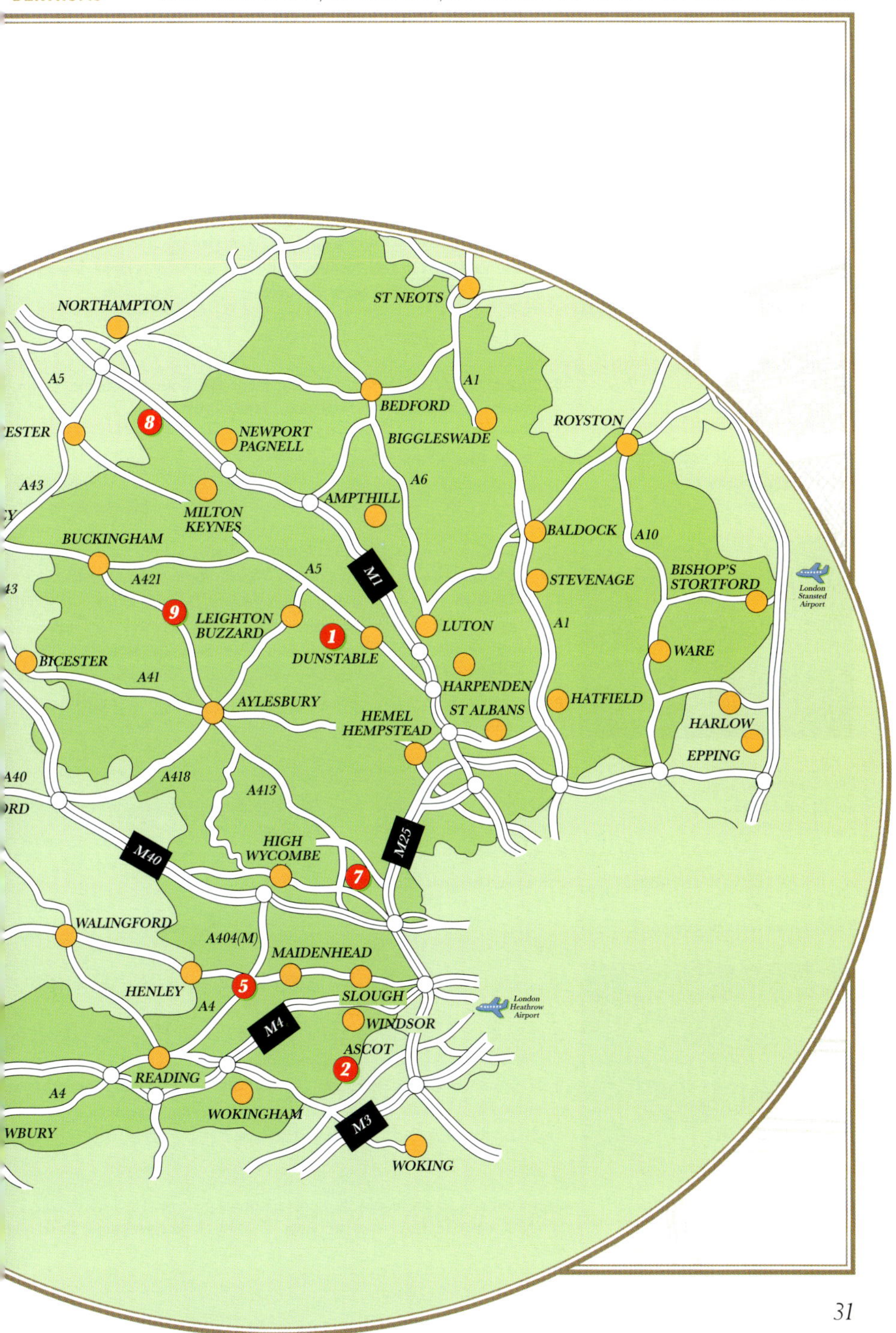

NORTHAMPTON
ST NEOTS
A5
A1
BEDFORD
8
NEWPORT PAGNELL
BIGGLESWADE
ROYSTON
A43
A6
AMPTHILL
MILTON KEYNES
BALDOCK
A10
BUCKINGHAM
A5
M1
STEVENAGE
BISHOP'S STORTFORD
London Stansted Airport
A421
9
LEIGHTON BUZZARD
1
LUTON
A1
DUNSTABLE
WARE
BICESTER
A41
HARPENDEN
AYLESBURY
HATFIELD
HEMEL HEMPSTEAD
ST ALBANS
HARLOW
EPPING
A40
A418
A413
HIGH WYCOMBE
M25
M40
7
WALINGFORD
A404(M)
MAIDENHEAD
HENLEY
5
SLOUGH
A4
London Heathrow Airport
M4
WINDSOR
ASCOT
2
READING
A4
WOKINGHAM
M3
WOKING

BELLOWS MILL, Eaton Bray, Dunstable, Bedfordshire LL6 1QZ
Email rachael@bellowsmill.co.uk
Website www.bellowsmill.co.uk

Map Ref 1
Nearest Road B489, A5

A warm welcome awaits you at this secluded water mill set in 21 acres of picturesque grounds on the outskirts of the village. The attractively furnished rooms in the converted stable block all have en-suite bathrooms and TVs. A Kitchenette is available for making tea/coffee. Guests may like to relax in the small sitting room or conservatory which overlooks the lake. Other facilities include a games room with pool/football table and table tennis, all weather tennis court and fly fishing, (rods not supplied). Credit cards accepted.

Rachael Hodge
Tel: 01525 220548
Fax: 01525 222536

B&B from £35-£75pr, Dinner by arrangement £18, Rooms 4 double, 4 twin, all en-suite, Children & dogs welcome, Open all year.

LYNDRICK GUEST HOUSE, The Avenue, Ascot, Berkshire SL5 7ND
Email mail@lyndrick.com
Website www.lyndrick.com

Map Ref 2
Nearest Road A30

An Edwardian house in tree lined avenue. A warm welcome is assured with friendly help and advice on places to visit. Well equipped bedrooms with colour TV, radio alarm, hair dryer and tea/coffee making facilities. Enjoy a delicious breakfast in pleasant conservatory overlooking the garden. Ideal base for various tourist attractions. Windsor is only four miles away and is close to Ascot racecourse, Wentworth, Sunningdale, Swinley Mill Ride, Berkshire Golf clubs nearby. Easy access by train to London for day trips. Heathrow 25 minutes by car. Credit cards accepted.

Mrs Chapman
Tel: 01344 883520
Fax: 01344 891243

B&B from £35-£60pp, Rooms 1 single, 2 double en-suite, 2 twin en-suite, No smoking or pets, Children welcome, Open all year.

MARSHGATE COTTAGE HOTEL, Marsh Lane, Hungerford, Berkshire RG17 0QX
Email reservations@marshgate.co.uk
Website www.marshgate.co.uk

Map Ref 3
Nearest Road A339, M4 J14

Full page photo opposite

Marshgate Cottage is tucked away at the end of a quiet country lane just half a mile from Hungerford and four miles from the M4. Guest rooms are in a traditionally designed addition to the original canal side 17th century thatched cottage. All rooms have en-suite shower and toilet, TV, phone and tea/coffee making facilities. Guests lounge and bar. Car park. The town has an abundance of antique and speciality shops, canal trips, pubs and restaurants. Ideal base for touring southern England. Superb walking area.

Carole Ticehurst
Tel: 01488 682307
Fax: 01488 685475

B&B from £36.50 single, £58.00 double, Rooms 1 single, 2 twin, 5 double, 2 family, all en-suite, Restricted smoking, Children & pets welcome, Open all year.

WOODPECKER COTTAGE, Warren Row, near Maidenhead, Berkshire RG10 8QS
Email power@woodpecker.co.uk
Website www.woodpeckercottage.com

Map Ref 5
Nearest Road A4, M40 jct 4, M4 jct 8/9

A tranquil woodland retreat away from crowds and traffic yet within half an hour of Heathrow, Windsor, Henley and Oxford. Set in a delightful garden of about 1 acre and surrounded by woods where deer abound. The ground floor comprises en-suite double room with its own entrance, en-suite single, and a twin room with private bathroom. All have tea/coffee making facilities and TV. There is a cosy sitting room with wood burning stove in winter. A full English breakfast includes home made bread and jam made from fruit grown in the garden. Local pubs and restaurants are within easy reach.

Michael & Joanna Power
Tel: 01628 822772
Fax: 01628 822125

B&B from £25pp, Rooms 1 twin with private bathroom, 1 en-suite single, 1 en-suite double, No smoking, Children over 8, Open all year except Christmas & New Year.

WHITEWEBBS, Grange Road, off Lower Road, Chalfont St Peter, Buckinghamshire SL9 9AQ

Map Ref 7
Nearest Road A413

Whitewebbs has been our family home for over 45 years. There are large gardens back and front with fields beyond. Guests enjoy tea and home made cakes under the Willow tree in summer and preserves made from our own fruit at breakfast. The village centre is 2 minutes away. Both bedrooms are en-suite and furnished in a cottagey style. Guests may browse and buy paintings in my studio. Good local walks. Explore the Chiltern Hills, Amersham, Beaconsfield and Windsor. London is 30 minutes away by train.

Mrs Maureen Marsh
Tel: 01753 884105

B&B from £33-£35pp, Single occupancy £45, Rooms 1 double, 1 twin, both en-suite, No smoking or pets, Children over 7, Open all year except Christmas & New Year.

SPINNEY LODGE FARM, Forest Road, Hanslope, Milton Keynes, Buckinghamshire MK19 7DE

Map Ref 8
Nearest Road A508, M1

Spinney Lodge Farm is a sheep, beef and arable farm with a very attractive farm house, surrounded by delightful gardens in a secluded position. Yet only 8 minutes from junction 15, M1, Northampton and 15 minutes from Milton Keynes. Ideal base for touring Silverstone, Woburn Abbey and Stowe Gardens. Closed for Christmas.

Mrs Christina Payne
Tel: 01908 510267

B&B from £22-£30pp, Dinner £12.50, Rooms 4 double, 2 twin, all en-suite, No smoking or pets, Children over 12, Open all year except Christmas & New Year.

THE CONGREGATIONAL CHURCH, 15 Horn Street, Winslow, Buckinghamshire MK18 3AP

Map Ref 9
Nearest Road A421

A fascinating church has been turned into a fascinating home. Each bedroom has an original stained glass, stone-mullion window. Bedrooms on one side of the church aisle and two bathrooms, including a shower, on the other side of the aisle. One bathroom has painted fish swimming round the walls. Under the gallery is the hall for tea and coffee. The high ceiling room has been decorated to make a cosy sitting room with television. Sarah serves a delicious breakfast in the magnificent kitchen/school room.

Sarah Hood
Tel/Fax: 01296 715717

B&B from £22.50-£30pp, Rooms 1 single, 1 double, 1 twin, 2 private bathrooms, Restricted smoking, Children over 10, No pets, Open all year.

"There's our road" said Bertie "Past Snowdon, and on to Anglesey"

BELLE & BERTIE IN WALES

Cambridgeshire & Northamptonshire

Best known for its world-famous university town, Cambridgeshire is a predominantly flat county covered by the unique Cambridgeshire Fens – a former wet wilderness tamed and drained from Roman times and now heralded as the best agricultural land in Britain.

Situated on the River Cam and just north of the Gog Magog Hills, Cambridge is a charming town, fiercely proud of its academic prowess and brimming with history and character. The university's many historic colleges – some founded as early as 1284 – include Trinity College with its enormous Great Court and Sir Isaac Newton tree; Christ's College which is entered by way of a superbly carved heraldic gateway; and of course the Gothic masterpiece that is King's College Chapel with its extraordinary fan-vaulted ceiling. The impressive-looking Fitzwilliam Museum in Trumpington Street is the art museum of the University. Founded by 1816 by the bequest of the seventh Viscount Fitzwilliam of Merrion, it contains over half a million artefacts spanning many civilisations and millennia. Other Cambridge highlights include the beautiful water meadows of 'The Backs'; the Botanic Gardens, featuring a lake, many glasshouses and no less than nine National plant collections; and just eight miles out of town, the magnificent Wimpole Hall set in recently restored formal gardens.

A short drive north from Cambridge, the attractive town of Ely – once an island before the Fens were drained – is crammed with narrow streets and historic buildings, including the former home of Oliver Cromwell. It is, however, the magnificent cathedral which dominates here – situated slightly above the surrounding plains and known as 'the ship of the fens'.

To the west of the county, Peterborough is another town boasting an impressive cathedral featuring fine Norman architecture and a unique 13th century timber ceiling.

The distinctive Eton Hall, home to the Proby family for over 350 years, can also be found close by. A fascinating mix of architectural styles, Eton houses some fine 15th century furniture and paintings and an extensive private library containing the prayer book of Henry VIII.

To escape the stresses of everyday life, the neighbouring county of Nothamptonshire provides the perfect backdrop of rolling countryside, leafy bridlepaths and tranquil villages. It is also a county historically dominated by the estates of great landowners, described as many as four hundred years ago as "passing well furnished with noblemen's and gentlemen's houses". The same can certainly be said of the county today, with many of its great country houses still lived in as much loved family homes.

Seat of the Isham family for over four centuries, Lamport Hall – just north of Northampton – contains a wealth of books, paintings, furniture and some particularly fine rooms, including the High Room of 1655 with magnificent plasterwork and the Cabinet Room, featuring rare Venetian cabinets. The tranquil gardens were much influenced by Sir Charles Isham, the eccentric 10th Baronet, who created the Italian Garden and Rockery featuring England's very first garden gnomes. Also situated near Northampton is Althorp, the celebrated home of the Spencer family where Diana, Princess of Wales is laid to rest in the grounds.

Near the more northerly town of Kettering, Boughton House has been home to the Duke of Buccleuch and his Montagu ancestors since 1528 and represents an original Tudor building much enlarged over the centuries. Indeed it was after the French style addition of 1695 that Boughton was described as 'England's Versailles'. Deene Park near Corby also represents another fine family home to the north of the county, originally designed as a typical medieval manor house and evolving into first a Tudor and then fine Georgian mansion. There is a delightful ambience both in and around this home – still occupied by the Brudenell family, ancestors to seventh Earl of Cardigan who led the charge of the Light Brigade at Balaclava.

Cambridgeshire & Northamptonshire

Olla & David Hindley, Purlins
Tel: 01223 842643
Map Ref 1 *see page 41*
Jenny & Robin Farndale, Cathedral House
Tel: 01353 662124
Map Ref 2 *see page 41*
Jan Roper, Queensberry
Tel: 01638 720916
Map Ref 4 *see page 41*
Mr & Mrs Hartland, The Watermill
Tel: 01223 891520
Map Ref 5 *see page 43*
Phyllis King, Astwell Mill
Tel: 01295 760507
Map Ref 6 *see page 43*
Mrs Sue Hill-Brookes, The Old Vicarage
Tel: 01780 450248
Map Ref 7 *see page 43*

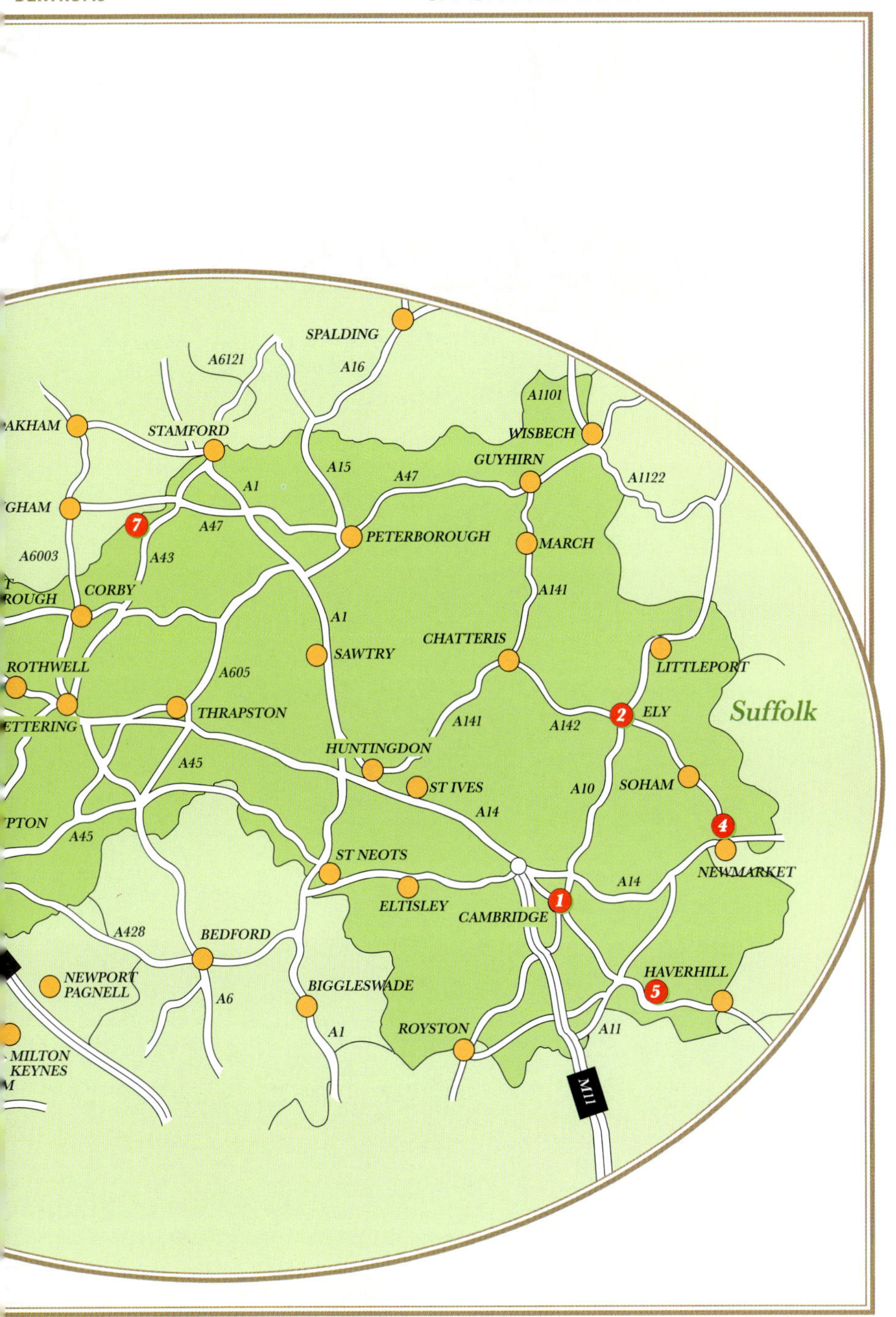
SPALDING
A6121
A16
A1101
STAMFORD
WISBECH
GUYHIRN
A1122
A15
A47
A1
A47
PETERBOROUGH
MARCH
A6003
A43
CORBY
A141
A1
CHATTERIS
SAWTRY
ROTHWELL
A605
LITTLEPORT
THRAPSTON
ELY
Suffolk
A141
A142
HUNTINGDON
A45
ST IVES
A10
SOHAM
A14
A45
ST NEOTS
A14
NEWMARKET
ELTSILEY
CAMBRIDGE
A428
BEDFORD
HAVERHILL
NEWPORT PAGNELL
A6
BIGGLESWADE
ROYSTON
A11
A1
MILTON KEYNES
M11

PURLINS, 12 High Street, Little Shelford, Cambridge, Cambridgeshire CB2 5ES
Email dgallh@ndirect.co.uk

Map Ref 1
Nearest Road A10, A1301

Elegant house of 25 years old, set in two acres of mature woodland, meadow and gardens in quiet, picturesque village on the Cam, four miles south of Cambridge. Ideal centre for visiting colleges, country houses, cathedrals, the Imperial War Museum. Three comfortable bedrooms, (two on the ground floor) have colour TV, radio and tea/coffee making facilities. Large conservatory with exotic plants is the guests' sitting room. Varied breakfasts are served in the galleried dining hall. Restaurants nearby. On drive parking for three cars.

Full page photo opposite

Olla & David Hindley
Tel/Fax: 01223 842643

B&B from £24-£33pp, Rooms 2 double, 1 twin, all en-suite, No smoking or pets, Children over 8, Open February to mid December.

CATHEDRAL HOUSE, 17 St Mary's Street, Ely, Cambridgeshire CB7 4ER
Email farndale@cathedralhouse.co.uk
Website www.cathedralhouse.co.uk

Map Ref 2
Nearest Road A10

Cathedral House is in the centre of Ely within the shadow of its famous cathedral known as 'the ship of the Fens' and within 2 minutes walk of Cromwell's House, the museums, shops and restaurants. A Grade II listed house retaining many of its original features, accommodation comprises 1 twin en-suite, a family suite and a luxurious double en-suite. All have TV and tea/coffee trays and overlook the tranquil walled garden. A choice of full English or continental breakfast is served at a farmhouse table by an open fire (lit when cold). Ely is an ideal base to tour East Anglia, Cambridge and Newmarket are close by. Free parking.

Full page photo on page 42

Jenny & Robin Farndale
Tel/Fax: 01353 662124

B&B from £30pp, Rooms 1 twin, 1 double, 1 family, all en-suite, No smoking, No pets, Open mid January to December.

QUEENSBERRY, 196 Carter Street, Fordham, Cambridgeshire CB7 5JU
Email queensberry@queensberry196demon.co.uk

Map Ref 4
Nearest Road A14, A142, A10

So peaceful this very English Georgian home on edge of village, as featured on television, large gardens and safe parking. Well located for touring East Anglia, Newmarket (horse racing centre of the world), Cambridge, Ely, Bury-St-Edmunds, the attractive old Suffolk wool towns, Norfolk coast, even London, all within easy reach. Jan attends to detail-delightful bedrooms, a wide selection of local produce cooked to order. Malcolm a tour guide will advise and arrange tours, race meetings etc. So do book early. Good restaurants within walking distance.

Jan Roper
Tel: 01638 720916
Fax: 01638 720233

B&B from £25-£30pp, Rooms 1 single, 1 double, 1 twin, 2 en-suite, No smoking, Children welcome, Pets by arrangement, Open all year.

THE WATERMILL, Linton Road, Hildersham, Cambridgeshire CB1 6BS
Email mGey04@dial.pipex.com

Map Ref 5
Nearest Road A1307

There is a watermill recorded here in the Domesday Book although the present buildings are 18th and 19th century. Set in 6 acres on the River Granta, the house has views across the garden and water meadows to the village where meals can be taken in the Pear Tree. As well as Cambridge, Ely and Saffron Walden many other beautiful towns and villages of Suffolk and Essex are within easy reach.

Mr & Mrs Hartland
Tel: 01223 891520

B&B from £22pp, Rooms 1 en-suite double/family, No smoking or pets, Children welcome, Open all year except Christmas & New Year.

ASTWELL MILL, Helmdon, Brackley, Northamptonshire NN13 5QU
Email astwell01@aol.com
Website www.astwellmill.co.uk

Map Ref 6
Nearest Road A43, B4525, M1, M40

Astwell Mill is a converted watermill set in the heart of the countryside, between Helmdon and Wappenham. Magnificent views overlooking a large millpond and garden with stream and waterfalls, which provide an abundance of wildlife. Well situated, with the M1 12 miles away and M40 10 miles; Blenheim, Oxford and Stratford can be reached in under an hour. Local attractions including Silverstone (4 miles), Althorp, Sulgrave Manor, Canons Ashby are nearby. Lounge for guests' use. 3 double (1 en-suite), all with private facilities plus TV.

Phyllis King
Tel: 01295 760507
Fax: 01295 768602

B&B from £22.50-£28pp, Rooms 3 double (1 en-suite), No smoking, Children welcome, Open all year.

THE OLD VICARAGE, Laxton, near Corby, Northamptonshire NN17 3AT
Email susan@marthahill.co.uk
Website www.marthahill.co.uk/bed-breakfast/

Map Ref 7
Nearest Road A43

Comfortable home, full of character, designed by Repton (1805) in hamlet bordering Rutland/Lincs. Stamford, Corby, Oundle and Upppingham our local towns. House is beautifully decorated and situated in large gardens with woods opposite. Our Martha Hill herbal beauty products in your bedrooms. 'Real' organic food cooked on Aga. 'Home from home' atmosphere. All sorts of extras include video, library, magazines, games, wine, papers etc. All rooms have colour TV, tea/coffee facilities. Very good restaurants nearby. Ample parking.

Mrs Sue Hill-Brookes
Tel: 01780 450248
Fax: 01780 450259

B&B from £22.50pp, twin/double with private bathroom and toilet washroom, family en-suite, (all rooms used as singles), Children & dogs welcome, Open all year.

left, Cathedral House, Ely - *please see page 41 for details*

Cheshire, Merseyside & Greater Manchester

Cheshire, Merseyside and Manchester are often collectively referred to as North-Western England and present a diverse mix of densely populated cityscapes, grand architecture, declining dockland and charming rural countryside.

Once a thriving port, the city of Liverpool enjoys a dramatic position over the River Mersey estuary and – although now home more to tourists than ships – the dockland area of the city still features a unique ambience and some particularly impressive waterfront buildings, especially around Pier Head. Other notable architecture within the city includes St George's Hall – with Grecian exterior, Roman interiors and a reputation as one of the world's finest neo-classical structures – and the twin cathedrals of the Roman Catholic and Anglican churches both vying for supremacy on the Liverpool skyline. Music lovers may also want to visit the Victorian warehouse in Mathew Street that was once the Cavern Club; and for those who enjoy the unusual, the Tudor Speke Hall features concealed priest holes where Roman Catholic priests could hide when forbidden to hold Mass in the 16th century.

A commercial hub since Roman times, Manchester's fortunes amassed in the 18th century around its weaving tradition, accessible coal supplies and convenient canal network. Despite the city's industrial decline after the Second World War, it still remains an important financial and cultural centre today, boasting many prestigious city centre buildings. Dominating Albert Square, the Victorian Gothic Town Hall features an 85 metre tower and some fine interior baroque decoration; while from the same period, John Rylands Library on Deansgate provides a stunning façade and houses a renowned collection of manuscripts. Also on Deansgate, the fascinating 15th century cathedral provides a fine spectacle of medieval engineering – and architecture enthusiasts will certainly appreciate the City Art Gallery, designed by Houses of Parliament architect Charles Barry in 1824.

Within a short drive of Manchester city centre and actually situated within the neighbouring county of Cheshire, a number of fine country homes are also to be found – many a reflection of the wealth that the manufacturing industry brought to the area. Both Dunham Massey, near Altrincham and Tatton Park in Knutsford provide particularly fine examples of Georgian manor houses; while the gloriously situated Arley Hall – rebuilt between 1832 and 1845 – represents the epitome of elegant country living. History lovers will also delight in Capesthorne Hall, an imposingly situated lakeside estate near Macclesfield which has been touched by nearly 1000 years of English occupation and nobility.

The county town of Cheshire is Chester – a particularly attractive town almost entirely encircled by a red sandstone wall dating back to Roman times. A walk along the wall offers fine views over the River Dee and the rolling countryside beyond, and also rewards with a series of ancient gates, towers and even the ruins of a Roman amphitheatre situated around its circumference. Other highlights of the town include Chester Cathedral, built between 1250 and 1540 but occupying the site of a more ancient Saxon church, and The Rows – Chester's unique two level shopping streets thought to date back to post Roman times.

Just to the south of Chester Cholmondleley Castle Garden is situated near the village of Malpas and represents a rare ornamental delight. Dominated by a romantic Gothic Castle built in 1801, these extensive grounds include fine roses, mixed herbaceous borders and an idyllic temple water garden that exudes peace and tranquillity.

CHESHIRE, MERSEYSIDE & GREATER MANCHESTER

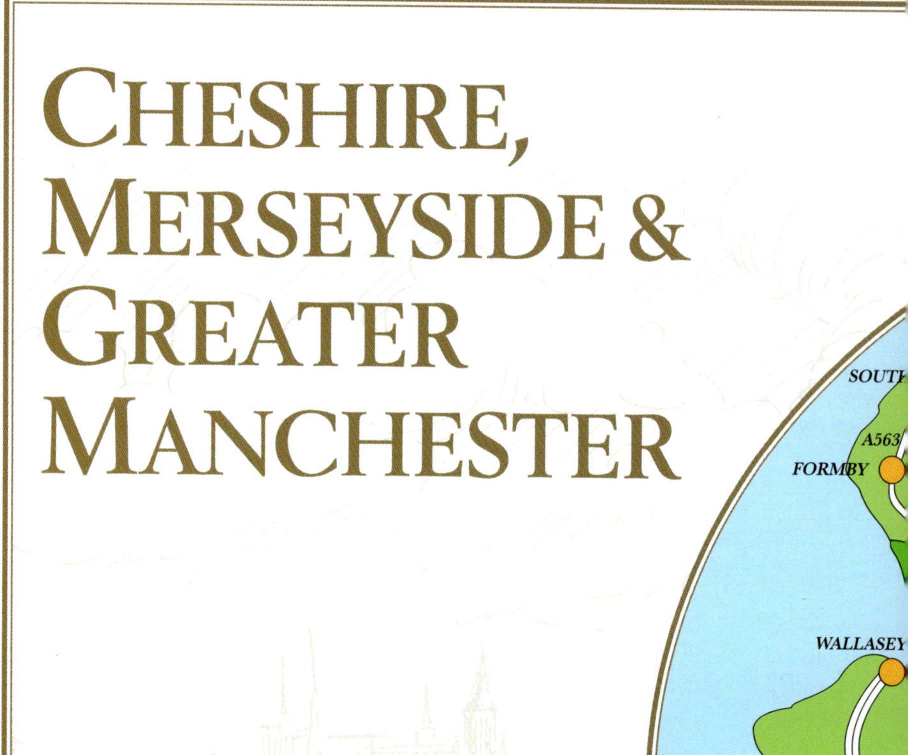

Mrs Ann Ikin, Golborne Manor
Tel: 01829 770310
Map Ref 1 *see page 48*

Johnathan & Rachel Major, The Mount
Tel/Fax: 01244 660275
Map Ref 2 *see page 48*

Charlotte Walsh, Needhams Farm
Tel: 0161 3684610
Map Ref 3 *see page 48*

Mrs Georgina West, Stoke Grange Farm
Tel/Fax: 01270 625525
Map Ref 4 *see page 51*

Mrs Jean Callwood, Lea Farm
Tel: 01270 841429
Map Ref 5 *see page 51*

Mrs Sutcliffe, Roughlow Farm
Tel: 01829 751199
Map Ref 6 *see page 51*

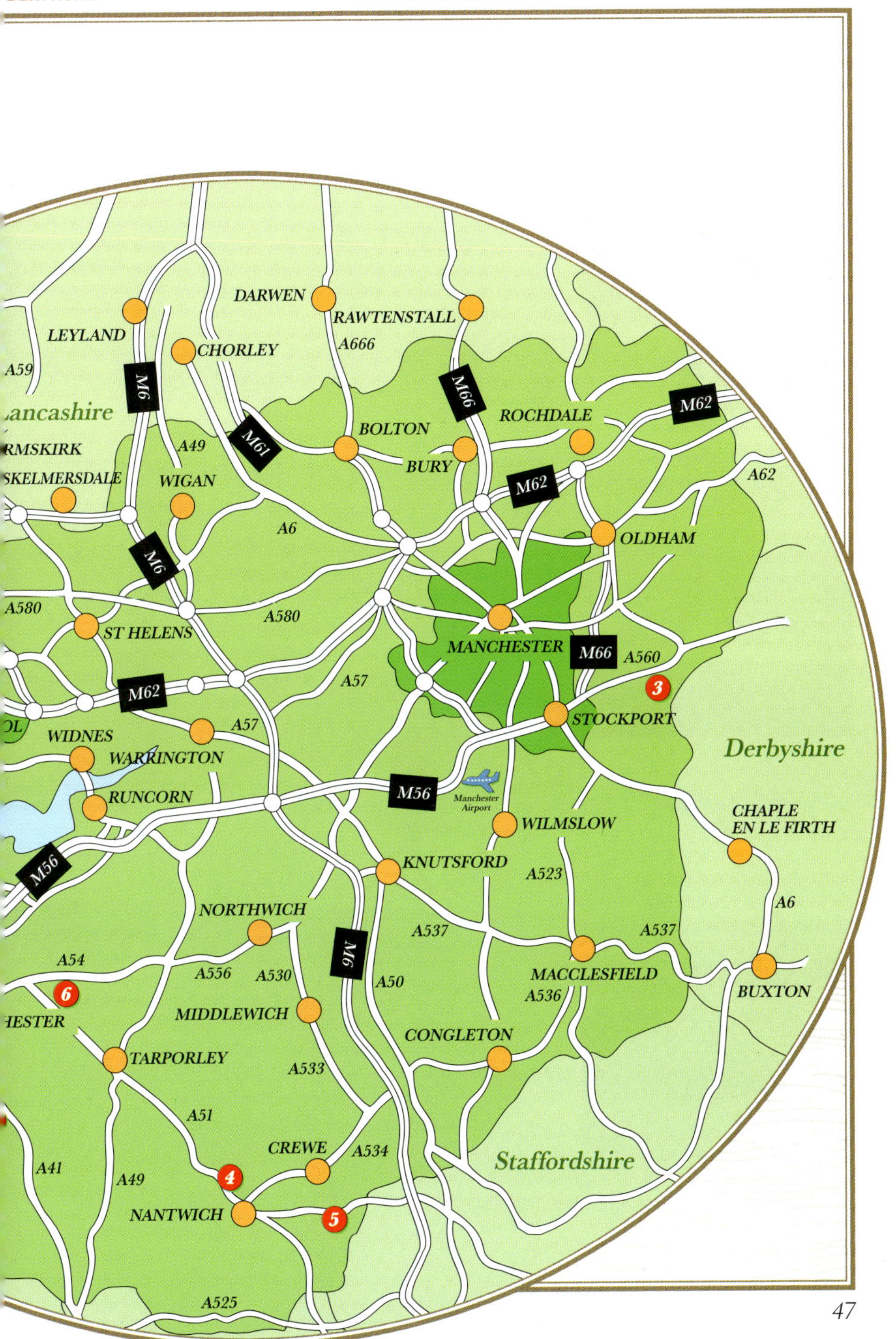
DARWEN
RAWTENSTALL
LEYLAND
CHORLEY
A666
A59
M6
M66
Lancashire
M61
BOLTON
ROCHDALE
M62
RMSKIRK
A49
BURY
SKELMERSDALE
WIGAN
M62
A62
A6
OLDHAM
M6
A580
A580
ST HELENS
MANCHESTER
M66
A560
A57
M62
STOCKPORT
WIDNES
A57
Derbyshire
WARRINGTON
RUNCORN
M56
Manchester Airport
WILMSLOW
CHAPLE EN LE FIRTH
M56
KNUTSFORD
A523
NORTHWICH
A6
A537
A537
M6
A54
A556
A530
A50
MACCLESFIELD
A536
BUXTON
HESTER
MIDDLEWICH
CONGLETON
TARPORLEY
A533
A51
CREWE
A534
Staffordshire
A41
A49
NANTWICH
A525
3
4
5
6

GOLBORNE MANOR, Platts Lane, Hatton Heath, Chester, Cheshire CH3 9AN
Email ann.ikin@golbornemanor.co.uk

Map Ref 1
Nearest Road A41

Golborne Manor is an elegant 19th century country residence with glorious views. Renovated to a high standard and set in three and a half acres of grounds and gardens. Beautifully decorated with spacious en-suite bedrooms. Farmhouse breakfast. Tea and coffee in room and colour TV. Guest lounge, piano, croquet and table tennis. Large car park. Easy access to motorway network and North Wales coast. Five and a half miles south of Chester off A41, turn right a few yards after D.P. Motors (on the left). AA, ETC Highly Commended 4 Diamonds.

Mrs Ann Ikin
Tel: 01829 770310
Fax: 01829 770370

B&B from £30, Rooms all en-suite, No smoking or pets, Children welcome, mini coaches, Open all year.

THE MOUNT, Lesters Lane, Higher Kinnerton, Cheshire CH4 9BQ
Email major@mountkinnerton.freeserve.co.uk

Map Ref 2
Nearest Road A55, A5104

Full page photo opposite

Victorian country house with spacious and imaginatively decorated rooms set in 12 acres on the edge of the village. Gardens with tennis court and croquet lawn. Spacious bedrooms with TV, tea/coffee facilities all en-suite. View over the surrounding country. An ideal place to relax and explore the North Wales coast and Cheshire countryside. 6 miles from Chester. 45 minutes to Liverpool and Manchester. 1 hour to Anglesey. Bodnant Gardens, Port Sunlight, historic Chester, Erdigg, Offas Dyke and Llangollen 20 minutes. Excellent pub in village quarter of a mile away.

Johnathan & Rachel Major
Tel/Fax: 01244 660275

B&B from £25pp, Dinner £24 (bring own wine) not Friday, Saturday or Sunday, Rooms 2 en-suite double, 1 en-suite twin, No smoking, Children over 12, Open all year.

NEEDHAMS FARM, Uplands Road, Werneth Low, Gee Cross, near Hyde, Cheshire SK14 3AG
Email charlotte@needhamsfarm.co.uk
Website www.needhamsfarm.co.uk

Map Ref 3
Nearest Road A560

Needhams Farm is a non working farm offering quality bed and breakfast with optional evening meals. This is complimented by a residential licence. The farm is situated only a few miles outside the Peak National Park, nestling between Werneth Faw and Etheraw Country Parks. The location provide easy access for Manchester city and airport, Stockport and surrounding areas including Ashton-under-Lynn, Oldham and Glossop. Credit cards accepted.

Charlotte Walsh
Tel: 0161 3684610
Fax: 0161 3679106

B&B from £20-£22pp, Dinner £8, Rooms 2 single, 3 double, 1 twin, 1 family, all en-suite, Children & pets welcome, Open all year.

STOKE GRANGE FARM, Chester Road, Nantwich, Cheshire CW5 6BT
Email stokegrange@freeuk.com
Website www.stokegrangefarm.co.uk

Map Ref 4
Nearest Road M6, A51

Attractive farmhouse in a picturesque canalside location. Hearty breakfast, vegetarians catered for. Individually styled en-suite rooms with colour TV. Four poster bedroom with balcony surveying Cheshire countryside also watch canal boats cruising the Shropshire Union. Relax in garden with lawns down to the canal. Pets corner and peacocks. First class service at B&B and self catering accommodation. Past Cheshire's Tourist Development Award winners. Chester 20 mins, Crewe 10 mins. Near to Stapeley Water Gardens, Beeston and Cholmondeley castles, Tatton Park and Chester Zoo. Which Good B&B Guide. Highly Commended, North West Tourist Board. 4 Diamonds Highly Commended.

Mrs Georgina West
Tel/Fax: 01270 625525

B&B from £25pp, Rooms 1 twin, 2 double, 1 family, Restricted smoking, Children welcome, No pets, Open all year.

LEA FARM, Wrinehill Road, Wynbunbury, Nantwich, Cheshire CW5 7NS
Email contactus@leafarm.co.uk

Map Ref 5

Charming farmhouse set in landscaped gardens where peacocks roam on a dairy farm. Ample car parking. In beautiful rolling countryside. Spacious bedrooms. Luxury lounge. Pool, snooker and fishing available. M6 Junction 16. Go along A500 towards Nantwich over the roundabout, still heading towards Nantwich. Go to traffic lights. Turn left to Wybunbury. Then turn left down Wrinehill Road by Church Tower, one and a half miles from B&B.

Mrs Jean Callwood
Tel: 01270 841429

B&B from £20pp (children half price if sharing with parents), Rooms 1 double, 1 family, 1 twin, 2 en-suite, Open all year.

ROUGHLOW FARM, Willington, Tarporley, Cheshire CW6 0PG
Email sutcliffe@roughlow.freeserve.co.uk
Website www.roughlow.freeserve.co.uk

Map Ref 6
Nearest Road A54

Roughlow Farm is a converted farmhouse built around 1800. It has wonderful views to Shropshire and Wales and was the location chosen for the recent filming of Soames's house "Robin Hill" in the Forsyte Saga on account of its lovely position. Friendly family home elegantly furnished to a high standard with 3 very comfortable en-suite bedrooms including one with private sitting room and entrance. Attractive garden with cobbled courtyard. Situated in peaceful rural surroundings yet handy for visiting Chester and North Wales. M6 25 minutes.

Full page photo opposite

Mrs Sutcliffe
Tel: 01829 751199

B&B from £30-£40pp, Rooms 2 double, 1 twin, all en-suite/private facilities, No smoking, Children welcome, Open all year.

CORNWALL

Cornwall lies at the extreme south western tip of Britain and from its jagged frame of windswept cliffs to the wild moors of its interior, the county offers a fascinating mix of dramatic land and seascapes that have inspired artists for generations. The last bastion of the Celts in England, Cornwall retained its own Cornish language until the end of the 18th century and, even today, the Cornish pride themselves in being somewhat 'culturally aloof' from the rest of the country. Throughout the 18th and 19th century Cornwall's tin mines thrived and became the lifeblood of the county. These days, tourism has replaced mining as the main industry in the area and western towns such as Bude, Newquay and Penzance are packed with holidaymakers in the summer months.

The famously beautiful fishing town of St Ives, with its fascinating harbour and winding streets, acts as a seasonal magnet to tourists and also attracts artists by the drove – many choosing to set up permanent home here. Inspired by the quality and brightness of the light, Turner painted in St Ives in 1811 and in 1993 the much-celebrated branch of London's Tate Gallery - which also includes the stunning Barbara Hepworth Sculpture Garden - opened its doors.

Just as the southern light is favourable to artists, so the climate of this southern corner of Cornwall is favourable to plant life, allowing many rare species to flourish. The award-winning millennium Eden Project is home to a huge variety of sub-tropical plants and, in the more established grounds of Trebah Garden near Falmouth, 100-year-old rhododendron trees have sprouted to almost Himalayan proportions. Additional delights in this stunning 25 acre subtropical ravine garden include huge Brazilian rhubarb plants, Australian tree ferns, Monterey Pines and two acres of white and blue hydrangeas. Other notable gardens in south Devon include Glendurgan Garden near Falmouth with its intriguing laurel maze, the tranquil Trelissick Garden just south of Truro and, to experience a living museum of superb 19th century holticulture, don't miss The Lost Gardens of Heligan near St Austell.

For lovers of Georgian architecture, Truro provides a good stopping point as the town's Lemon Street boasts some fine town houses of the period built during the prosperous heyday of tin mining. On Grampound Road the charming Trewithen manor house stands majestically in its setting of woods and parkland, providing a fine example of early 18th century design.

Although the West Country abounds with prominently positioned stately homes, it is always a delight to find those situated slightly off the beaten track. Two particularly fine Elizabethan hideaways include the small Arundell manor house of Trerice in Newquay, intriguingly reached via a web of narrow lanes, and Prideaux Place, discretely tucked away above the busy fishing village of Padstow and home to the Prideaux family for over 400 years.

Sometimes referred to as Cornwall's 'roof', Bodwin Moor presents wild heathland and mighty tors and rather enjoys its mysterious reputation, made famous by Daphne Du Maurier in her celebrated novel Jamaica Inn. Windswept and unkempt around the town of Bodwin it is not, however, as Cornwall's grandest and most welcoming house, Lanhyrock, proves beyond any doubt. With 50 rooms on show - and particularly beautiful gardens - it is a fascinating place to spend a day. Slightly smaller in proportion but equally impressive in its own right, the Georgian manor house of Pencarrow can be found just four miles to the north west of Bodwin. Pencarrow houses a superb collection of paintings, porcelain and furniture - including a suite in the rather impressive drawing room which is covered with Chinese silk captured from a Spanish treasure ship in 1762. Camellias, rhododendrons, azaleas and bluebells thrive in the grounds and, interestingly, Pencarrow claims to be home to the Monkey Puzzle tree. As the story goes, a young parliamentary lawyer, Charles Austin, stayed at the house in 1834 and on seeing the Araucaria Imbricata is said to have remarked: "That tree would puzzle a monkey!" The name stuck and has been associated with Pencarrow ever since.

CORNWALL

Muriel Fairhurst, Mellan House
Tel: 01326 280482
Map Ref 1 *see page 56*

Mrs Margaret Smith, Hurdon Farm
Tel: 01566 772955
Map Ref 2 *see page 56*

Mrs Hilary Lugg, Cobblers Cottage
Tel: 01326 241342
Map Ref 14 *see page 56*

Julie Tamblyn, Botelet
Tel: 01503 220225
Map Ref 3 *see page 57*

Kathy Woodley, Degembris Farmhouse
Tel: 01872 510555
Map Ref 4 *see page 57*

Sarah Furniss, Lancrow Farmhouse
Tel: 01726 814263
Map Ref 5 *see page 57*

Nuala Leeper, Quilkyns
Tel: 01736 719141
Map Ref 6 *see page 58*

Lynne & Anthony Tuckett, Trenderway Farm
Tel: 01503 272214
Map Ref 7 *see page 58*

Mr & Mrs Crawford, Long Cross Hotel & Victorian Gardens
Tel: 01208 880243
Map Ref 8 *see page 58*

Jane & Steve Epperson, Anchorage House
Tel: 01726 814071
Map Ref 9 *see page 61*

Charles & Mally Francis, The Wagon House
Tel: 01726 844505
Map Ref 10 *see page 61*

Mr Weston, Grey Mullet Guest House
Tel: 01736 796635
Map Ref 11 *see page 61*

Blue Hayes Private Hotel
Tel/Fax: 01736 797129
Map Ref 12 *see page 62*

ST JUST

Alison Swann, Penvith Barns
Tel: 01503 240772
Map Ref 13 *see page 62*

Clive & Button Poole, The Old Rectory
Tel: 01752 822275
Map Ref 15 *see page 62*

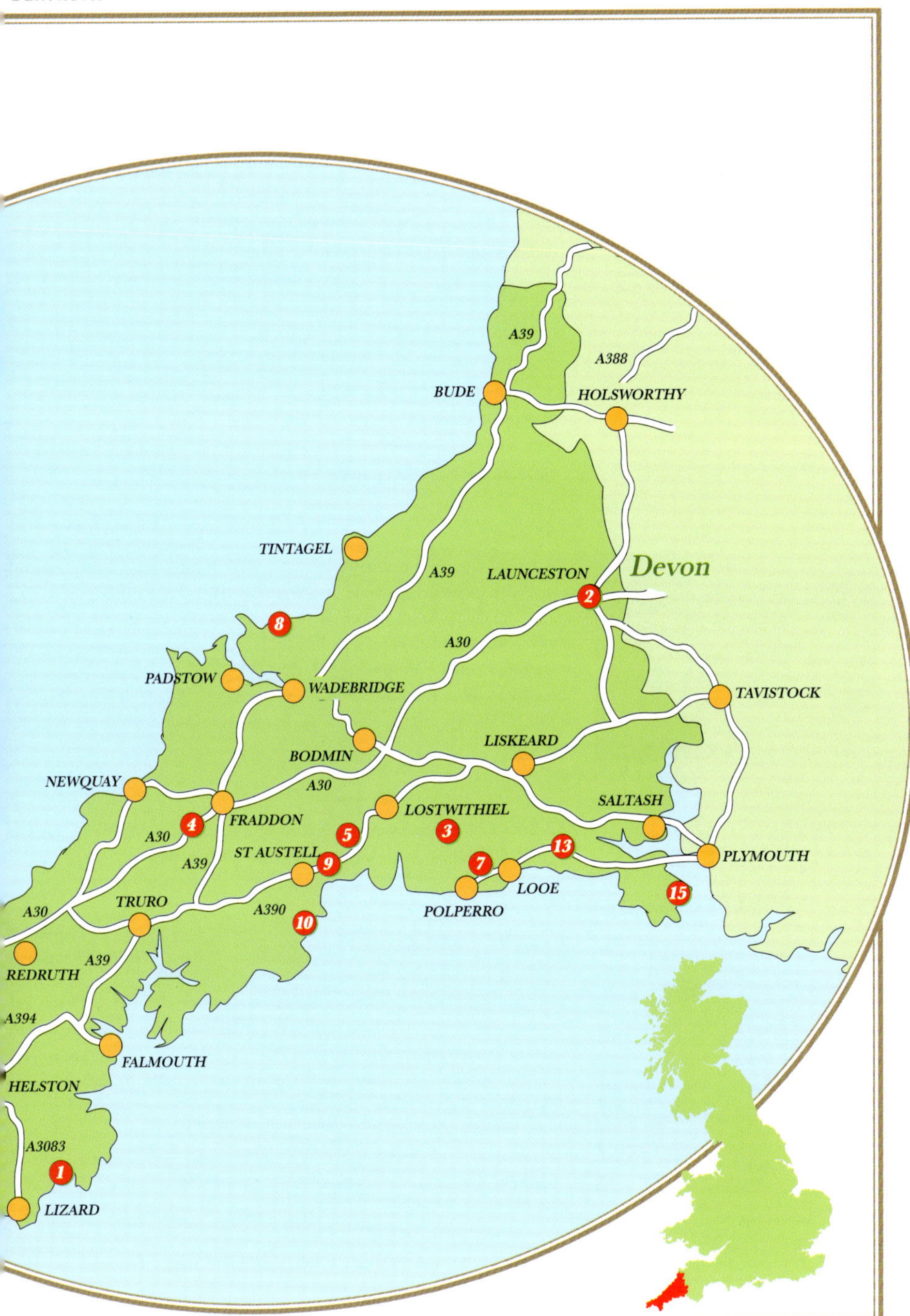
A39
A388
BUDE
HOLSWORTHY
TINTAGEL
A39
LAUNCESTON
Devon
2
8
A30
PADSTOW
WADEBRIDGE
TAVISTOCK
LISKEARD
BODMIN
NEWQUAY
A30
FRADDON
LOSTWITHIEL
SALTASH
4
5
3
A30
ST AUSTELL
9
13
A39
7
PLYMOUTH
LOOE
15
A30
TRURO
A390
POLPERRO
10
REDRUTH
A39
A394
FALMOUTH
HELSTON
A3083
1
LIZARD

MELLAN HOUSE, Coverack, Helston, Cornwall TR12 6TH
Email hmfmelcov@aol.com

Map Ref 1
Nearest Road B3294

Mellan House stands in a large garden and is 5 minutes from a safe sandy beach. Fishing, boating and windsurfing are available and a golf course is 6 miles away at Mullion. Coverack is a beautiful small fishing village in an area of outstanding natural beauty. Bedrooms have sea views and garden views and tea/coffee making facilities, and there is a comfortable lounge with colour television for guests' use.

Muriel Fairhurst
Tel: 01326 280482

B&B from £20pp, Rooms 2 double, 1 single, No smoking, Pets by arrangement, Open all year except Christmas.

COBBLERS COTTAGE, Nantithet, Cury, Helston, Cornwall TR12 7RB

Map Ref 14
Nearest Road A3083

This picturesque 17th century rose clad cottage is set in an acre of beautiful garden with meandering stream, in a sheltered valley 2 miles from the sea and coastal walks. This former shoemakers shop and kiddlewink has been carefully modernised, and still maintains its old world character, with beamed ceilings and interesting alcoves. Furnished to a high standard, all bedrooms en-suite with tea/coffee facilities and TV. Evening dinner optional. Ample parking. Sorry no smoking, children or pets. ETC 5 Diamonds Silver Award. A warm welcome awaits you.

Mrs Hilary Lugg
Tel/Fax: 01326 241342

B&B from £24-£25pp, Dinner £12, Rooms 2 double, 1 twin, all en-suite, No smoking, children or pets, Open all year except Christmas.

HURDON FARM, Launceston, Cornwall PL15 9LS

Map Ref 2
Nearest Road A30

Only 5 minutes from A30. Hurdon Farm is ideally situated to explore Devon and Cornwall. The north and south coast are within easy driving distance, as are Dartmoor and Bodmin Moor. The Eden Project, Lost Garden of Heligan are just two of the wonderful gardens to visit. There is also a number of National Trust properties in the area. The 18th century farmhouse is spacious and quietly located. All bedrooms are en-suite, centrally heated and have colour TV, hair dryer, hospitality tray and other thoughtful extras. We currently hold 4 Diamonds Award from the AA and RAC.

Mrs Margaret Smith
Tel: 01566 772955

B&B from £21-£24pp, Rooms 1 single, 2 double, 2 twin, 1 family, all en-suite, No smoking or pets, Children welcome, Open May to November.

BOTELET, Herodsfoot, Liskeard, Cornwall PL14 4RD
Email stay@botelet.co.uk
Website www.botelet.co.uk

Map Ref 3
Nearest Road B3359, A390, A38

Below the Neolithic hill fort of Burydown the Tamblyn family have preserved tradition at Botelet since 1860. Change has been slow over the generations with emphasis on preservation and simplicity. Within 250 acres of rolling farmland, trees and a threadwork of wild flowered lanes choose to stay in the farmhouse B&B or one of the original cottages. Crisp summer linen, winter log fires. The enthusiastic young generation offer pure food using home grown and local organic suppliers. For ultimate relaxation, aromatherapy and reflexology treatments are available.

Julie Tamblyn
Tel/Fax: 01503 220225

B&B from £25-£40pp, Dinner £25, Rooms 1 double, 1 twin, No smoking or pets, Children over 12, Open all year except Christmas & New Year.

DEGEMBRIS FARMHOUSE, St Newlyn East, Newquay, Cornwall TR8 5HY
Email kathy@degembris.co.uk
Website www.degembris.co.uk

Map Ref 4
Nearest Road A30, A3058

Degembris inspires imagination of former times remaining an unspoilt gem of Cornish history. Built on the site of Degembris Manor, the present farmhouse was constructed in the 16th to early 17th century. From the parking area a few steps lead up to the pretty front garden which overlooks a beautiful wooded valley. The attractive, individually furnished bedrooms vary in size from small flowery single to spacious family rooms. The natural environment is enhanced by a country trail, this preserving wildlife and bluebell walks in the spring. Credit cards accepted.

Kathy Woodley
Tel: 01872 510555
Fax: 01872 510230

B&B from £25-£28pp, Rooms 1 single, 2 double, 1 twin, 1 family, No smoking or pets, Open all year.

LANCROW FARMHOUSE, Penpillick, near Par, Cornwall PL24 2SA
Email sarahfurniss@aol.com
Website www.foweyvacations.com

Map Ref 5
Nearest Road A390

Delightful 700 year old listed farmhouse. Peaceful rural setting close to coast, Fowey, the Eden Project and Lost Gardens of Heligan. One double en-suite and twin with private facilities. Adjacent barn has three double en-suite rooms with self catering if required. Dinner available with emphasis on fish and local produce. Informal, friendly atmosphere, a tranquil home from home, with a warm welcome.

Sarah Furniss
Tel: 01726 814263
Fax: 01726 813428

B&B from £30-£40pp, Dinner £22, Rooms 3 double, 2 twin, all en-suite, No smoking, Children & pets welcome, Open all year.

QUILKYNS, 1 St Pirans Way, Perranuthnoe, Penzance, Cornwall TR20 9NJ
Email paul@quilkyns.co.uk
Website www.quilkyns.co.uk

Map Ref 6
Nearest Road A394, A30

Quilkyns is a small family run B&B. The rooms have a warm sunny atmosphere with views to the sea. TV, tea/coffee and clock radio in rooms. Access to laundry room. Children welcome if family occupying both rooms. The village pub, with family dining room, serves excellent food. Excellent beach within easy walking distance.

Nuala Leeper
Tel: 01736 719141

B&B from £20-£30pp, Rooms 2 twin, 1 family, No smoking or pets, Children welcome, Open February to November.

TRENDERWAY FARM, Pelynt, Polperro, Cornwall PL13 2LY
Email trenderwayfarm@hotmail.com
Website www.trenderwayfarm.co.uk

Map Ref 7
Nearest Road A387

Built in the late 16th century, this attractive award winning farmhouse is set in peaceful, beautiful countryside at the head of the Polperro Valley, 5 minutes from the fishing ports of Looe and Polperro. Bedrooms here are superb, individually decorated with the flair of a interior designer. A wide choice of breakfasts are offered. Excellent restaurants and inns nearby. Perfectly located to visit historic houses, Lost Gardens of Heligan and Eden Project. Credit cards accepted.

Lynne & Anthony Tuckett
Tel: 01503 272214
Fax: 01503 272991

B&B from £35-£40pp, Rooms 5 double, 1 twin, No smoking, children or pets, Open all year except Christmas.

LONG CROSS HOTEL & VICTORIAN GARDENS, Trelights, Port Isaac, Cornwall PL29 3TF

Map Ref 8
Nearest Road B3314

One of Cornwalls most unusual hotels, a character Victorian country house with a unique garden and its own free house tavern. The Long Cross has 12 en-suite rooms all with TV's and tea/coffee facilities, some ground floor rooms, some sea views. The hotel retains many of the original Victorian features and the Victorian gardens are open to the public. The free house Tavern is a popular drinking and dining spot with an extensive menu and a famous beer garden. Ideal spot for walkers, near surfing beaches.

Mr & Mrs Crawford
Tel: 01208 880243

B&B 3 nights from £55pp, Dinner available, Rooms 4 twin, 8 double, 3 family, all en-suite/private facilities, Children & pets welcome, Open all year except Christmas.

---

right, Anchorage House, Boscundle - please see page 61 for details

ANCHORAGE HOUSE, Nettles Corner, Boscundle, Tregrehan Mills, St Austell, Cornwall PL25 3RH
Email Anchoragehse@aol.com
Website www.anchoragehouse.co.uk

Map Ref 9
Nearest Road A390

Full page photo on page 59

Every attention has been paid to the smallest detail in this impressive house, it's the only establishment in Cornwall awarded the AA's highest rating (5 Red Diamonds) and one of only 35 in the UK. It is modern and unpretentious, but has a traditional feel with all the luxurious conveniences of jacuzzi, outdoor heated lap pool, satellite TV, luxury king and super king-sized beds and beautifully decorated, clean rooms filled with everything to make you happy and comfortable. 5 minutes from the Eden Project, 15 minutes to the Lost Gardens of Heligan. Steve, a retired US Navy Special Operations Commander and his English wife Jane, lived in Virginia and Hawaii before settling in Cornwall, where they also own a hotel.

Jane & Steve Epperson
Tel: 01726 814071

B&B from £39-£47pp, singles £65, Dinner by arrangement £27, Rooms 3 double, all en-suite, No smoking, children or pets, Open all year except December.

THE WAGON HOUSE, Heligan Manor, St Ewe, Cornwall PL26 6EW
Email thewagonhouse@macace.co.uk

Map Ref 10
Nearest Road B3273

An ideal B&B for garden lovers. Make the most of your visit to Heligan by staying in the former wagon house at the centre of the Gardens, a short walk from the entrance. Charles and Mally are respectively photographer and botanical artist to Heligan Gardens and the Eden Project and they can provide useful information about both venues through their connections as well as on other gardens to visit in the area. Courses in photography and botanical painting are held periodically in their large studio.

Charles & Mally Francis
Tel: 01726 844505
Fax: 01726 844525

B&B from £35pp, Rooms 2 twin, No smoking, children or pets, Open all year except Christmas & New Year.

GREY MULLET GUEST HOUSE, 2 Bunkers Hill, St Ives, Cornwall TR26 1LJ
Email greymulletguesthouse@lineone.net
Website www.touristnetuk.com/sw/greymullet

Map Ref 11
Nearest Road A30, A3074

Full page photo opposite

Full of interest and character, 20 yards from the harbour, the Grey Mullet Guest House lies in the heart of St Ives' old fishing and artists quarter. Glorious beaches nearby. Minutes from car parks, restaurants, pubs, shops and art galleries - including the Tate Gallery and Barbara Hepworth Museum. Ideal for south west coastpath. Comfortable en-suite bedrooms, some with 4-poster beds, have TV and tea/coffee making facilities. There is a cosy guest lounge. An excellent English or vegetarian breakfast is served in the oak beamed cellar dining room. Credit cards accepted.

Mr Weston
Tel: 01736 796635
Fax: 01793 828267

B&B from £22-£26pp, Rooms 1 single, 5 double, 1 twin, all en-suite, No smoking or pets, Children over 12, Open all year.

BLUE HAYES PRIVATE HOTEL, Trelyon Avenue, St Ives, Cornwall TR26 2AD
Email malcolm@bluehayes.fsbusiness.co.uk
Website www.bluehayes.co.uk
Map Ref 12
Nearest Road A30, A3074

Country House by the sea, within its own grounds and car park, overlooking St Ives Bay and Harbour. Recently extended and completely refurnished to provide a higher standard and elegant relaxation. Five luxury rooms: Master Suite with balcony overlooking Bay and Harbour, and four poster bed; Godrevy Suite and Bay Suite both have sea views; Garden Suite with direct access to Garden; Trelyon Suite with roof garden and balcony overlooking woodlands and with sea views. Private licensed bar with terrace overlooking Bay and Harbour. Credit cards accepted.

Tel/Fax: 01736 797129

B&B from £45-£65pp, Rooms 6 double, all en-suite, No smoking or pets, Children over 10, Open February to November.

PENVITH BARNS, St Martin by Looe, Cornwall PL13 1NZ
Email penvith@btinternet.com
Website www.penvith.users.btopenworld.com
Map Ref 13
Nearest Road A387

Bed & Breakfast with a difference in Grade II Listed 16th century converted barns exc en-suite facilities. Situated in acres of glorious countryside, close to coastal paths. Penvith is ideally placed for touring Cornwall and Devon. Three miles away from the historic port of Looe. Two bedroom self catering apartment also available.

Alison Swann
Tel: 01503 240772

B&B from £20pp, Rooms 1 double, 1 family, all en-suite, No smoking or pets, Open all year.

THE OLD RECTORY, St John-in-Cornwall, near Torpoint, Cornwall PL11 3AW
Email clive@oldrectory-stjohn.co.uk
Website www.oldrectory-stjohn.co.uk
Map Ref 15
Nearest Road A374

Regency listed country house with beautifully appointed and romantic bedrooms set in a quiet valley of this 'forgotten corner of Cornwall' with subtropical garden and millpond located by tidal creek. A warm welcome, inspirational breakfasts and relaxing drawing room. Coastal walks, beaches, NT and Eden Project. 3 miles from chain ferry. NB: Water surrounds this property, therefore we cannot accept responsibility for the safety of children.

Clive & Button Poole
Tel: 01752 822275
Fax: 01752 823322

B&B from £40-£50pp (min 2 nights), Rooms 1 double, 1 twin, 1 family, all en-suite/private, No smoking, Children & pets by arrangement, Open all year.

Full page photo opposite

CUMBRIA

Scenic Cumbria is perhaps the north's most-visited county, thanks mainly to its celebrated Lake District where England's highest mountains tower over scenic stretches of water and rolling fells. On the quieter, eastern side of the county, fine rural vistas run for miles to meet the Yorkshire Dales and the brooding Pennine Hills, while the beautiful Eden Valley offers the visitor some interesting market towns – as well as some welcome tranquillity.

To the north lies the border town of Carlisle, once the Roman administrative centre for the north-east and scene to much warring and siege over the centuries. Not surprisingly, Carlisle has been home to a fine Norman castle since 1092, featuring a great maze of passageways and chambers and stunning views from its ramparts. For those particularly interested in the Roman history of the area – and that of Hadrian's Wall slightly to the north – Tullie House Museum on the corner of Castle Street and Finkle Street is both informative and well presented.

Also of particular note in Carlisle is the magnificent red sandstone cathedral dating from 1122 and incorporating some of the very finest stained glass; and the town's historic market cross – the exact spot where Bonnie Prince Charlie proclaimed his father king during the Jacobite rebellion of 1745.

In the very heart of Cumbria lies the magnificent Lake District National Park, containing over 1800 miles of footpaths through some of Britain's best-walked countryside. In the words of celebrated local poet William Wordsworth, the spectacular mountains, lakes and fells of the area are there for everyone "with an eye to perceive and a heart to enjoy".

The same could be said, of course, for practically all of Cumbria's fine stately homes and while in the national park there is one gem in particular that should not be missed. Muncaster Castle lies near the coastal town of Ravenglass on the park's western periphery and has been owned by the Pennington family since 1208. Oustanding features of this impressive house include the Great Hall, Salvin's Octagonal Library and the Drawing Room with its wonderful barrel ceiling. Although said to be haunted, the castle retains a pleasant ambience and the resident family are happy to greet and entertain visitors. Extensive woodland gardens offer good views of the Esk valley, fine specimen trees and a riot of azaleas, camellias and magnolias in spring – while in May the spectacular colours of the cherry and maple trees complement the rhododendrons to perfection.

Again on the outskirts of the national park, but this time to the east, Levens Hall near Kendal also rates as a must-see Elizabethan country home. Offering a welcoming and friendly atmosphere, this much loved home of the Bagot family boasts fine panelling and plasterwork and some exquisite collections of furniture and art. It is, however, the world famous topiary gardens that have put Levens Hall on the map, and indeed among the top ten favourite gardens in the UK. Designed by Monsieur Guillaume Beaumont in 1694, the grounds feature over 90 individual pieces of topiary – some large, some small but all demanding the unflinching attention of four full-time gardeners.

CUMBRIA

Alan Rhone, Riverside Lodge
Tel: 015394 34208
Map Ref 1 *see page 68*

Roy & Barbara Hood, The Fairfield
Tel: 015394 46565
Map Ref 2 *see page 68*

Marjorie Stobart, Cracrop Farm
Tel: 016977 48245
Map Ref 3 *see page 68*

Jack & Margaret Sisson, Bessiestown Farm Country Guest House
Tel: 01228 577219
Map Ref 4 *see page 71*

Evelyn & Yvonne Cervetti, Lightwood Country Guest House
Tel: 015395 31454
Map Ref 5 *see page 71*

Hazel Thompson, New House Farm
Tel: 01900 85404
Map Ref 6 *see page 71*

Mr Chris Varley, Aynsome Manor Hotel
Tel: 015395 36653
Map Ref 7 *see page 72*

Lyn & John Kirkbride, Ryelands
Tel: 015394 35076
Map Ref 8 *see page 72*

Sylvia Beaty, Garnett House Farm
Tel: 01539 724542
Map Ref 9 *see page 72*

Mrs D M Swindlehurst, Tranthwaite Hall
Tel: 015395 68285
Map Ref 10 *see page 73*

Chris Beaty, Willow Cottage
Tel: 017687 76440
Map Ref 11 *see page 73*

Tony Sawyer, Ing Hill Lodge
Tel: 017683 71153
Map Ref 13 *see page 73*

Mrs C.Weightman, Near Howe Farm Hotel
Tel: 017687 79678
Map Ref 14 *see page 74*

Eleanor & David Lines, Castlemont
Tel: 016973 20205
Map Ref 15 see page 74

Arnold & Nan Savage, Swaledale Watch
Tel: 016974 78409
Map Ref 16 see page 74

Janine & Duncan Hatfield, Braemount House Hotel
Tel: 015394 45967
Map Ref 2 see page 75

Brenda Butterworth, Orrest Head House
Tel: 015394 44315
Map Ref 17 *see page 75*

Mrs Joanne Furness, Cuddy's Hall Holiday Cottage
Tel: 016977 48160
Map Ref 18 *see page 75*

WO
WHIT
E

Scotland
CANONBIE
GRETNA
LONGTOWN
BRAMPTON
CARLISLE
A69
A689
Northumberland
WIGTON
THURSBY
ASPATRIA
A596
A6
M6
ALSTON
A686
B6277
MIDDLETON IN TEESDALE
66
OCKERMOUTH
PENRITH
County Durham
A66
KESWICK
A592
APPLEBY
A591
GRASMERE
SHAP
BROUGH
A66
AMBLESIDE
A6
KIRKBY STEPHEN
WINDERMERE
TEBAY
A685
A593
KENDAL
SEDBERGH
A684
M6
HAWES
KIRKBY LONSDALE
ULVERSTON
Yorkshire
A6
A65
BARROW IN FURNESS
1
2
3
4
5
6
7
8
9
10
11
13
14
15
16
17
18

RIVERSIDE LODGE, Rothay Bridge, Ambleside, Cumbria LA22 0EH
Email alanrhone@riversidelodge.co.uk
Website www.riversidelodge.co.uk

Map Ref 1
Nearest Road A593

Riverside Lodge is a house of immense charm and character offering quality bed and breakfast and self-catering accommodation in an idyllic riverside setting at Ambleside in the heart of the English Lake District. All rooms are en-suite but vary in size and outlook which is reflected in the room tariff. Credit cards accepted.

Alan Rhone
Tel: 015394 34208

B&B from £27.50-£33pp, Rooms 4 double, all en-suite, No smoking, children or pets, Open all year except Christmas.

THE FAIRFIELD, Brantfell Road, Bowness on Windermere, Cumbria LA23 3AE
Email Roy&barb@the-fairfield.co.uk
Website www.the-fairfield.co.uk

Map Ref 2
Nearest Road A591

Fairfield is a small friendly, family run, 200 year old Lakeland hotel found in peaceful garden setting. 200 metres from Bowness village, 400 metres from the shores of Windermere and at the end of the Dales Way (an 81 mile walk from Ikley to Bowness). The Beatrix Pottery Exhibition is within easy walking distance. The well appointed and tastefully furnished bedrooms all have colour television. Breakfast are a speciality. Leisure facilities available. On site car parking. Genuine hospitality and warm welcome. Credit cards accepted.

Roy & Barbara Hood
Tel/Fax: 015394 46565

B&B from £27-£34pp, Rooms 1 single, 5 double, 1 twin, 2 family, all en-suite, No smoking or pets, Children welcome, Open February to November.

Full page photo opposite

CRACROP FARM, Kirkcambeck, Brampton, Cumbria CA8 2BW
Email cracrop@aol.com
Website www.cracrop.co.uk

Map Ref 3

If you want your holiday to be something special then Cracrop Farm is an excellent choice. A spacious distinguished farm house, sit in a lovely garden on a working farm with breathtaking views. The en-suite guest rooms are tastefully furnished to a high standard each with colour TV, central heating and hospitality trays. Breakfasts are a feast. Guests can relax in sauna or spa bath or exercise in gym. Places to visit Hadrians Wall, Scottish Borders, Carlisle and Lake District. Excellent walking. Farm trail. Wildlife abounds.

Marjorie Stobart
Tel: 016977 48245
Fax: 016977 48333

B&B from £25-£30pp, Rooms 1 single, 1 twin, 2 double, all en-suite, No smoking or pets, Children over 12, Open all year except Christmas.

BESSIESTOWN FARM COUNTRY GUEST HOUSE, Catlowdy, Longtown, Carlisle, Cumbria CA6 5QP
Email info@bessiestown.co.uk
Website www.bessiestown.co.uk
Map Ref 4

Booker prize for Excellence UK, Best Guest House. Cumbria for Excellence and AA Best B&B for England Award Winner. AA, ETC 5 Diamonds, Silver Award. One of the nicest farm guest houses offering many of the delights of a small country hotel with the relaxed atmosphere of a family home. Delightfully decorated public rooms and pretty en-suite bedrooms with colour TV, radio and hostess tray. Delicious traditional home cooking using fresh produce whenever possible. Residential licence. Stop off for England, Scotland and N. Ireland. The indoor heated swimming pool is open from mid May to mid September. Beautiful honeymoon suite. Family accommodation is in comfortable courtyard cottages.

Jack & Margaret Sisson
Tel: 01228 577219
Fax: 01228 577019

B&B from £27.50pp, Dinner from £14, Rooms 2 double 1 family, 1 twin, also 3 courtyard cottages, No smoking, Open all year.

LIGHTWOOD COUNTRY GUEST HOUSE, Cartmel Fell, Cumbria LA11 6NP
Email enquiries@lightwoodguesthouse.com
Website www.lightwoodguesthouse.com
Map Ref 5
Nearest Road A590

Lightwood is a charming 17th century farmhouse retaining original oak beams and staircase. Standing in 2 acres of beautiful, natural and landscaped gardens with unspoilt views of the countryside. 2 1/2 miles from the southern end of Lake Windermere. Excellent fell walking area. Maps provided. All rooms are en-suite, tastefully decorated and furnished with central heating, tea/coffee making facilities and all with colour TV. Cosy lounge with log fire and colour TV. We serve a good high standard of home cooking with seasonal home grown produce. Fully licensed. ETC 4 Diamonds. RAC listed. Which? Guide recommended.

Evelyn & Yvonne Cervetti
Tel/Fax: 015395 31454

B&B from £26pp, Dinner from £17.50, Rooms 2 twin, 2 double, 2 family, all en-suite, Restricted smoking, Children welcome, Pets by arrangement, Open February to mid December & New Year.

NEW HOUSE FARM, Lorton, nr Cockermouth, Cumbria CA13 9UU
Email hazel@newhouse-farm.co.uk
Website www.newhouse-farm.co.uk
Map Ref 6
Nearest Road A66, B5289

This is the "real lakes' with all the peace and beauty of the fells, valleys and lakes, but without the crowds. New House Farm is a 17th Century Grade II listed farmhouse offering luxury accommodation. The bedrooms are all en-suite with many little extras. There are two residents' lounges, both with open fires and a cosy dining room where delicious five course evening meals are served and hearty breakfasts enjoyed in the morning. Fabulous views from every window. Which? Hotel of the Year Award Winner. AA 5 Diamonds.

Hazel Thompson
Tel: 01900 85404
Fax: 01900 85421

B&B from £42pp, Dinner £22, Rooms 3 double, 2 twin, all en-suite, No smoking, Children over 6, Open all year.

Full page photo opposite

AYNSOME MANOR HOTEL, Cartmel, near Grange over Sands, Cumbria LA11 6HH
Email info@aynsomemanorhotel.co.uk
Website www.aynsomemanorhotel.co.uk

Map Ref 7
Nearest Road A590, M6

The age of elegance is not past; it still lives on at this lovely old manor house where the Varley family have created a special atmosphere of warmth and comfort. Located in the still untouched Vale of Cartmel, Aynsome is an ideal centre from which to explore the richness of the English lakes. Newby Bridge at the southern tip of lake Windermere is just 4 miles away. Five course dinners are superbly prepared and served in an elegant candlelit Georgian dining room using fresh local produce. Credit cards accepted.

Mr Chris Varley
Tel: 015395 36653
Fax: 015395 36016

DB&B from £56-£72pp, Rooms 5 double, 6 twin, 1 family, all en-suite, Restricted smoking, Children over 5, Open all year except January.

RYELANDS, Grasmere, Cumbria LA22 9SU
Email kirkbride.ryelands@virgin.net
Website www.ryelandsgrasmere.co.uk

Map Ref 8
Nearest Road A591

Ryelands, a delightful Victorian country house in 3 acres of peaceful and pleasant gardens on the edge of one of the most beautiful villages in Lakeland. Your friendly, helpful hosts have lovingly restored their home to create elegant, spacious and comfortable rooms for discerning guests, the perfect retreat from which to enjoy the Lake District. You can walk from the house into the beautiful countryside, relax as you row round the Lake or make a pilgrimage to Wordsworth's Homes. Exclusively for non smokers. Brochure available.

Lyn & John Kirkbride
Tel/Fax: 015394 35076

B&B from £30-£35pp, Rooms 3 double, all en-suite, No smoking or pets, Children over 10, Open mid March to end October.

GARNETT HOUSE FARM, Burneside, Kendal, Cumbria LA9 5SF
Email info@garnetthousefarm.co.uk
Website www.garnetthousefarm.co.uk

Map Ref 9
Nearest Road A591

AA/RAC inspected farmhouse on dairy sheep farm. 10 minutes from Windermere and 5 minutes Kendal. A 15th century house with oak panelled lounge, 4ft thick walls. Separate tables in dining room for help yourself starters and choice of cooked breakfast. All bedrooms are en-suite with colour TV, tea making facilities and hairdryers. On the edge of the village-walk to inn, shops, public transport or on the footpaths or Dalesway. Good parking. An old house worth a visit. £57 winter 3 night breaks. No smoking. Cleanliness, comfort and a warm welcome awaits you. Credit cards accepted.

Sylvia Beaty
Tel/Fax: 01539 724542

B&B from £19pp, Rooms 5 double, 1 twin, 2 family, all en-suite, No smoking or pets, Children welcome, Open all year.

TRANTHWAITE HALL, Underbarrow, near Kendal, Cumbria LA8 8HG
Email tranthwaitehall@aol.com
Website www.tranthwaitehall.co.uk

Map Ref 10
Nearest Road A591, M6 jct 36

Getting on for a thousand years old now, this magnificent farmhouse shows many signs of its long history in the form of ancient woodwork and weathered stone. The evidence is most striking in the guest lounge, with its great oak beams and massive door with a huge inglenook fireplace. Richly furnished with lovely antiques, china and pretty en-suite bedrooms with TV, hairdryer, hostess tray and little extras for your comfort. After a good night sleep in the comfortable beds enjoy a scrumptious farmhouse-breakfast. Free range eggs and all local produce are used. Enjoy Doreen's home-made jam or marmalade. This 300 acre dairy and sheep farm is tucked away in beautiful south Lakeland between Kendal and Windermere.

Mrs D M Swindlehurst
Tel: 015395 68285

B&B from £22pp, Rooms 2 double, 1 twin, 1 family room, all en-suite, No smoking, Open all year.

WILLOW COTTAGE, Bassenthwaite, near Keswick, Cumbria CA12 4QP
Website www.willowbarncottage.co.uk

Map Ref 11
Nearest Road A591, A66, M6

We welcome guests to our tastefully converted barn where we have retained many original featured which combined with stencilling, patchwork and painted furniture gives a comfortable country atmosphere. Our bedrooms have tea trays, radios and are en-suite. We are no smoking and have no TV, but guests enjoy our books, music and games as they relax by the wood-stove or in the cottage garden (with views towards Skiddaw). Country lanes are beautiful with wild flowers and ducks roam by the stream. Come and try us.

Chris Beaty
Tel/Fax: 017687 76440

B&B from £22.50-£27pp, Rooms 1 double, 1 twin, both en-suite, No smoking or pets, Children over 12, Open February to end of November.

ING HILL LODGE, near Outhgill, Mallerstang Dale, Kirkby Stephen CA17 4JT
Email IngHill@FSBDial.co.uk

Map Ref 13
Nearest Road B6259, M6

Unwind in comfort at this small Georgian house in Mallerstang, a little known Dale on the fringe of the National Park. Superb views, quiet and peaceful for your preferred form of relaxation. Excellent en-suite shower rooms, comfortable bedrooms with Sealy beds (most are king-size). Colour TV and radio alarms. The 'Butlers Pantry' is popular for making tea and coffee at any time. You get to choose your own breakfast! Lounge with books, maps, open fire and central heating throughout. A warm welcome assured.

Tony Sawyer
Tel: 017683 71153
Fax: 017683 72710

B&B from £20-£25pp, Rooms 2 double, 1 twin, all en-suite, No smoking or children, Pets welcome, Open March to December & New Year.

NEAR HOWE FARM HOTEL, Mungrisdale, Penrith, Cumbria CA11 0SH
Email nearhowe@btopenworld.com
Website www.nearhowe.co.uk

Map Ref 14
Nearest Road A6, A66

A Cumbrian family home which is situated amidst 300 acres of moorland. Five of the 7 bedrooms have private facilities and all have tea/coffee making facilities. Meals are served in the comfortable dining room and great care is taken to produce good home cooking with every meal freshly prepared. Comfortable residents lounge with colour TV, games room, smaller lounge with well stocked bar and for the cooler evenings an open log fire. The surrounding area can provide many activities and past-times including golf, fishing, pony trekking, boating and walking. Commended 3 Crowns.

Mrs Christine Weightman
Tel: 017687 79678
Fax: 017687 79678

B&B from £20-£25pp, Dinner £10, Rooms 3 double, 3 family, 1 twin, Also cottages to let sleep up to 7, Dogs welcome, Open February to November.

CASTLEMONT, Aspatria, Wigton, Cumbria CA7 2JU
Email castlemont@tesco.net
Website www.tuckedup.com/castlemont.html

Map Ref 15
Nearest Road A596

Castlemont is a large Victorian family residence set in 2 acres of garden with unrestricted views of the Northern Lakeland fells and Solway Firth. Built of Lazonby stone, Castlemont combines the best of old world gracious living with the benefits of modern facilities. Start your day with a traditional English breakfast of an oak smoked kipper or perhaps a poached egg with haddock or ham. Loads of toast, butter, marmalade and homemade jam, pots of tea or coffee all made on the ever willing AGA. Credit cards accepted.

Eleanor & David Lines
Tel: 016973 20205

B&B from £20-£24pp, Rooms 1 double, 1 twin, 1 family, all en-suite, No smoking or pets, Children welcome, Open all year.

SWALEDALE WATCH, Whelpo, Caldbeck, Wigton, Cumbria CA7 8HQ

Map Ref 16
Nearest Road B5299

Swaledale Watch is a busy sheep farm just outside the picturesque village Caldbeck, situated within the Lake District National Park. Enjoy great comfort, excellent food, a warm welcome and peaceful unspoilt surroundings. Central for touring, walking or discovering the rolling Northern fells. All rooms have private facilities, are tastefully decorated, have colour TV, radio, tea-tray, clean fluffy towels daily and books for every interest in the lounges. Walk into Caldbeck via the Howk, a wooded limestone gorge, guaranteed to be memorable. Your happiness is our priority.

Arnold & Nan Savage
Tel/Fax: 016974 78409

B&B from £17pp, Dinner £11, Rooms 2 double, 2 family/twin, 1 double/twin, all private facilities, No smoking or pets, Children welcome, Open all year except Christmas Eve, Day & Boxing Day.

ORREST HEAD HOUSE, Kendal Road (A591), Windermere, Cumbria LA23 1JG
Email bjb@orrest.co.uk
Website www.orrest-head.co.uk

Map Ref 17
Nearest Road A591, M6 jct 36

Orrest Head House is a charming country house dating back to the 17th century. These are bedrooms are en-suite and comfortably furnished, with TVs, tea/coffee facilities and hairdryers. It is set in 3 acres of garden woodland. Only a 5 minute walk from the village of Windermere station and buses. Distant views to the lake. Private parking. A homely atmosphere and friendly welcome assured.

Brenda Butterworth
Tel/Fax: 015394 44315

B&B from £23-£30pp, Rooms 3 double, 2 twin, all en-suite, No smoking or pets, Children over 8, Open all year.

BRAEMOUNT HOUSE HOTEL, Sunny Bank Road, Windermere, Cumbria LA23 2EN
Email enquiries@braemount-house.co.uk
Website www.braemount-house.co.uk

Map Ref 2
Nearest Road A591

ETC 4 Diamonds. Our rooms, breakfast and hospitality are second to none. But don't just take our word for it....our guest book reads: 'Immaculate accommodation and lots of extras not normally available!' 'Lovely rooms, brilliant hospitality, yummy breakfast, we'll be back.' 'Excellent, especially breakfast in bed.' 'Simply the best.' And many more, why not come and read it? Call for a brochure or visit our website.

Janine & Duncan Hatfield
Tel/Fax: 015394 45967

B&B from £22pp, Rooms 1 twin, 2 double, 3 family, 3 four poster, all en-suite, Exclusively non smoking, Children & pets welcome, Open all year.

CUDDY'S HALL HOLIDAY COTTAGE, Bailey, Newcastleton, Roxburghshire
Email joannafurness@btopenworld.com
Website www.cuddys-hall.co.uk

Map Ref 18

Cumbrian/Scottish borders. Traditional family cottage, well maintained and equipped throughout. Set amidst beautiful forest and winding streams (part of Kielder Forest Park) abundant with wildlife. Superb forest walks/cycle routes, start right at the door. Private garden, patio and barbecue/lockable shed for cycles, fishing tackle etc. On the 'Reivers Cycle Route'. Bed linen, duvets, towels, electricity, central heating and a welcome food pack inclusive. Good base to explore - Hadrians Wall, the Lakes and Scotland. Pony trekking, fishing and golf nearby. Short breaks available.

1 cottage, sleeps up to 5, Price per week £200 to £300 (at peak times), No smoking, Children over 7, No pets, Available all year.

Contact: Mrs Joanna Furness, No. 2 Cuddy's Hall, Bailey, Newcastleton, Roxburghshire TD9 0TP
Tel/Fax: 016977 48160

Derbyshire & Staffordshire

Situated between Sheffield and Manchester to the east and west and the industrial towns of Yorkshire and the Midlands to the north and south, visitors could be forgiven for writing Derbyshire off as a mainly commuter county. Nothing, however, could be further from the truth as Derbyshire is home to the glorious Peak District, one of the most beautiful, wild and unspoilt areas of England.

Although the county also features the attractive towns of Derby and Chesterfield to the south, there is no doubt that it is the sprawling Peak District National Park that attracts nature lovers, walkers and tourists by the drove. Wild moorland, rolling hills, emerald fields, dry stone walls and picturesque villages are all here to be savoured and photographed – not to mention the Park's abundance of particularly fine country estates.

Small but perfectly formed is Eyam Hall, a small manor house situated in the famous plague village of Eyam. Home to the Wright family since 1671, it enjoys a wonderful ambience and features an impressive Jacobean staircase and fine tapestries. In complete architectural contrast, the celebrated country house of Chatsworth stands vast and imposing near the village of Bakewell. First built in 1552, this grand home of the Cavendish family has been remodelled and significantly added to over the centuries – while its 105 acre gardens have enjoyed the magical touches of both Lancelot Capability Brown and Sir Joseph Paxton.

Just south of Bakewell, Haddon Hall presents another imposing home, this time in unmistakable Tudor style. Although occupied until around 1703, the Hall actually lay deserted for 200 years and thus missed any of the architectural changes so popularly undertaken in the 18th and 19th centuries. The resulting house was therefore sympathetically restored in the 20th century to reflect its charming Tudor proportions – much to the delight of the many film producers who have used this splendid location since.

Travelling to the southern reaches of the Park and situated close to the border of Staffordshire, Tissington Hall is situated in a superbly maintained estate featuring a 10 acre garden and a fine arboretum. Home to the FitzHerbert family for over 500 years, the homely interiors include wonderful oak beams and panelling, a particularly handsome staircase and a notable collection of paintings.

Derbyshire's neighbouring county, Staffordshire, is possibly most famous for its many Potteries (porcelain factories which include Wedgwood and Royal Doulton) around Stoke-on-Trent, and the three-spired medieval cathedral in the attractive town of Lichfield. Staffordshire does, however, feature some fine rural retreats amid its more open countryside, most notably the neo-Jacobean Sandon Hall situated in the heart of the county; and Shugborough, the elegant 18th century home of the Earl of Lichfield on the outskirts of Stafford. Also well worth a visit is Little Moreton Hall near the village of Congleton, England's most spectacular black and white timbered house dating back to the 15th century and, within the same village, Biddulph Grange Garden – a beautifully restored High Victorian garden featuring Chinese and Egyptian influences and some quite delightful walks.

Derbyshire & Staffordshire

Mrs Sue Prince, Beechenhill Farm
Tel: 01335 310274
Map Ref 1 *see page 81*
Naomi Chambers & Nick Lourie, Stanshope Hall
Tel: 01335 310278
Map Ref 2 *see page 81*
Mrs Round, Jasmine Cottage
Tel: 01335 350465
Map Ref 3 *see page 81*
Mr J M Moffett, Biggin Hall
Tel: 01298 84451
Map Ref 4 *see page 82*
Mrs Hull-Bailey, Cressbrook Hall
Tel: 01298 871289
Map Ref 5 *see page 82*
Jane Gibbs, Wolfscote Grange
Tel: 01298 84342
Map Ref 6 *see page 82*
Philip & Vivienne Taylor, Underleigh House
Tel: 01433 621372
Map Ref 7 *see page 84*
Mr & Mrs Groom, Littlemoor Wood Farm
Tel: 01629 534302
Map Ref 8 *see page 84*
Mrs Anne Hodgson, The Hollies
Tel: 01782 503252
Map Ref 9 *see page 84*
Josie & Jim Little, Leehouse Farm
Tel: 01538 308439
Map Ref 10 *see page 85*
Ken & Evelyn Meredith, Bank End Cottages
Tel: 01782 502160
Map Ref 11 *see page 85*

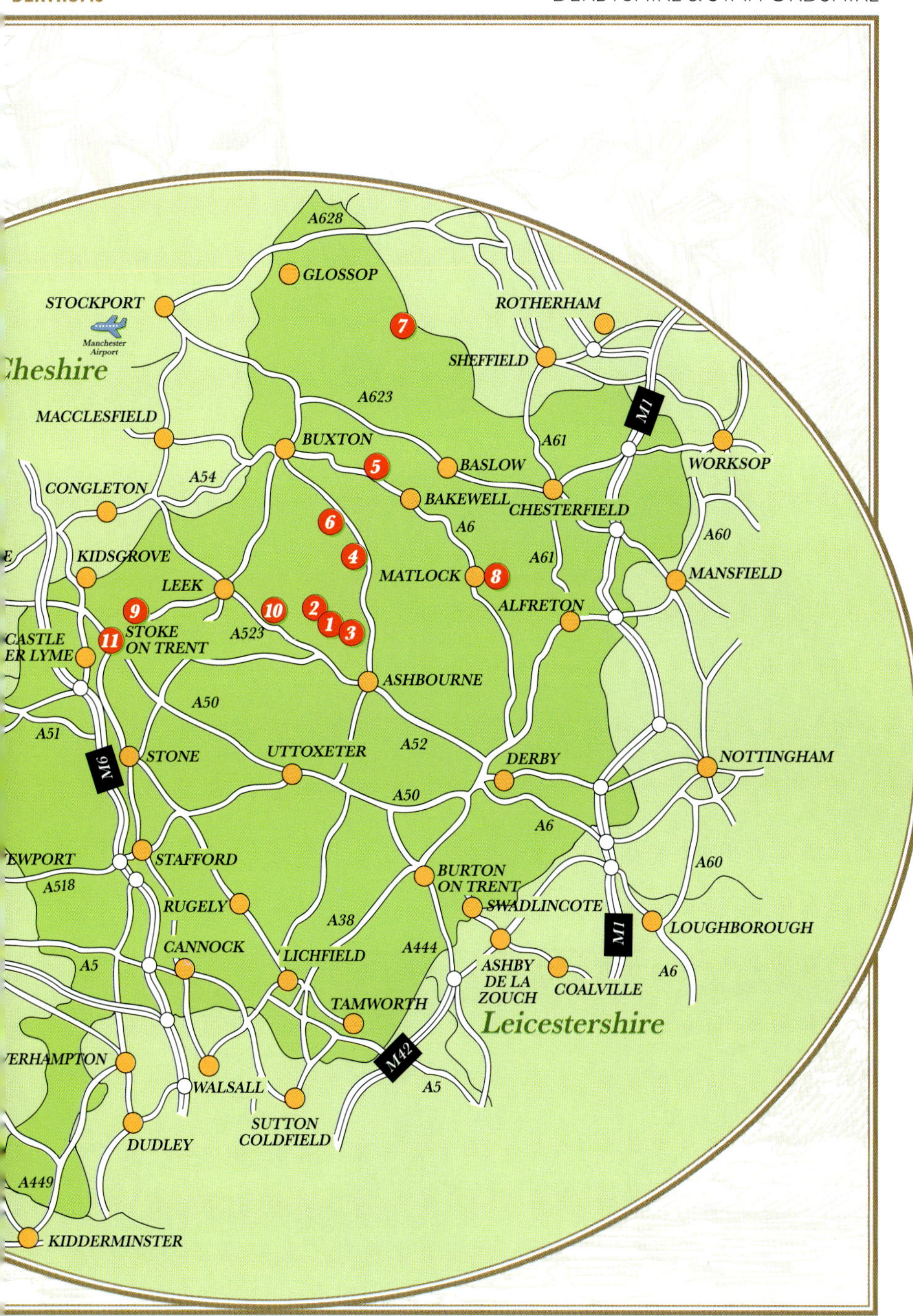
A628
GLOSSOP
STOCKPORT
Manchester Airport
ROTHERHAM
7
SHEFFIELD
Cheshire
A623
MACCLESFIELD
M1
BUXTON
A61
WORKSOP
5
BASLOW
A54
CONGLETON
BAKEWELL
CHESTERFIELD
6
A6
A60
4
A61
KIDSGROVE
MATLOCK
8
MANSFIELD
LEEK
ALFRETON
9
10
2
1
3
11
STOKE ON TRENT
CASTLE
ER LYME
A523
ASHBOURNE
A50
A51
A52
M6
STONE
UTTOXETER
DERBY
NOTTINGHAM
A50
A6
EWPORT
STAFFORD
BURTON ON TRENT
A60
A518
RUGELY
SWADLINCOTE
A38
M1
LOUGHBOROUGH
CANNOCK
LICHFIELD
A444
A5
ASHBY DE LA ZOUCH
COALVILLE
A6
TAMWORTH
Leicestershire
M42
ERHAMPTON
WALSALL
A5
SUTTON COLDFIELD
DUDLEY
A449
KIDDERMINSTER

BEECHENHILL FARM, Ilam Moor Lane, Ilam, Ashbourne, Derbyshire DE6 2BD
Email beechenhill@btinternet.com
Website www.beechenhill.co.uk

Map Ref 1
Nearest Road A515

Wake up to beautiful views over a country garden and the scent of fresh organic bread. We offer two delightful en-suite rooms, a double with a canopied bed, and a lovely family room in our ivy-clad farmhouse at our organic dairy farm. Local and organic foods are used in carefully cooked farmhouse breakfasts with famous porridge and homemade yoghurt. Beechenhill Farm is near Dovedale in the Peak District National Park with many walks from the door, including farm trail, Chatworth and attractions within easy reach.

Mrs Sue Prince
Tel: 01335 310274
Fax: 01335 310467

B&B from £26-£30pp, Rooms 1 double, 1 family, both en-suite, No smoking or pets, Children welcome, Open March to November.

STANSHOPE HALL, Stanshope, near Ashbourne, Derbyshire DE6 2AD
Email naomi@stanshope.demon.co.uk
Website www.stanshope.net

Map Ref 2

Stanshope Hall, dating from the 16th century, stands on the brow of a hill between the Manifold and Dovedale in the Peak District. The hall faces south across rolling landscape. Lovingly restored and retaining many of its original features. All bedrooms are en-suite with direct dial phone and tea/coffee making facilities. There is a guests' drawing room with piano and record player and local information table. Centrally heated throughout. Home cooked dinners with garden and local produce and a residents licence. Extensive breakfast menu. Brochure available.

Full page photo opposite

Naomi Chambers & Nick Lourie
Tel: 01335 310278
Fax: 01335 310127

B&B from £30pp, Dinner £22, Rooms 1 twin with en-suite facilities, 2 en-suite double, Restricted smoking, Open all year except Christmas.

JASMINE COTTAGE, Thorpe, Ashbourne, Derbyshire DE6 2AW

Map Ref 3
Nearest Road A515, A52

Pretty detached stone cottage in own grounds, offers very comfortable accommodation for a maximum of four guests. Quiet village and lovely walks from the house. Ideally situated for exploring the many villages, market towns and stately homes of Derbyshire. The cottage is cosy and warm with beams, wood burner and full central heating. Excellent breakfasts. Good local pubs and restaurants in the area. A warm welcome is assured.

Mrs Round
Tel: 01335 350465

B&B from £20-£25pp, Dinner £12.50, Rooms 1 double en-suite, 1 twin, No smoking or pets, Children over 12, Open all year except Christmas & New Year.

Full page photo opposite

BIGGIN HALL, Biggin-by-Hartington, Buxton, Derbyshire SK17 0DH
Email enquiries@bigginhall.co.uk

Map Ref 4
Nearest Road A515

Beautifully restored, this stone built house dating from the 17th century, set 1,000 feet up in the Peak District National Park, is delightful in every way. Antiques, a log fire, a 4 poster bed give this home a wealth of charm. The food is outstanding with the owners priding themselves on the use of only the freshest and best produce available. The home baked bread is excellent! Perfect in every way. Easy access to the Spa town of Buxton, Chatsworth House, Haddon Hall, etc. Beautiful uncrowded footpaths from the grounds.

Mr J M Moffett
Tel: 01298 84451

B&B from £21pp, Dinner £15.50, Winter Breaks, Children over 12, Pets in annexe by arrangement, Open all year.

CRESSBROOK HALL, Cressbrook, near Buxton, Derbyshire SK17 8SY
Email stay@cressbrookhall.co.uk
Website www.cressbrookhall.co.uk

Map Ref 5
Nearest Road A623, A6

Perched high on the south face of the Wye Valley adjoining Monsal Dale and with spectacular views around the compass, historic Cressbrook Hall is an impressive family residence. Surrounded by seven holiday cottages in 30 acres. The perfect base to explore the Peaks. Elegant en-suite B&B is offered in the Hall, with cottages for families, corporate events, celebrations and wedding receptions in the recently restored orangery. For self catering or B&B try Cressbrook Hall. Credit cards accepted.

Mrs Hull-Bailey
Tel: 01298 871289
Fax 01298 871845

B&B from £37.50-£47.50pp, Dinner available £18.50, Rooms 1 double, 1 twin, 1 family, all en-suite, No smoking, Children welcome, Open all year.

WOLFSCOTE GRANGE, Hartington, near Buxton, Derbyshire SK17 0AX
Email wolfscote@btinternet.com
Website www.wolfscotegrangecottages.co.uk

Map Ref 6
Nearest Road B5054, A515

A more beautiful setting would be hard to find, Wolfscote Grange set beside the Dove Valley with stunning scenery. The farmhouse steeped in history dates back to the Doomsday book and is full of fine oak. The lounge and well appointed bedrooms have views of the hills enveloping the valley. Separate dining room with antique fireplace and oak mullioned window seat. Pretty bedrooms, with en-suite and tea/coffee facilities, fresh linen/towels; warm welcome; freedom to roam miles of unspoilt walks and central to Peak District attractions.

Jane Gibbs
Tel/Fax: 01298 84342

B&B from £27-£30pp, Rooms 2 double, 1 twin, 1 family, all en-suite, No smoking or pets, Children welcome, Open all year except Christmas & New Year.

UNDERLEIGH HOUSE, off Edale Road, Hope, Hope Valley, Derbyshire S33 6RF
Email Underleigh.House@btinternet.com
Website www.underleighhouse.co.uk

Map Ref 7
Nearest Road A6187

Set in an idyllic and peaceful location amidst glorious scenery, this extended cottage and barn conversion (dating from 1873) is the perfect base for exploring the Peak District. Nestling under Lose Hill, Underleigh is in the heart of magnificent walking country. Each of the 6 en-suite rooms is furnished to a high standard with many thoughtful extras included. Delicious breakfasts in the flagstoned dining hall feature local and home-made specialities. The beamed lounge, with a log fire on chilly evenings, is the perfect place to relax after a delightful day in the Peak National Park.

Philip & Vivienne Taylor
Tel: 01433 621372
Fax: 01433 621324

B&B from £34.50pp, Rooms 1 twin, 4 double, 1 suite, all en-suite, No smoking or pets, Children over 12, Open all year except Christmas & New Year.

LITTLEMOOR WOOD FARM, Littlemoor Lane, Riber, near Matlock, Derbyshire DE4 5JS
Email gillygroom@ntlworld.com
Website www.derbyshireheaven.co.uk

Map Ref 8
Nearest Road A6, A615

This peaceful and informal farmhouse lies at the edge of the Derbyshire Dales and the Peak Park. Set among 20 acres of meadows with wonderful open views it is the perfect place to unwind. Rooms are attractive and comfortable with TV and tea/coffee trays. We provide hearty breakfasts including home-produced bacon and sausages, and cater for vegetarian and special diets. Many stately homes including Chatsworth House and other popular places of interest are nearby. Ashbourne, Bakewell and M1 Junction 28 all within 20 minutes. VISA/Mastercard.

Simon & Gilly Groom
Tel: 01629 534302
Fax: 01629 534008

B&B from £25pp, Rooms 1 double/twin, 1 double both with private facilities, No smoking, Children over 8, Open all year except Christmas & New Year.

THE HOLLIES, Clay Lake, Endon, Stoke-on-Trent, Staffordshire ST9 9DD

Map Ref 9
Nearest Road A53, B5051

A warm welcome awaits you in this Victorian house which has been sympathetically developed to its present comfortable standard. Situated in a quiet country setting in Endon and within easy reach of The Potteries, Staffordshire Moorlands and Alton Towers. Bedrooms are spacious, comfortable and have central heating, shaver points, colour TV and tea/coffee making facilities. The dining room overlooks a secluded garden. There is a choice of breakfast and home made preserves. Private parking.

Mrs Anne Hodgson
Tel: 01782 503252

B&B from £20pp, Rooms 5 en-suite, double, twin or family, No smoking, Open all year.

LEEHOUSE FARM, Leek Road, Waterhouses, Stoke-on-Trent, Staffordshire ST10 3HW

Map Ref 10

Josie and Jim welcome you to their lovely Georgian farmhouse, providing excellent accommodation in the centre of a village in the Peak Park. Ideally situated for cycling, walking or touring the beautiful valleys of the Manifold Dove and Churret. Convenient for visiting Stately Homes, Alton Towers and the potteries. The business traveller will find it well situated on the A523. Midway between Derby, Manchester. Our spacious bedrooms are centrally heated with TV and tea/coffee making facilities. Private parking and secure parking for bicycles. ETC 4 Diamonds Silver Award.

B&B from £20pp, Rooms 1 twin, 2 double, all en-suite, Restricted smoking, Children over 8, Pets by prior arrangement, Open all year except Christmas Day.

Josie & Jim Little
Tel: 01538 308439

BANK END COTTAGES, Stoke-on-Trent, Staffordshire
Email pjmeredith@btinternet.com

Map Ref 11

Two warm welcoming stone cottages set in pleasant countryside. Each sleeping 5 to 6 in family room with double and single bed, and twin room, with 2 extra put-up beds downstairs. Ample parking, garden. Fully equipped including colour TV, microwave and washing machine. Children welcome. Ideal for visiting the potteries, Peak District and Alton Towers. Village amenities, country pubs and takeaways five minutes' walk away. Owner managed.

2 cottages, sleeps 5-6, Price per week from £215 low season, £280 high season (linen included), Children welcome, Pets by arrangement, Available all year.

Contact: Ken & Evelyn Meredith, Bank End Farm, Hammond Avenue, Brown Edge, Stoke-on-Trent, Staffordshire ST6 8QU
Tel: 01782 502160

"Over the Menai Bridge" said Belle, map reading, "and on to Anglesey, now where is Rhosneigt and our bed and breakfast?"

BELLE & BERTIE IN WALES

DEVON

Boasting the much-visited English Riviera towns of Torquay, Paignton and Brixham along its impressive coastline, Devon is one of Britain's most popular seaside holiday destinations - and also a county whose history is inextricably linked to the sea. It was from the mouth of the River Tamar at Plymouth that Sir Frances Drake first embarked to circumnavigate the globe in the Golden Hind in 1577, and then again eleven years later to successfully fend off the might of the Spanish Armada. In 1620 the Pilgrim Fathers set sail for America in the Mayflower and in 1768 one Captain James Cook set out from The Barbican in search of a southern continent. Drake, Raleigh and Frobisher were all reputed to live in Devon - yet there is certainly more to this area than fine beaches and unrivalled maritime heritage.

Two national parks are situated within the county - Exmoor in the north featuring England's highest cliffs and impressively undulating headland scenery – and Dartmoor, just a short drive from Exeter and encompassing some of Britain's wildest and bleakest terrain (so inspired was Arthur Conan Doyle by the eeriness of the place that he made it the setting for the Hound of the Baskervilles). Looming monuments to ancient man can be found on Dartmoor in the shape of Neolithic tombs such as Spinster's Rock and the ceremonial stone rows at

Drizzlecombe. In sharp contrast, Devon also delights with quaint thatched villages, serpentine lanes, high hedgerows and some of the most clement horticultural conditions to be found in the British Isles.

To the east of the county, Bicton Park Botanical Gardens at Budleigh Salterton are situated in the picturesque Otter Valley and house one of the country's most comprehensive outdoor and indoor collections of trees, shrubs and flowers. Of particular interest in the 63-acre park are the axial style Italian ornamental garden and the stunning high-domed Palm House – arguably one of the world's most beautiful garden buildings. Moving north, Garden Rosemoor in Great Torrington - formerly owned by Lady Anne Berry - is home to spectacular examples of established West Country roses as well as many new Mediterranean plantings. Hartland Abbey, Bideford is also well worth a visit, featuring recently discovered Victorian fernery, fine woodland walks and exquisite murals within its Augustinian interior.

Buckland Abbey, Yelverton, dating from the 13th century, was once home to Sir Francis Drake and now stands as a fascinating testimony to the great man's life. Highlights include Drake's ghostly drum, the decorated plaster ceiling in the Tudor Drake Chamber and a fine new Elizabethan garden within the grounds.

If the clean lines of Georgian architecture appeal, don't leave the Plymouth area without visiting Puslinch at Yelampton. Built in 1720 by the Yonge family in the Queen Anne tradition, this stunning home features contemporary-style interiors that are still enthusiastically embraced by architects and builders today.

The city of Exeter was founded by the Romans in 50 AD and many fine examples of stately residences can be found around this historic hub of the West Country. Powderham Castle is situated on the River Exe just eight miles from Exeter and dates in part from the 14th century. The gardens and grounds include a terraced Rose Garden, an ancient and currently stocked deer park, a Victorian walled garden known as the Children's Secret Garden and the renowned Powderham Country Store. The castle itself is home to the Courtenay Family and features collections of French porcelain and Stuart and Regency furniture, along with fine examples of grand rococo ceilings. Also within the Exeter area, Bickleigh Castle offers 900 years of history for the visitor to ponder, as well as some extremely impressive Tudor furniture – and to experience a truly charming period country home set in commanding hillside gardens, Killerton House, Broadclyst remains beautiful throughout the year.

DEVON

Susan Grey, Wellpritton Farm
Tel: 01364 631273
Map Ref 1 *see page 90*

Jackie & Antony Payne, Huxtable Farm
Tel: 01598 760254
Map Ref 2 *see page 90*

Brenda & Colin Goode, Lufflands
Tel: 01395 568422
Map Ref 3 *see page 90*

Tim Daniel, Parford Well
Tel: 01647 433353
Map Ref 4 *see page 93*

Caroline & Douglas Pye,
The Barn - Rodgemonts
Tel: 01769 580200
Map Ref 5 *see page 93*

Mrs Jackie Bolt, Wood Barton
Tel: 01395 233407
Map Ref 6 *see page 93*

Mrs Nova Easterbrook, Drakes Farm House
Tel: 01392 256814 & 495564
Map Ref 7 *see page 94*

Katie Bunn, Whitstone Farm
Tel: 01626 832258
Map Ref 8 *see page 94*

Janice Wiemeyer, The Thatched Cottage
Tel: 01626 365650
Map Ref 9 *see page 94*

Mrs Mandy Tooze, Elberry Farm
Tel: 01803 842939
Map Ref 10 *see page 95*

John & Penny Adie,Barkham
Tel: 01643 831370
Map Ref 11 *see page 95*

Hilary Tucker ,Beera Farm
Tel: 01822 870216
Map Ref 12 *see page 95*

Jennifer & Michael Britton, Virginia Cottage
Tel: 01626 872634
Map Ref 13 *see page 96*

RSH Cochrane, Bickleigh Cottage Hotel
Tel: 01884 855230
Map Ref 14 *see page 96*

Mrs Sylvia Hann, Great Bradley Farm
Tel: 01884 256946
Map Ref 15 *see page 96*

Leon Butler, Lanscombe House Hotel
Tel: 01803 606938
Map Ref 16 *see page 98*

David Miller & Christine Hillier,
The Old Forge at Totnes
Tel: 01803 862174
Map Ref 17 *see page 98*

Helen Baker,
Higher Torr Farm
Tel: 01548 521248
Map Ref 18
see page 98

Mrs Steer, Preston Farm
Tel: 01803 862235
Map Ref 19 *see page 99*

Mrs Sylvia Hamm,
Cider Cottage
Tel: 01884 256946
Map Ref 15 *see page 99*

ILFRACOMBE
LYNTON
MINEHEAD
WATCHET
A39
A361
SIMONSBATH
A39
A396
A358
BARNSTAPLE
B3223
Somerset
SOUTH MOLTON
BIDEFORD
A361
B3227
B3227
TAUNTON
GREAT TORRINGTON
BAMPTON
A361
A377
TIVERTON
M5
A386
ILMINSTER
A3072
HATHERLEIGH
COPPLESTONE
CULLOMPTON
A373
A30
CHARD
A3072
CREDITON
HONITON
A30
A35
Dorset
A30
EXETER
A3052
LYME REGIS
SIDMOUTH
A386
EXMOUTH
TAVISTOCK
TEIGNMOUTH
NEWTON ABBOT
A386
TOTNES
TORQUAY
PLYMOUTH
A38
BRIXHAM
A379
DARTMOUTH
A379
KINGSBRIDGE
SALCOMBE
1
2
3
4
5
6
7
8
9
10
11
12
13
14
15
16
17
18
19

WELLPRITTON FARM, Holne, Ashburton, Devon TQ13 7RX
Email info@wellprittonfarm.com
Website www.wellprittonfarm.com

Map Ref 1
Nearest Road A38

Relax in a lovely Dartmoor farmhouse with lovely views set in the heart of the countryside, yet only half an hour to Exeter/Plymouth/Torbay. Mouth watering food and Devonshire cream every day as featured in the West country Good Food Guide 2002. Most rooms en-suite. Tea/coffee facilities. Satellite TV in all rooms. Central heating. Original character residents lounge. Garden. Pet goats, horses, dogs and chickens. Most country pursuits nearby. ETB 4 Crowns Highly Recommended.

Susan Grey
Tel: 01364 631273

B&B from £22.50pp, Dinner £15, Rooms 2 twin, 1 double, 2 family, all en-suite or private bathrooms, No smoking, Open all year.

HUXTABLE FARM, West Buckland, Barnstaple, Devon EX32 0SR
Email tu@huxtablefarm.co.uk
Website www.huxtablefarm.co.uk

Map Ref 2
Nearest Road A361

Full page photo opposite

Enjoy a memorable candlelit dinner of farm/local produce with a complimentary glass of homemade wine in this wonderful mediaeval (1520) Devon longhouse. With modern facilities Huxtable still retains such delights as original oak panelling, beams and bread ovens. A secluded sheep farm with abundant wildlife and panoramic views ideally situated for exploring Exmoor National Park and North Devon's dramatic coastline. There is a tennis court, sauna, farm/wildlife trail, fitness and games room and log fires to be enjoyed in winter. A cream tea awaits you. Credit cards accepted.

Jackie & Antony Payne
Tel/Fax: 01598 760254

B&B from £25-£35pp, Rooms 3 double, 1 twin, 2 family, No smoking or pets, Children welcome, Open February to November & New Year.

LUFFLANDS, Yettington, Budleigh Salterton, Devon EX9 7BP
Email stay@lufflands.co.uk
Website www.lufflands.co.uk

Map Ref 3
Nearest Road B3180

A warm welcome and friendly atmosphere can be found at Lufflands, a 17th century former farmhouse set in the hamlet of Yettington, three miles from the sea at Budleigh Salterton. It is ideal for a relaxing break with excellent walking nearby or as a location for touring with easy access to Exeter and the M5. All rooms are equipped to a very high standard. Your breakfast is freshly cooked to order and served in the original farmhouse kitchen. Off street parking. ETC/AA 4 Diamonds, Silver Award.

Brenda & Colin Goode
Tel: 01395 568422
Fax: 01395 568810

B&B from £24pp, Rooms 1 single, 1 double, 1 family, all en-suite/private facilities, No smoking, Children welcome, Pets restricted, Open all year.

PARFORD WELL, Sandy Park, Chagford, Devon TQ13 8JW

Map Ref 4
Nearest Road A30, A382

Parford Well. A comfortable house set in a walled garden within the Dartmoor National Park. There are wonderful walks on the doorstep both in the wooded valley of the River Teign and on the open moor yet it is only 3 miles from the A30. It's the ideal place for a few days break if you want to "get away from it all", relax and be well looked after. Parford Well is AA 5 Diamond placing it in their Premier collection.

Tim Daniel
Tel: 01647 433353

B&B from £27.50-£37.50pp, Rooms 2 double, 1 twin, all en-suite, No smoking or pets, Children over 8, Open all year except Christmas & New Year.

THE BARN - RODGEMONTS, Chawleigh, Chulmleigh, Devon EX18 7ET
Email pyerodgemonts@btinternet.com

Map Ref 5
Nearest Road A377, B3042

Rodgemonts - a 17th century thatched property overlooking the little Dart Valley, lies within an 'island' of fields and woods, bordered by typical Devon lanes. The converted barn offers, peace, tranquility and complete privacy. Come and go as you please with your own key to the comfortable and attractive accommodation with balcony overlooking woods and farmland. We welcome you into our adjoining thatched cottage for delicious breakfast including home produced apple juice, soft fruit and preserves. AA 4 Diamonds.

Caroline & Douglas Pye
Tel: 01769 580200

B&B from £20-£24pp, Dinner by arrangement £12, Rooms 1 double, 1 twin, both en-suite, No smoking, Open all year.

WOOD BARTON, Farringdon, Exeter, Devon EX5 2HY
Email jackie_bolt@hotmail.com
Website www.smoothhound.co.uk/hotels/woodbar.html

Map Ref 6
Nearest Road A3052, M5 jct 30

Wood Barton is a 17th century farmhouse in quiet countryside, yet only 3 miles from the M5 junction 30. An excellent traditional English breakfast is served cooked on an Aga. Spacious en-suite bedrooms with central heating, hospitality trays, colour TV's and radios. Within 6 miles are the city of Exeter, sandy beaches, National Trust houses and golf course. Good local eating places. Easy access.

Mrs Jackie Bolt
Tel: 01395 233407
Fax: 01395 227 226

B&B from £21pp, Rooms 1 twin, 1 double, 1 family, all en-suite, No smoking, Children welcome, No pets, Open all year except Christmas & New Year.

DRAKES FARM HOUSE, Drakes Farm, Ide, near Exeter, Devon EX2 9RQ
Email drakesfarm@hotmail.com
Website www.drakesfarm.fsnet.co.uk

Map Ref 7
Nearest Road A30, B3212

Drakes Farm House is a listed old oak beamed house with full central heating set in a large garden in the centre of quiet village, with a listed public house and one of the longest road fords in the country. Situated just 2 miles from M5 and cathedral city of Exeter. Convenient for coast and moors. Two pubs and two restaurants within 5 minutes easy walking distance. Separate TV lounge for guests. Laundry facilities. Minimum 2 nights. Tea/coffee, TV, in all rooms. Ample off street private parking. VISA and Mastercard accepted.

Mrs Nova Easterbrook
Tel: 01392 256814 & 495564
Fax: 01392 495564

B&B from £20-£22.50pp, Rooms 1 twin en-suite, 2 double, 1 en-suite, 1 family en suite, No smoking, Children welcome, No pets, Open all year.

WHITSTONE FARM, Bovey Tracey, Newton Abbot, Devon TQ13 9NA
Email katie@reynolds2000.co.uk
Website www.whitstonefarm.co.uk

Map Ref 8
Nearest Road A38, A382

A truly great place to stay! A warm welcome awaits you at this lovingly restored house overlooking Dartmoor. Offering luxurious en-suite bedrooms equipped with TV, hairdryer, tea/coffee etc, guests may enjoy the cosy guest lounge or our three acres of spectacular garden. Choice of breakfasts and special diets catered for. Ideally situated for all parts of Devon from coasts to moors, with wonderful gardens, walking, National Trust properties all nearby. Come and be pampered and unwind in this relaxing home. Special rates longer stays.

Katie Bunn
Tel: 01626 832258
Fax: 01626 836494

B&B from £27.50-£32.50pp, Dinner by prior arrangement £18, Rooms 2 double, 1 twin, all en-suite, No smoking or pets, Children over 15, Open all year except Christmas.

THE THATCHED COTTAGE, 9 Crossley Moor Road, Kingsteignton, Newton Abbot, Devon TQ12 3LE
Email bestthatch-janice@fsmail.net

Map Ref 9
Nearest Road A38, A380

A charming 16th century thatched longhouse situated in the ancient heart of England's largest village. Our rooms are nicely furnished and have central heating, colour TVs and tea/coffee trays. You can dine in our superb restaurant where local produce, some home grown, is prepared to your order, and served with care. Ideal base to travel from - just ten minutes away from the coast down the Teign Estuary or up the river to Dartmoor. Exeter is only 15 minutes and Plymouth 45 minutes away. Credit cards accepted.

Janice Wiemeyer
Tel: 01626 365650

B&B from £25pp, Dinner from £10, Rooms 1 single, 2 double/twin, all en-suite, No smoking or pets, Children welcome, Open all year.

ELBERRY FARM, Broadsands, Paignton, Devon TQ4 6HJ
Email tooze_elberryfarm@fsmail.net
Website www.elberryfarm.co.uk

Map Ref 10
Nearest Road A3022

Elberry Farm is a working farm with beef, poultry and arable production. The farmhouse is between 2 beaches both within a 2 minute walk. Broadsands being a safe bathing beach has been awarded the European Blue Flag 1994. As an alternative there is a 9 hole pitch and putt golf course opposite; and a short drive away is the zoo, town centre and the National Park. The comfortable bedrooms all have tea/coffee making facilities. Guests are welcome to relax in the lounge; stroll around the secluded garden. Baby sitting available by arrangement.

Mrs Mandy Tooze
Tel: 01803 842939

B&B from £15.50pp, Dinner from £7.50, Rooms 1 twin, 2 double/family, 1 en-suite double, Restricted smoking, Pets by arrangement, Open January to November.

BARKHAM, Sandyway, South Molton, Devon EX36 3LU

Map Ref 11
Nearest Road A361

Tucked away in a hidden valley in the heart of the Exmoor National Park you can relax and enjoy the tranquillity of our licenced Georgian farmhouse. Dine by candlelight in the oak panelled dining room and then relax on the patio and watch the sun go down. In winter log fires in the drawing room and old paintings.

John & Penny Adie
Tel/Fax: 01643 831370

B&B from £23pp, Dinner £18, Rooms 1 twin, 2 double (1 en-suite), No smoking or pets, Children over 12, Open all year except Christmas.

BEERA FARM, Milton Abbot, Tavistock, Devon PL19 8PL
Email Hilary.Tucker@farming.co.uk
Website www.beera-farm.co.uk

Map Ref 12
Nearest Road B3362, A30

A warm friendly welcome awaits your arrival and a delicious home baked cream tea served in the lounge. We have three spacious en-suite rooms, all tastefully decorated and generously equipped, with colour TV, tea/coffee facilities with home made biscuits and many other little extras for your comfort and convenience. Beera provides excellent base for touring the west country with the famous Eden Project, The Lost Gardens of Heligan, north and south coasts, Dartmoor, National Trust properties all within easy reach. Credit cards accepted.

Hilary Tucker
Tel: 01822 870216

B&B from £23-£40pp, Dinner £14, Rooms 2 double, 1 twin, all en-suite, No smoking or pets, Children welcome, Open all year except Christmas & New Year.

VIRGINIA COTTAGE, Brook Lane, Shaldon, Teignmouth, Devon TQ14 0HL

Map Ref 13

Virginia Cottage is a Grade II listed 17th century house set within a peaceful, partly walled, garden offering a delightful and relaxing place to stay. The pretty bedrooms with en-suite/private facilities, and tea/coffee makers, overlook the gardens and there is an attractive sitting room with large inglenook fireplace. A short walk to the coastal village of Shaldon where good pubs and restaurants are to be found. This is an ideal location for walking or exploring the Dartmoor National Park, Cathedral city of Exeter and delights of Devon. Car parking in grounds.

Jennifer & Michael Britton
Tel: 01626 872634
Fax: 01626 872634

B&B from £25pp, Rooms 1 twin, 2 double, all en-suite or private bathroom, No smoking, Children over 12, No Pets, Open April to November.

BICKLEIGH COTTAGE HOTEL, Bickleigh Bridge, Tiverton, Devon EX16 8RS

Map Ref 14
Nearest Road A396, M5

Full page photo opposite

Situated on the bank of the River Exe, near Bickleigh Bridge, a famous beauty spot. Bickleigh Cottage owned by the Cochrane family since 1933. We offer en-suite cottage style bedrooms in a pleasant surrounding in the centre of Devon, the whole of the country being reachable on half or one day tours. From here there are pub and restaurants facilities available within 100 yards in the evening. Credit cards accepted.

RSH Cochrane
Tel: 01884 855230

B&B from £25-£30pp, Rooms 1 single, 2 double, 2 twin, all en-suite, Restricted smoking, Children over 12, No pets, Open April to October.

GREAT BRADLEY FARM, Withleigh, Tiverton, Devon EX16 8JL
Email hann@agriplus.net
Website www.smoothhound.co.uk/hotels/grbrad.html

Map Ref 15
Nearest Road M5 jct 27, B3137

Lovely 16th century farmhouse overlooking the gentle hills of Devon. Offering rest and relaxation in peaceful surroundings. Guests lounge with wonderful views, books, television and local information. The comfortable bedrooms are centrally heated and have private bathrooms. Extensive breakfast menu including local produce and our own free-range eggs. Special diets catered for. Lovely gardens and farm walk. Exmoor and National Trust properties within easy reach. Safe parking. Sorry no pets or smoking. ETC 4 Diamonds, Silver Award.

Mrs Sylvia Hann
Tel/Fax: 01884 256946

B&B from £24-£28pp, Rooms 1 single, 1 double, 1 twin, all with private bathroom, No smoking, children or pets, Open April to October.

LANSCOMBE HOUSE HOTEL, Cockington Village, Torquay, Devon TQ2 6XA
Email Enquiries@LanscombeHouse.co.uk
Website www.LanscombeHouse.co.uk

Map Ref 16
Nearest Road A359

A small, friendly run hotel located within the preserved village of Cockington; offering a relaxed, country house atmosphere and providing you with a comfortable and enjoyable stay in a rural location, close to sea and centre of Torquay but 'a world apart'. The six en-suite bedrooms have all those modern conveniences you expect and most rooms overlook the beautiful walled gardens. Enjoy a complimentary cream tea - the famous Devon speciality with hand made jam, clotted cream and home made scones from our traditional tearooms. Credit cards accepted.

Leon Butler
Tel: 01803 606938

B&B from £27.50-£42.50pp, Rooms 4 double, 1 twin, 1 family, all en-suite, No smoking or pets, Children over 12, Open all year except Christmas & New Year.

THE OLD FORGE AT TOTNES, Seymour Place, Totnes, Devon TQ9 5AY
Email enq@oldforgetotnes.com
Website www.oldforgetotnes.com

Map Ref 17
Nearest Road A38, A384, A381

A warm welcome is assured at this 600 years old creeper clad building with cobbled drive and coach arch leading to delightful walled garden. Rooms are newly refurbished with all amenities. Quiet, peaceful yet only 4 minutes walk from town centre and riverside. Extensive breakfast menu including vegetarian. Conservatory lounge with whirlpool spa. Licensed with meals by prior arrangement. No smoking indoors. Good golfing area and excellent base for visiting beaches, Dartmoor, Torbay, Eden Project (1 ½ hours drive). Featured on BBC TV "Holiday" programme. Visit the Blacksmiths Prison Cell. Credit cards accepted.

David Miller & Christine Hillier
Tel: 01803 862174
Fax: 01803 865385

B&B from £27-£39pp, Dinner by prior arrangement, Rooms 6 double, 2 twin, 2 family, all en-suite, No smoking, Children welcome, Open all year.

HIGHER TORR FARM, East Allington, Totnes, Devon TQ9 7QH
Email helen@hrtorr.freeserve.co.uk

Map Ref 18
Nearest Road A381

Relax and unwind in a spacious old farmhouse, set in the South Devon hills, with panoramic views of Dartmoor. Central for Salcombe, and Dartmouth, the sandy beaches and coastal walkways. Higher Torr is ideal for that long weekend or short mid-week break you have been looking to take! Guests can enjoy the farm walks and neighbouring bridle paths plus horse riding nearby. On the cooler evenings the log fire is lit for guests' comfort. Traditional farmhouse accommodation with choice of breakfast.

Helen Baker
Tel/Fax: 01548 521248

B&B from £20-£22pp, Rooms 1 double, 1 twin, 1 family, all en-suite, Children welcome, Open all year except Christmas & New Year.

PRESTON FARM, Harberton, Totnes, Devon TQ9 7SW

Map Ref 19
Nearest Road A381

A warm welcome and excellent food awaits you at this 300 year old farmhouse, situated in the heart of an unspoilt village, with Egon Ronay Inn, just south of Totnes, close to coast and moors. Generous English breakfasts are served from help-yourself platters in the cosy, beamed dining room. Relax in the large, attractive sitting room, with a woodburners for those chilly evenings. Bedrooms are spacious and beautifully furnished, with big beds. They have beverage trays, TV, central heating and good sized bathrooms.

Mrs Steer
Tel: 01803 862235
Fax: 01803 847933

B&B from £21-£25pp, Dinner by prior arrangement £15, Rooms 3 double, all en-suite, No smoking or pets, Children welcome, Open all year except Christmas & New Year.

CIDER COTTAGE, Great Bradley Farm, Withleigh, Tiverton, Devon
Email hann@agriplus.net
Website www.cider-cottage.co.uk

Map Ref 15

Charming cottage, originally a 17th century cider barn, providing every comfort for a happy farm holiday. Wonderful views over peaceful countryside, dotted with sheep and cows. Friendly hosts. Good pubs nearby. Wildlife, birds and wildflowers on your doorstep. Microwave and dishwasher to make life easy. Children welcome and safe parking. Beaches and moors within an hour. Local antique and craft markets. ETC 4 Stars. Highly Recommended.

1 cottage, sleeps 5+cot, Price per week from £180 low season, £425 high season, No smoking, Children welcome, No pets, Available all year.

Contact: Sylvia Hamm, Great Bradley Farm, Withleigh, Tiverton, Devon EX16 8JL
Tel/Fax: 01884 256946

"My goodness, that was quite a breakfast" said Bertie, next morning
"You'll need some stamina for all those castles" replied Mrs Thomas

BELLE & BERTIE IN WALES

DORSET

Arguably one of the most beautiful counties in England, Dorset has been a jewel in the country's crown since Roman Times. Priding itself in being able to offer the visitor 'the best of both worlds', Dorset has a varied topography that includes magnificent beaches, rolling hills, secluded valleys and extensive heathland. Its award winning heritage coastline offers some of the most dramatic coastal walking in the British Isles while, inland, views of up to seven surrounding counties can be enjoyed from Bulbarrow – a huge ridge of chalk at Dorset's heart. To the west, quaint, sleepy villages proliferate, many lying hidden in quiet valleys yet hiding a wealth of history and character – perhaps the most notable being Cerne Abbas where the famous 180-foot Cerne Giant can be found cut into the chalk downs and towering above the 15th century village.

Dorset also enjoys great literary connections, being a favourite haunt of Jane Austen and home to William Barnes and Thomas Hardy – Dorset's most famous son. Rural Dorset provided the inspiration for many of Hardy's novels, and it was his hometown of Dorchester that Hardy immortalized in The Mayor of Casterbridge. Literary enthusiasts still flock by the thousand to see the local settings for the great author's books and to pay homage at Max Gate – home to Hardy from 1885 to 1928 and where many of his

great works were penned.
Although Hardy helped to put the Roman town of Dorchester on the map, the town itself is steeped in history and its environs include some exquisite stately homes and gardens – a particularly fine specimen being Wolfeton House. Set amid water-meadows and dating back to the 15th century, this manor house was much embellished in the Elizabethan era and includes an impressive great hall, splendid plaster ceilings and an interesting gatehouse. Athelhampton House, another fine example of 15th century building in the area, is surrounded by one of the great architectural gardens of England and contains the world-renowned topiary pyramids. Equally impressive but in marked contrast, the informal Minterne Gardens at Minterne Magna offer visitors 20 wild acres of cascading valley garden to explore, where magnolias, rhododendron, water lilies and rare trees thrive in abundance.
To the north east of Dorchester and two miles north of Wimborne Minster, the grand 17th century home of Kingston Lacy also enjoys a relaxed wooded location offering waymarked walks and an Iron Age fort within its estate grounds. The house itself, which was radically altered by Sir Charles Barry in the 19th century, contains an outstanding collection of paintings and artefacts accumulated by William Bankes and a dramatic Spanish Room – the walls of which are hung in magnificent gilded leather.
Moving north, Sandford Orcas Manor House near Sherborne is a real Tudor find. Set in charming terraced gardens, complete with a topiary and delightfully fragranced herb beds, the house offers some fine examples of furniture, pictures and panelling from the period. Equally charming, and certainly not to missed during a visit to the county's western region, Mapperton manor house in Beaminster not only boasts fine Tudor features but also enjoys one of the finest situations in Dorset. Infact, so breathtaking is the setting of the formal Italianate upper garden descending to fish ponds and beyond to a vista of woods and hills that Mapperton was chosen as the location for the film Emma. Local girl Jane Austen would have undoubtedly approved.

DORSET

Mr Hardy, Britmead House
Tel: 01308 422941
Map Ref 1 *see page105*

Anita & Anore Millorit, Brambles
Tel: 01935 83672
Map Ref 2 *see page 105*

Mr & Mrs O B N Paine, Muston Manor
Tel: 01305 848242
Map Ref 4 *see page 105*

Michael & Jane Deller ,
Churchview Guest House
Tel: 01305 889296
Map Ref 5 *see page 106*

Jorgen Kunatha & Anthony Ma,
The Old Vicarage
Tel: 01963 251117
Map Ref 6 *see page 106*

Jill & Ken Hookham-Bassett, Stourcastle Lodge
Tel: 01258 472320
Map Ref 7 *see page106*

Nicky Willis, Lamperts Cottage
Tel: 01300 341659
Map Ref 8 *see page 109*

Sara Turnbull, Thornhill
Tel: 01202 889434
Map Ref 9 *see page 109*

Mrs Garvey, Primrose Cottage
Tel: 01300 341352
Map Ref 10 *see page 109*

MERE
WINCANTON
A303
Wiltshire
SHAFTESBURY
A30
B3081
A354
RBORNE
6
A3030
Hampshire
7
CRANBORNE
A357
A352
BLANDFORD
FORUM
B3078
RINGWOOD
A37
CERNE
ABBAS
8
A31
9
10
WIMBORNE
MINSTER
BERE
REGIS
A31
4
A35
A338
A35
A35
PUDDLETOWN
5
POOLE
DORCHESTER
BOURNEMOUTH
WAREHAM
A352
33157
A353
CORFE CASTLE
A351
SWANAGE
WEYMOUTH
FORTUNEWELL
BILL OF
PORTLAND

BRITMEAD HOUSE, 154 West Bay Road, Bridport, Dorset DT6 4EG
Email britmead@talk21.com
Website www.britmeadhouse.co.uk

Map Ref 1
Nearest Road A35, M5

An elegant Edwardian house situated just off the A35 between the historic market town of Bridport and the harbour at West Bay, the ideal location for exploring the beautiful Dorset countryside. We offer family run comfortable en-suite accommodation with many thoughtful extras. 10 minutes walk to the harbour, beaches, golf courses and the Dorset coast path, now part of the World Heritage Coast Site. Spacious rooms, south facing dining room and lounge, private parking. AA and ETC 4 Diamond guest accommodation. Credit cards accepted.

Mr Hardy
Tel: 01308 422941
Fax: 01308 422516

B&B from £24-£44pp, Rooms 3 double, 2 twin, 2 family, all en-suite, Restricted smoking, Children & pets welcome, Open all year.

BRAMBLES, Woolcombe, Melbury Bubb, near, Dorchester Dorset DT2 0NJ

Map Ref 2
Nearest Road A37

A warm welcome awaits you in this delightful thatched cottage. Set in beautiful countryside, this centrally heated home offers every comfort. Bedrooms are traditionally pretty with old beams, fresh flowers, tea/coffee making facilities and colour television. You will enjoy a beautifully cooked breakfast of your choice in a sunny dining room with old beams and an inglenook fireplace where log fires crackle into life on chilly mornings. There are many places of interest to visit and lovely walks. Parking within grounds.

Anita & Anore Millorit
Tel: 01935 83672

B&B from £20-£28pp, Rooms 2 single, 1 en-suite double, 1 en-suite twin, No smoking or pets, Children welcome, Open all year except Christmas & New Year.

Full page photo opposite

MUSTON MANOR, Piddlehinton, Dorchester, Dorset DT2 7SY

Map Ref 4
Nearest Road B3143

Originally built in 1609 by the Churchill family, it remained in their ownership until bought by the present owners in 1975. Situated in the peaceful Piddle Valley with its many good pubs, the house is set in five acres, surrounded by farmland. Large comfortable, well furnished rooms with tea/coffee making facilities and central heating. Heated swimming pool in season.

Mr & Mrs O B N Paine
Tel: 01305 848242

B&B from £23pp, Rooms 2 double, 1 en suite, No smoking, Children over 10, Pets by arrangement, Open all year except Christmas.

Full page photo opposite

CHURCHVIEW GUEST HOUSE, Winterbourne Abbas, Dorchester, Dorset DT2 9LS
Email stay@churchview.co.uk
Website www.churchview.co.uk

Map Ref 5
Nearest Road A35

Our 17th century guest house noted for warm, friendly hospitality, traditional breakfasts and delicious evening meals, make an ideal base for exploring beautiful West Dorset. Our character bedrooms are comfortable, well appointed and include televisions and hospitality trays. Meals taken in our period dining room feature local produce, cream and cheeses. Relaxation is provided by two attractive lounges and licensed bar. Your hosts will give every assistance with local information on attractions, walks and touring to ensure you of a memorable stay. Credit cards accepted. 4 Diamonds ETC.

Michael & Jane Deller
Tel: 01305 889296

B&B from £30-£36pp, Dinner £12-£15, Rooms 1 single, 4 double, 3 twin, 1 family, all en-suite, No smoking, Children over 5, Pets welcome, Open all year except Christmas & New Year.

THE OLD VICARAGE, Sherborne Road, Milborne Port, Sherborne, Dorset DT9 5AT
Email theoldvicarage@milborneport.freeserve.co.uk
Website www.miborneport.freeserve.co.uk

Map Ref 6
Nearest Road A30

Situated at the edge of a charming village overlooking open country at the far side of the Sherborne Castle estate. The entire town of Sherborne has that olde world' feel and is well worth a visit, so are the many houses and gardens in the area. It's ideal for hiking, cycling, golf and walking. The Old Vicarage is spacious and elegantly furnished with antiques. On Friday and Saturday evenings the former owners of a highly acclaimed London restaurant serve delicious food - ask for sample menu. On other nights you can eat in an excellent pub restaurant, 200 yards from the Old Vicarage. Weekend breaks from £46pppn DB&B.

Jorgen Kunatha & Anthony Ma
Tel: 01963 251117
Fax: 01963 251515

B&B from £30pp, Dinner from £23, Rooms 2 double, 3 family, all en-suite, Restricted smoking, Children over 5, Pets restricted, Open February to December.

STOURCASTLE LODGE, Gough's Close, Sturminster Newton, Dorset DT10 1BU
Email enquiries@stourcastle-lodge.co.uk
Website www.stourcasle-lodge.co.uk

Map Ref 7
Nearest Road A357

Jill and Ken Hookham-Bassett have run Stourcastle Lodge for twenty years. They offer a very high standard of accommodation serving excellent food. The house, dating back from 17th century, looks on to the south facing garden, which has an abundance of herbaceous plants and shrubs making it an ideal place to relax in after a day visiting the outstanding countryside of Dorset. Credit Cards accepted.

Jill & Ken Hookham-Bassett
Tel: 01258 472320
Fax: 01258 473381

B&B from £33-£40pp, Dinner £20, Rooms 4 double, 1 twin, all en-suite, Restricted smoking, No children or pets, Open all year.

Churchview
GUEST
HOUSE
Licensed
VACANCIES
Church View
GUEST
HOUSE

LAMPERTS COTTAGE, Sydling St Nicholas, Dorset DT2 9NU
Email nickywillis@tesco.net

Map Ref 8
Nearest Road A37

Stay in idyllic 16th century thatched cottage in beautiful village. The cottage is bounded front and back by streams. Accommodation in three prettily furnished double/twin/family rooms with Dormer windows under the eaves. Breakfast is served in dining room, with its enormous inglenook fireplace, with bread oven and original beams. There is a comfortable sitting room for guests' use. Ideal touring area with coast 25 minutes by car. Walking superb. Perfect for those wishing peace and quiet. Excellent food at local pubs. Credit cards accepted.

Nicky Willis
Tel: 01300 341659
Fax: 01300 341699

B&B from £22pp, Rooms 2 double, 1 twin, 1 family/double, Children & pets welcome, Open all year.

THORNHILL, Holt, Wimborne, Dorset BH21 7DJ
Email scturnbull@lineone.net

Map Ref 9
Nearest Road A31, B3078

A thatched family home in a peaceful rural location. There is a large garden with a hard tennis court which may be used by guests. A twin, a double and a single room are available, together with two bathrooms, which can be for private use only. Tea/coffee making facilities are provided and there is a sitting room with colour TV. The New Forest, Dorset coast and Salisbury area are all within easy reach as are plenty of local pubs for meals. Ample parking.

Sara Turnbull
Tel: 01202 889434

B&B from £23-£25pp, Rooms 1 single, 1 double, 1 twin, 1 family, No smoking or pets, Children over 10, Open all year.

PRIMROSE COTTAGE, Milton Abbas, Dorset
Email tgarvey@ragtime99.freeserve.co.uk
Website www.miltonabbas-primrosecottage.co.uk

Map Ref 10

Primrose Cottage is one of the semi-detached cob and thatched houses that make up a unique village created around 1770 by Lord Milton and landscaped by Capability Brown. The cottage has everything you would expect from a Grade II listed building. The beamed sitting room, with Inglenook fireplace and wood stove. Low doors remind you of the buildings age but the 21st century has taken over everywhere else from a modern kitchen and bathroom to the 2 bedrooms.

1 cottage, sleeps 4-6, Price per week £195 low season, £445 high season, Children & pets welcome, Available all year.

Contact: Mrs Garvey, Brook Cottage, 1 Long Street, Cerne Abbas, Dorchester, Dorset DT2 7JF
Tel/Fax: 01300 341352

ESSEX

Situated on the south east coast of England, Essex is a large geographical county featuring an extensive coastline, fine arable land and considerable areas of woodland. It is also a county many people may unwittingly recognise thanks to one John Constable who drew inspiration from his local surroundings of Dedham in the 19th century to paint the romantic, bucolic landscapes we all know and love today. Essex is also home to Epping Forest and the ancient dwelling place of Colchester - founded by the emperor Claudius in AD 49 and once the capital of Roman Britain, it is now heralded as England's oldest recorded town. The villages of Thaxted and Saffron Walden also enjoy an ancient history dating back to medieval times, the latter – rather interestingly – taking its name from the saffron crocus which was prolifically cultivated in nearby fields.

Particularly prominent in the neihbourhood of Saffron Walden stands the Jacobean mansion of Audley End House, originally built in the 17th century for James I and a palace in all but name. King James didn't ever stay in the house, however, describing it as 'too big for a king', and it was Charles II who actually bought and made use of the property from 1668 (he aquired it for the princely sum of £50,000). The house – now much reduced in size from the original – is surrounded by a fine 18th century landscaped park laid out by the much celebrated Capability Brown.

For lovers of rich horticultural history, a trip to the inland Gardens of Easton Lodge near Great Dunmow is an absolute must. The fascinating history of the house and especially the gardens – originally designed by Harold Pinto for 'Daisy' Countess of Warwick and undergoing a painstaking restoration process thanks to current owners Diana and Brian Creasey – can be found in the dovecote and makes fascinating reading. Highlights include the Italian garden and Glade, Peto's original brick and cobbled courtyard and the Rose Walk.

Also currently enjoying huge restoration work is Hylands House, Chelmsford – a Grade II listed villa with a fine neo-classical frontage. Set in 500 acres of parkland which includes formal gardens, the main public rooms of the house have been delightfully returned to their original Victorian splendour. Somewhat different in style but certainly rich in family history, the nearby Ingatestone Hall stands as another fine example of an ancient Essex home. Set in 11 acres of grounds, this 16th century mansion was built for Sir William Petre – Secretary of State to four Tudor monarchs – and it still remains in the hands of his family today. Significant furniture, portraits and memorabilia have been amassed by the family over the generations and can be enjoyed at leisure in these particularly convivial surroundings.

ESSEX

Mrs Blackie, Ollivers Farm
Tel: 01787 237642
Map Ref 1 *see page 114*

Elizabeth & Tony Dickinson, Yew Tree House
Tel: 01277 352580
Map Ref 2 *see page 114*

Marilyn & James Butler, Beech Villa
Tel: 01799 516891
Map Ref 3 *see page 114*

Mrs Linda Tritton, Live & Let Live
Tel: 01206 823100
Map Ref 4 *see page 117*

Mr Kiddy, Little Bulls Farmhouse
Tel: 01799 599172/599272
Map Ref 5 *see page 117*

HAVERHILL
Suffolk
SUDBURY
SAFFRON WALDEN
5
1
A131
A12
B184
HALSTEAD
A1017
BRAINTREE
A120
GREAT DUNMOW
A130
A131
A12
A120
HARWICH
COLCHESTER
B1015
A133
4
WALTON ON THE NASE
TIPTREE
WITHAM
ST OSYTH
CLACTON ON SEA
WEST MERSEA
CHELMSFORD
MALDON
BRADWELL ON SEA
A414
2
A414
B1021
BILLERICAY
A130
B1010
BRENTWOOD
BURNHAM ON CROUCH
RAYLEIGH
BASILDON
M25
A13
SOUTHEND ON SEA
A1089
TILBURY
Kent
SHEERNESS
GRAVESEND

OLLIVERS FARM, Toppesfield, Halstead, Essex CO9 4LS
Website www.essex-bed-breakfast.co.uk

Map Ref 1
Nearest Road A1124, M11, A12

17th century farmhouse, quiet rural location. Two acres of landscaped gardens, vineyard, lime avenue, stunning views, white border, herbaceous borders and orchard. Home made brown bread and home made jam from our own organic fruit. Locally cured bacon, free range eggs. One twin bedroom with en-suite shower, one double with private bath. Stansted 45 minutes. Cambridge 40 minutes. Beth Chattos Garden approx one hour. Within easy reach Audley End, Hyde Hall, Long Melford, Lavenham, Thaxted, Sudbury, Saffron Walden, Colchester, Freeport, Braintree and Bury Saint Edmunds. Excellent restaurants nearby. Good walks.

Mrs Blackie
Tel: 01787 237642
Fax: 01787 237602

B&B from £50-£55pr (£10 single supplement), Rooms 1 double with private bathroom, 1 en-suite twin, No smoking or pets, Children over 10, Open all year except Christmas & New Year.

YEW TREE HOUSE, Mill Green Road, Fryerning, Ingatestone, Essex CM4 0HS
Email yewtree@amserve.com
Website www.SmoothHound.co.uk/hotels/yewtreehouse.html

Map Ref 2
Nearest Road A12

Full page photo opposite

The house nestles behind Yew hedges in peaceful countryside. Guests have their own lounge, with TV, looking on to a secluded walled garden. Bedrooms are luxurious and beautifully decorated with tea/coffee facilities. Elizabeth is a trained cook and enjoys serving interesting evening meals in the dining room which reflects her enthusiasm for gardening. We are only 5 miles from M25 and London is 30 minutes by train. Local places to visit include Ingatestone Hall, Hyde Hall, RHS Garden and many other interesting nurseries and gardens.

Elizabeth & Tony Dickinson
Tel: 01277 352580

B&B from £40pp, Dinner from £15, Rooms 2 double en-suite/private bathroom, Restricted smoking, Children over 12, No pets, Open all year except Christmas & New Year.

BEECH VILLA, 1 Borough Lane, Saffron Walden, Essex CB11 4AF
Email marilynjbutler@hotmail.com

Map Ref 3
Nearest Road M11, B184

Full page photo on page 116

A charming regency villa five minutes walk from the centre of the busy market town of Saffron Walden and two minutes from lovely walks in the Audley End estate. Conveniently situated for Stansted Airport and Cambridge, both less than 30 minutes drive and London, (one hour by train). Close to picturesque countryside with delightful villages, also Duxford Air Museum, Newmarket and Wimpole Mall. Three bedrooms with comfortable guest sitting room, dining room and an attractive conservatory where breakfast is served. Close by are excellent pubs and restaurants or evening meals by arrangement.

Marilyn & James Butler
Tel: 01799 516891
Fax: 01799 521390

B&B from £20-£30pp, Dinner £15pp, Rooms 1 single, 2 twin 1 en-suite, No smoking or pets, Children over 5, Open all year except Christmas & New Year.

LIVE & LET LIVE, No 2 Alma Street, Wivenhoe, Essex CO7 9DL
Email linda_tritton@hotmail.com

Map Ref 4
Nearest Road A133

Live and Let Live is a Grade II listed early Victorian house. It is set in the heart of a conservation area and within yards of the quayside and a beautiful river walk. Your hostess is a keen cook and offers a comprehensive breakfast menu. Delicious meals, available on request, are a speciality, or there are excellent pubs nearby. Tea making facilities and TV are provided and guests have use of a sitting room overlooking the river. Parking with free premit.

Mrs Linda Tritton
Tel: 01206 823100
Mobile: 07976 246082

B&B from £23-£25, Dinner available on request, Rooms 1 single, 1 twin, Restricted smoking, Children over 12, No pets, Open all year.

LITTLE BULLS FARMHOUSE, Radwinter End, near Saffron Walden, Essex
Email ajkiddy@cambridge-vacation-homes.com

Map Ref 5

Recently renovated farmhouse in rural location on private farm, no neighbours. Has farmhouse kitchen with aga, full central heating, separate dining room and lounge. Three doube bedrooms, two bathrooms, dishwasher, tumbledrier, fridge freezer, washing machine, garden and barbeque. Near Cambridge and historic Saffron Walden. Excellent walking, cycling and riding stables nearby. Ideally situated for safe family holiday or business use. Weekend to one month.

1 farmhouse, sleeps 9, Price per week £450 low season, £600 high season, No smoking or pets, Children welcome, Available all year.

Contact: Mr A.J. Kiddy, Radwinter Park, Radwinter End, near Saffron Walden, Essex CB10 2UE
Tel/Fax: 01799 599172/599272
Mobile: 07802 599372

"Beaumaris Castle" said Bertie "what did the guide book say, the last of the great royal castles of Edward 1st. I'd like a more distant view when we've gone around."

BELLE & BERTIE IN WALES

left, Yew Tree House, Fryerning - please see page 114 for details

GLOUCESTERSHIRE

Often referred to as that most English of England's counties, Gloucestershire exudes rustic charm thanks largely to its geographic domination by the beautiful Cotswolds. An area of gentle hills with stone walls criss-crossing the landscape, hidden river valleys and distinctive medieval villages, the Cotswolds run practically the length and breadth of Gloucestershire and attract visitors from around the world. Hardly surprisingly, this naturally beautiful area has also attracted the rich and famous over the centuries and as a result the Cotswolds boast some world-famous historic houses and gardens. Among the most grand – and certainly the most historic – is Sudeley Castle near the Saxon village of Winchcombe. Home to Lord and Lady Ashcombe, this influential house enjoys royal connections that stretch back 1000 years. Queen Katherine Parr, Henry VIII's sixth wife, lived here – and indeed is buried in St Mary's church in the grounds – while Anne Boleyn, Lady Jane Grey and Charles I are all known to have stayed here. Sudeley also features award-winning gardens with particularly fine topiary and a stunning old-fashioned rose collection. Moving slightly north near Chipping Campden, Hidcote Manor Garden has been described as one of England's most delightful and is well worth making a detour for; while hidden within a six acre Cotswold combe near the more southerly picture perfect village of the same name, Painswick Rococo Garden offers a unique 18th century restoration featuring delightful woodland walks and fine vistas. Tree lovers may also be interested in Westonbirt Arboretum on the outskirts of Tetbury – begun in 1829 and now featuring an impressive 18,000 catalogued trees.

Gloucester, the main town of the county, is situated within the beautiful Severn Valley to the west of Gloucestershire and has played host to many different peoples over the centuries. Celts, Romans and Saxons have all settled here, but it was the Normans who left the city with its most lasting legacy in the form of the wonderful Gothic cathedral. A must for any visitor, this fine building features a magnificent east window with medieval glass and glorious fan-vaulted cloisters. Also in the Severn Vale is the glamorous Regency town of Cheltenham, a joy for enthusiasts of 19th century architecture, grand terraces and handsome squares. Originally a spa town, the waters can still be tried at the Pittville Pump Room situated in parkland just a mile from the town centre. Also of interest in this elegant town is the Holst Birthplace Museum on Clarence Road. As the name suggests, this was where composer Gustav Holst (1874-1934) was born and where his personal memorabilia and piano are still kept today. The museum also presents a fine example of a Regency/Victorian home and includes a working kitchen, elegant drawing room and charming nursery.

GLOUCESTERSHIRE

Helen Adams, Upper Farm
Tel: 01451 820453
Map Ref 1 *see page 122*

Mrs Pam Hutcheon, Burhill Farm
Tel/Fax: 01386 858171
Map Ref 2 *see page 122*

Robert & Barbara Millar, Guiting Guest House
Tel: 01451 850470
Map Ref 3 *see page 122*

Pauline Loving, Northfield B&B
Tel/Fax: 01451 860427
Map Ref 4 *see page 124*

Andrew & Jane O'Dell, The Masons Arms
Tel/Fax: 01285 850164
Map Ref 5 *see page 124*

Clive & Anna Rooke, Frogfurlong Cottage
Tel/Fax: 01452 730430
Map Ref 6 *see page 124*

David & Rosie Lucas, Gunn Mill House
Tel/Fax: 01594 827577
Map Ref 7 *see page 125*

Mrs Simmonds, Gower House
Tel: 01242 602616
Map Ref 10 *see page 125*

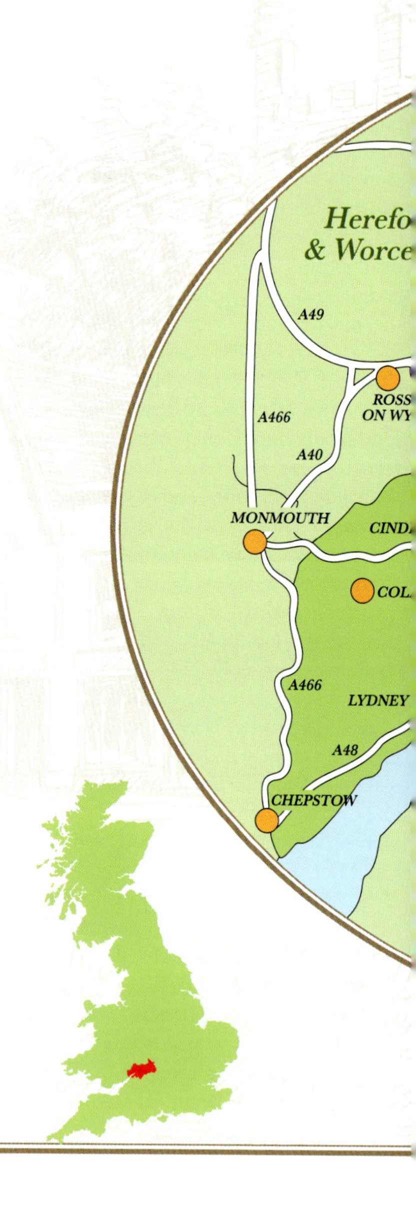

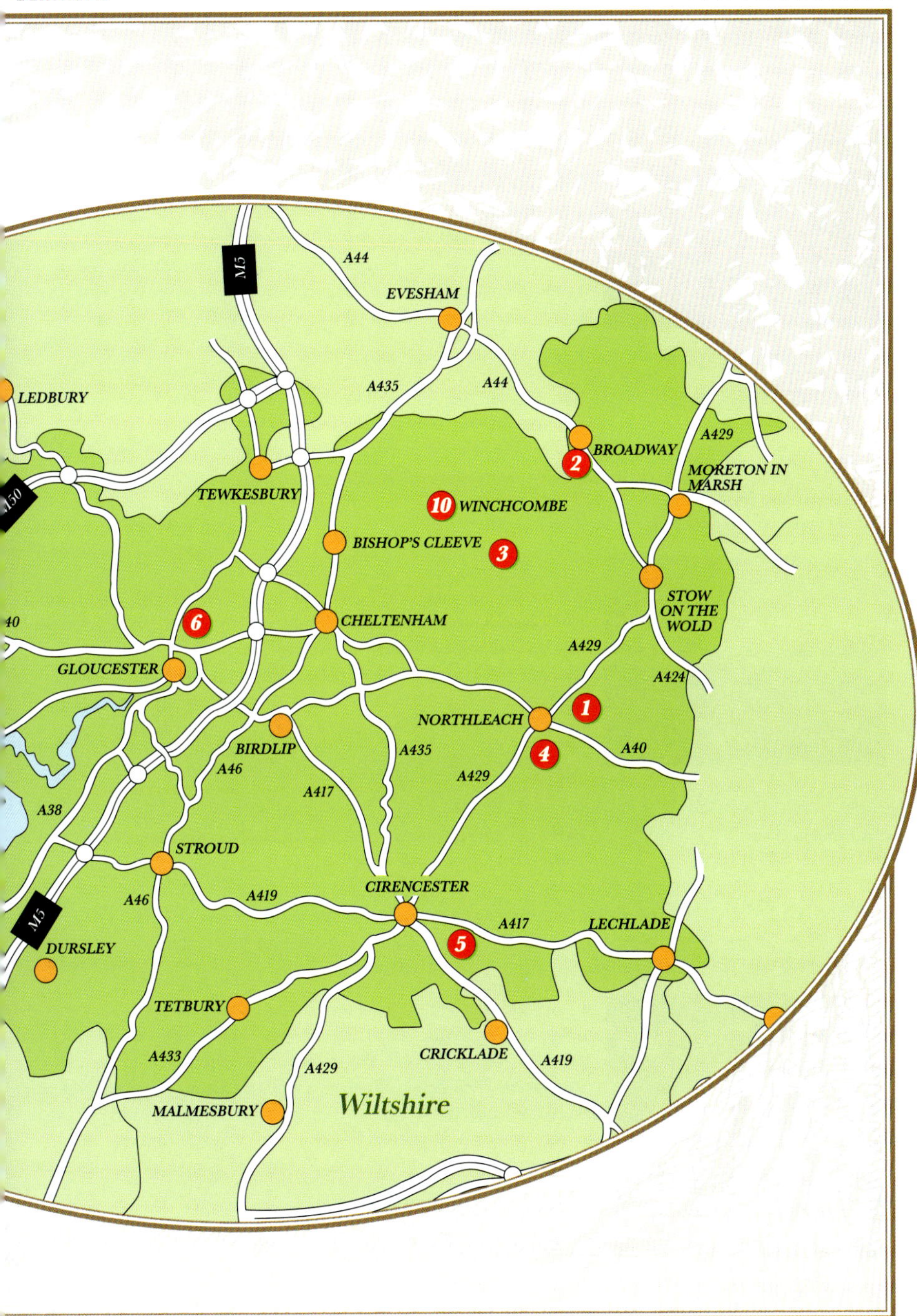
M5
A44
EVESHAM
LEDBURY
A435
A44
A429
BROADWAY
MORETON IN MARSH
TEWKESBURY
WINCHCOMBE
BISHOP'S CLEEVE
STOW ON THE WOLD
CHELTENHAM
A429
GLOUCESTER
A424
NORTHLEACH
A40
BIRDLIP
A435
A46
A429
A417
A38
STROUD
CIRENCESTER
A46
A419
A417
LECHLADE
M5
DURSLEY
TETBURY
A433
CRICKLADE
A419
A429
MALMESBURY
Wiltshire

Full page photo opposite

UPPER FARM, Clapton on the Hill, Bourton-on-the-Water, Gloucestershire GL54 2LG

Map Ref 1
Nearest Road A429, A40

A working family farm of 140 acres in a peaceful undiscovered Cotswold village 2 miles from the famous Bourton-on-the-Water. The listed 17th century farmhouse has been tastefully restored and offers a warm and friendly welcome with exceptional accommodation and hearty farmhouse fayre. The heated bedrooms are of individual character some are en-suite with TV and one is ground floor. From its hill position Upper Farm enjoys panoramic views of the surrounding countryside and being centrally located makes it an ideal base for touring, walking or merely relaxing. Brochure available. ETC 5 Diamonds.

Helen Adams
Tel: 01451 820453
Fax: 01451 810185

B&B from £23pp, Rooms 3 double, 1 family, 1 twin, some en-suite, No smoking, Children over 5, Open February to December.

BURHILL FARM, Buckland, near Broadway, Worcestershire WR12 7LY
Email burhillfarm@yahoo.co.uk
Website www.burhillfarm.co.uk

Map Ref 2
Nearest Road B4632

A warm welcome awaits our guests at our mainly grass farm lying in the folds of the Cotswolds just 2 miles south of Broadway. Both guest rooms are en-suite and have TV and hospitality trays. The Cotswolds Way runs through the middle of the farm providing many lovely walks. There are many pretty villages to visit nearby and Stratford-upon-Avon is about 30 minutes drive. Come and enjoy the peace and quiet with breakfast on the patio if the weather is fine.

Mrs Pam Hutcheon
Tel/Fax: 01386 858171

B&B from £25pp, Rooms 2 en-suite double, No smoking or pets, Open all year except Christmas & New Year.

GUITING GUEST HOUSE, Post Office Lane, Guiting Power, near Cheltenham, Gloucestershire GL54 5TZ
Email info@guitingguesthouse.com
Website www.guitingguesthouse.com

Map Ref 3
Nearest Road A429

A lovely old 16th century building of mellow Cotswold stone, this house retains many original features including exposed beams, inglenook fireplace and polished wooded floors. Public areas have a warm, comfortable and cosy atmosphere. Fresh flowers, fruit and a teddy are among the thoughtful extras when combined with four poster beds, quality toiletries and bathrobes give this establishment a well deserved Five Star rating which is complimented by the food and hospitality of your hosts Barbara and Robert Millar. Credit cards accepted.

Robert & Barbara Millar
Tel: 01451 850470
Fax: 01451 850034

B&B from £30pp, Dinner £25, Rooms 1 single, 5 double, 1 twin, 1 family, most en-suite, No smoking or pets, Children welcome, Open all year.

NORTHFIELD B&B, Cirencester Road, Northleach, Cheltenham, Gloucestershire GL54 3JL
Email nrthfield0@aol.com

Map Ref 4
Nearest Road A429, A40

Beautifully located in the Cotswolds and handy for visiting local villages. This delightful property is built of the honeyed local stone set in immaculate gardens. It offers tastefully furnished bedrooms with good home comforts, and plenty of extras in the spacious bathrooms. Two rooms have direct access to the garden. Breakfast is taken overlooking the open countryside. While delicious and imaginative evening meals using plenty of fresh vegetables from the garden are served in the elegant dining room. Credit cards accepted.

Pauline Loving
Tel/Fax: 01451 860427

B&B from £25-£27pp, Dinner available £8, Rooms 2 double, 1 twin/family, all en-suite, No smoking or pets, Children welcome, Open all year Christmas & New Year.

THE MASONS ARMS, 28 High Street, Meysey Hampton, near Cirencester, Gloucestershire GL7 5JT
Email jane@themasonsarms.freeserve.co.uk
Website www.smoothhound.co.uk/hotels/mason

Map Ref 5
Nearest Road A417

With origins dating from the 17th century. The Masons Arms is situated on the southern fringe of the Cotswold. The Cotswold stone building beside the village green has something to offer both the discerning traveller and tourist. Ideally placed for Cheltenham, Bath, Oxford and a host of local Cotswold beauty spots. Only 30 minutes from Swindon. Cirencester is six miles to the west. Golf, windsurfing, fishing, horse riding, cycle trails and walks provide a host of activities. A village local is the Masons Bar. Credit cards accepted.

Andrew & Jane O'Dell
Tel/Fax: 01285 850164

B&B from £32.50-£40pp, (£45 single room occupancy), Dinner from £7.95, Rooms 1 single, 4 double, 4 twin, 2 family, all en-suite, Children over 3, Pets welcome (£5 per night), Open all year.

FROGFURLONG COTTAGE, Frogfurlong Lane, Down Hatherley, Gloucester, Gloucestershire GL2 9QE
Email nostalgia.frogs@ukonline.co.uk

Map Ref 6
Nearest Road A38

At Frogfurlong Cottage we have two self-contained suites offering tranquility and a truly "get away from it all" break. The accommodation comprises a double en-suite with jacuzzi and direct access to the 30ft indoor heated swimming pool, and a twin/king size en-suite with shower. Both have colour television and tea/coffee tray facilities. The 18th century cottage surrounded by fields, is situated in the green belt area within the triangle formed by Cheltenham, Gloucester and Tewkesbury. Local attractions include Cotswolds, Malverns and Royal Forest of Dean.

Clive & Anna Rooke
Tel/Fax: 01452 730430

B&B from £22pp, Rooms 1 double, 1 twin/king size, all en-suite, No smoking or pets, Children by prior arrangement, Open all year except Christmas.

GUNN MILL HOUSE, Lower Spout Lane, Mitcheldean, Gloucestershire GL17 0EA
Email info@gunnmillhouse.co.uk
Website www.gunnmillhouse.co.uk

Map Ref 7
Nearest Road A40, A48

Gunn Mill House is a fine Georgian country property standing by a mill stream in five acres of grounds, in the Royal Forest of Dean. The forest is ideal for walking, cycling, riding, or just admiring the beauty and tranquility. All rooms in the house and courtyard are en-suite, with bath or shower. One four poster with own sitting room. Meals are served in the gallery, two to four courses by arrangement. Local produce is used where possible and vegetarians are catered for. Credit cards accepted.

David & Rosie Lucas
Tel/Fax: 01594 827577

B&B from £25-£40pp, Dinner by arrangement £15, Rooms 4 double, 2 twin, 2 family, all en-suite, No smoking, Children & pets welcome, Open all year.

GOWER HOUSE, 16 North Street, Winchcombe, Gloucestershire GL54 5LH

Map Ref 10
Nearest Road B4632, M5

Gower House a 17th century town house is conveniently situated close to the centre of Winchcombe a small picturesque country town on the "Cotswold Way". It makes an ideal base for exploring the Cotswolds. Ramblers, cyclists and motorists all receive a warm welcome here. The three comfortable bedrooms have colour TV, tea/coffee making facilities and full central heating. There is also a lounge area with TV and a secluded garden available for guests use. Off street parking at the rear includes two garages.

Mrs Simmonds
Tel: 01242 602616
Mobile: 07811 387495

B&B from £45-£48pr, Rooms 1 double (private bathroom), 2 en-suite twin, Restricted smoking, No pets, Open all year except Christmas & New Year.

"What a view, Beaumaris and all the mountains beyond" said Belle

BELLE & BERTIE IN WALES

Hampshire & Isle of Wight

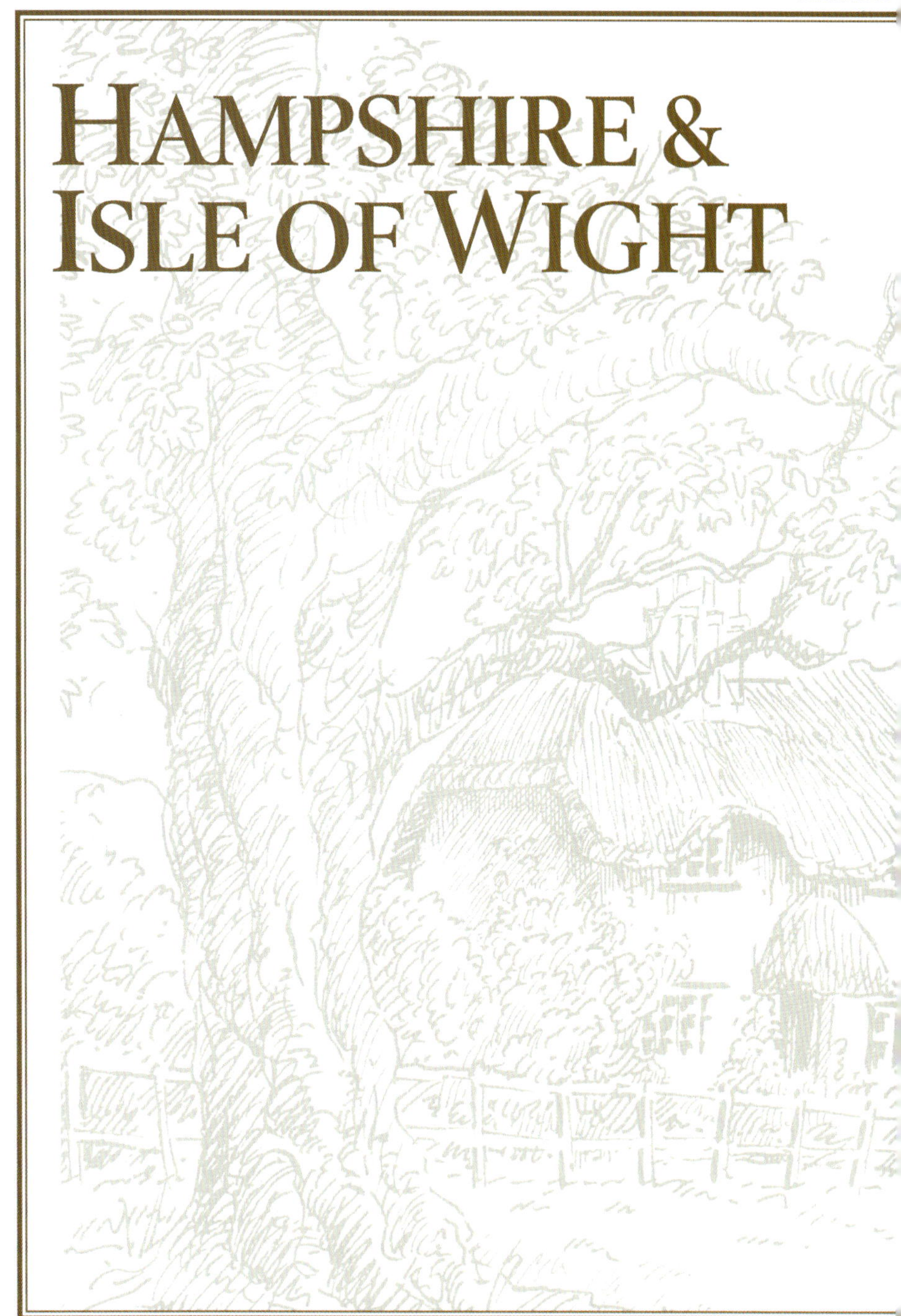

Set in the heart of the southern England, Hampshire offers the visitor a fine cathedral town in the shape of Winchester, the busy sea-faring ports of Southampton and Portsmouth and, to the west of the county, the New Forest – one of the most ancient and unspoilt areas of woodland in the British Isles. The county's rolling woodland topography has made Hampshire a particular favourite with nobility and gentry over the centuries and many fine stately homes and gardens can be found within this attractive pocket of rural England.

Situated upon the River Itchen to the north of the county, the city of Winchester was once the capital of Saxon England. Its fine ancient buildings include Winchester Cathedral founded in 1079; Winchester College dating from 1382 and thought to be the longest running school in the county; and Wolvesey Castle, one of England's finest medieval buildings and scene of the wedding feast of Philip of Spain and Mary Tudor in 1554.

Interesting country homes and gardens also abound around the city of Winchester, one of the finest horticultural specimens being that of Hinton Ampner Gardens at Bramdean. Created in the 20th century based on an existing Victorian layout, these gardens were the brainchild of the 8th Lord Sherbourne and are a masterpiece of design, blending parkland with woodland to absolute perfection.

Slightly south west, the village of Romsey also features two particularly fine gardens. Spellbinding by their sheer enormity of plant and tree species, The Sir Harold Hillier Gardens and Arboretum extend to 180 acres and enjoy world acclaim. Started by the late Sir Harold Hillier in 1953, the gardens provide a delightful mix of formal and informal and perfectly exemplify how knowledgeable planting can transform a varied landscape. Nearby Mottisfont Abbey House & Garden is a large estate centred around an impressive 12th century Augustinian Priory. The particularly tranquil grounds feature walled gardens, old fashioned roses, fine woodland and a tributary of the River Test. Situated on the same river, Broadlands Is a fine Palladian mansion set in beautiful landscaped grounds and famous home to the late Lord Mountbatten, Skirting the busy port of Southampton and moving to the south west of the county, the New Forest represents one of the last original areas of natural vegetation left in Britain and has justifiably been designated an Area of Outstanding Natural Beauty. Situated in the heart of the New Forest and representing one of the true jewels in Hampshire's crown, Beaulieu has been the ancestral seat of the Montagu family since 1538. Once the Great Gatehouse to the ancient Beaulieu Abbey, the Palace House features splendid monastic interiors; while the grounds now house the world famous National Motor Museum.

Nearby Furzey Gardens at Minstead also afford particularly fine views of the New Forest and the Isle of Wight beyond, while the gardens themselves delight with a heady mix of azaleas, rhododendrons, ferns and flaming Chilean Fire trees.

Lying just a couple of mile off the Hampshire coast, the Isle of Wight with its charming towns and many miles of unspoilt beaches makes for an interesting day trip. Highlights include Yarmouth Castle, Henry VIII's last great fortress, to the west of the island; the Georgian harbour town of Cowes to the north; and the ever-popular Osbourne House, much-loved rural retreat of Queen Victoria and Prince Albert.

Hampshire & Isle of Wight

David & Sue Lloyd-Evans, Thickets
Tel: 01962 772467
Map Ref 1 *see page 130*

Mrs Sinclair Vine, Farmhouse,
Tel: 01420 23262
Map Ref 2 *see page 130*

Mr & Mrs Blythe, The Ridge Cottage
Tel: 01425 672504
Map Ref 3 *see page 130*

Ken & Jean Kilford, Squirrels
Tel: 01590 683163
Map Ref 4 *see page 133*

The Penny Farthing Hotel & Cottages
Tel: 023 8028 4422
Map Ref 5 *see page 133*

Mrs D Matthews, Yew Tree Farm
Tel: 01425 611041
Map Ref 6 *see page 133*

Robin & Mary Ford, Holmans
Tel: 01425 402307
Map Ref 7 *see page 134*

Anthea & Bill Hughes, Ranvilles Farm House
Tel: 023 80 814481
Map Ref 8 *see page 134*

Vera Mc Mullan, Strang Hall
Tel: 01983 753189
Map Ref 9 *see page 134*

Carol Peace, Gleneagles
Tel: 01983 872285
Map Ref 10 *see page 135*

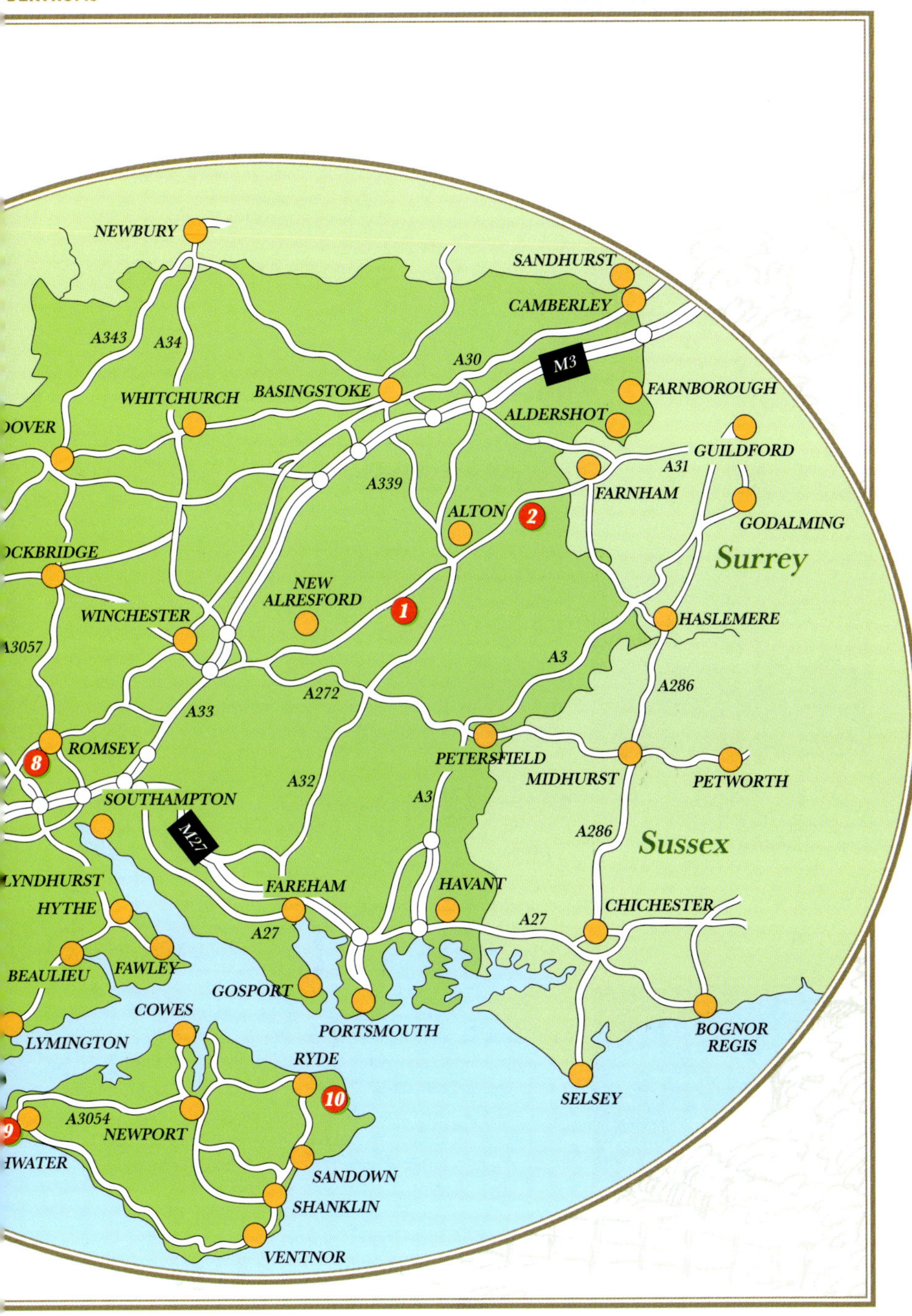
NEWBURY
SANDHURST
CAMBERLEY
A343
A34
A30
M3
WHITCHURCH
BASINGSTOKE
FARNBOROUGH
DOVER
ALDERSHOT
GUILDFORD
A31
A339
FARNHAM
ALTON
2
GODALMING
CKBRIDGE
Surrey
NEW
ALRESFORD
1
WINCHESTER
HASLEMERE
A3057
A3
A286
A272
A33
ROMSEY
8
PETERSFIELD
MIDHURST
PETWORTH
SOUTHAMPTON
A32
A3
M27
A286
Sussex
LYNDHURST
FAREHAM
HAVANT
HYTHE
CHICHESTER
A27
A27
FAWLEY
BEAULIEU
GOSPORT
COWES
PORTSMOUTH
BOGNOR
REGIS
LYMINGTON
RYDE
10
SELSEY
A3054
NEWPORT
9
IWATER
SANDOWN
SHANKLIN
VENTNOR

THICKETS, Swelling Hill, Ropley, Alresford, Hampshire SO24 0DA

Map Ref 1

This spacious country house surrounded by a two acre garden has fine views across the Hampshire countryside. There are two comfortable twin bedded rooms with private bath or shower room. Tea/coffee making facilities available. Guests sitting room with TV. Full English breakfast. Local attractions are Jane Austen's House ten minutes by car. Winchester with its fine cathedral twenty minutes away. Salisbury, Chichester and The New Forest within easy reach. Heathrow Airport one hour.

David & Sue Lloyd-Evans
Tel: 01962 772467

B&B from £23pp, Rooms 2 twin, both with private facilities, Restricted smoking, Children over 10, No pets, Open all year except Christmas & New Year.

VINE FARMHOUSE, Isington, Bentley, Alton, Hampshire GU34 4PN
Email vinefarm@aol.com

Map Ref 2
Nearest Road M3, A31

Vine Farmhouse, halfway between Alton and Farnham, is set in its own farmland overlooking the River Wey, an idyllic Hampshire chalk river. Gatwick and Heathrow are 1 hour by car, as is London by car or train. (Bentley station is 5 minutes away). Oxford, Winchester, Salisbury, Stonehenge, the New Forest and the coast are within 45 minutes. Local attractions are Farnham Castle, Birdworld, Jane Austen's house, a steam museum and railway, and numerous gardens open to the public. There are pubs and restaurants nearby.

Mrs Sinclair
Tel/Fax: 01420 23262

B&B from £17.50-£25pp, Rooms 1 single, 1 double, 1 twin, 1 family, most en-suite, No smoking or pets, Children welcome, Open all year except Christmas.

THE RIDGE COTTAGE, 164 Burley Road, Bransgore, (New Forest), Hampshire BH23 8DE
Email ridge.cottage@virgin.net

Map Ref 3
Nearest Road A31, A35, M27

The Ridge Cottage is situated in the New Forest 3 miles from Burley, 5 miles from Christchurch. Built in 1913, standing in 2/3 acres of secluded grounds. It has been extensively enlarged and tastefully modernised in keeping with the style of the property. There are 3 bedrooms served by a private bathroom plus 2 other toilets and a shower room. The garden is attractively landscaped with many flowering shrubs and ornamental trees. Facilities include outside Games room, abundant garden furniture, detached conservatory. Off road parking.

Mr & Mrs Blythe
Tel/Fax: 01425 672504

B&B from £20-£25pp, Dinner £10, Rooms 1 single, 1 double, 1 twin, 1 family, No smoking, Children welcome, Open all year, Christmas & New Year by arrangement.

Full page photo opposite

PENNY
FARTHING
HOTEL
BED & BREAKFAST
B & B
VACANCIES
AA
QUEENS PARADE

SQUIRRELS, Broadmead, off Silver Street, Sway, Lymington, Hampshire SO41 6DH
Email jean.kilford@lineone.net
Website www.squirrelsbandb.co.uk

Map Ref 4
Nearest Road A337, M27 jct 1

Modern spacious family home situated between forest and sea in a tranquil setting with one acre woodland garden, vehicle access via footpath and bridleway. Horse riding and cycle hire nearby. 1st floor, double has balcony overlooking garden, aviaries and fishpond. Family suite ground floor, consisting of two rooms plus bathroom, own entrance, use of fridge, ideal for the longer stays. All rooms have colour TV and tea/coffee making facilities. Welcome cuppa on arrival. 4 course English breakfast cooked by your friendly hosts. Off street parking. ETB 3 Diamonds.

Ken & Jean Kilford
Tel: 01590 683163

B&B from £22.50pp, Rooms 1 single, 1 twin, 1 double, 1 family, all en-suite, No smoking, Children over 8, Pets by arrangement, Open all year.

THE PENNY FARTHING HOTEL & COTTAGES, Romsey Road, Lyndhurst, Hampshire SO43 7AA
Email stay@pennyfarthinghotel.co.uk
Website www.pennyfarthinghotel.co.uk

Map Ref 5
Nearest Road M27 Jct 1, A337

Welcome to our cheerful "Four Diamonds" guesthouse ideally situated in Lyndhurst village centre, often referred to as the capital of the New Forest. Following a major extension during 2002 we now offer over twenty en-suite bedrooms and also some self-catering properties close by. All rooms have colour TV, tea/coffee tray, central heating and double glazing. The Hotel has a large private car park, bicycle store and garages for special cars and motorcycles. Credit cards accepted. Please see website for more details or call for a brochure.

Tel: 023 8028 4422
Fax: 023 8028 4488

B&B from £29.50-£45pp, Rooms 3 single, 12 double, 3 twin, 3 family, all en-suite, Restricted smoking, Children welcome, No pets, Open all year except Christmas & New Year.

Full page photo opposite

YEW TREE FARM, Bashley Common Road, New Milton, Hampshire BH25 5SH

Map Ref 6
Nearest Road B3058, A35

A very attractive thatched farmhouse and smallholding, 300 yards from open forest. Exceptional comfort in 2 double or twin rooms, 1 en-suite, 1 private bath. Superb beds, large armchairs fitted with and down and feather cushions. So much thought has been put into these rooms that it is impossible to list everything. Breakfast served in guest rooms between 7.30 and 11am, which is exceptional both for quality and choice as is the A La Carte dinner menu. Worthy of the highest praise so said the late Derek Johansen of Johansens Guide. Unsuitable for the disabled.

Mrs D Matthews
Tel/Fax: 01425 611041

B&B from £35-£40pp, Dinner by prior arrangement, Rooms 1 double, 1 twin, 1 en-suite, 1 private bathroom, No smoking, children or pets, Open all year.

HOLMANS, Bisterne Close, Burley, Ringwood, Hampshire BH24 4AZ

Map Ref 7
Nearest Road A31, A35

Holmans is a charming country house in the heart of the New Forest, set in four acres with stabling available for guests' own horses. Superb walking, horse riding and carriage driving. Golf course nearby. A warm friendly welcome is assured. All bedrooms are en-suite and tastefully furnished with tea/coffee making facilities, radio and hair dryer. Colour TV in guests lounge with adjoining orangery and log fires in winter.

Robin & Mary Ford
Tel/Fax: 01425 402307

B&B from £30pp, Rooms 1 twin, 2 double, all en-suite, No smoking, Children welcome, Open all year except Christmas.

RANVILLES FARM HOUSE, Romsey, Hampshire SO51 6AA
Email info@ranvilles.com
Website www.ranvilles.com

Map Ref 8
Nearest Road A3090, M27, Jct 2

Ranvilles Farm House dates from the 14th century when Richard de Ranville came from Normandy and settled with his family in this Grade 2 listed house provides a peaceful setting surrounded by 5 acres of gardens and paddock. All rooms with extra large beds are attractively decorated and furnished with antiques. Each room has its own en-suite bath/shower room. The house is only 3 miles from the New Forest and just over a mile from Romsey, a small market town. Equal distant from the two cathedral cities of Winchester and Salisbury. Close to Channel Ports.

Anthea & Bill Hughes
Tel/Fax: 023 80 814481

B&B from £25-£35pp, Rooms 3 double/twin 1 family, all en-suite, No smoking, Children & pets welcome, Open all year except Christmas & New Year.

STRANG HALL, Uplands, Totland Bay, Isle of Wight PO39 0DZ

Map Ref 9
Nearest Road B3322

Strang Hall is an Edwardian family home decorated in the arts and craft style with splendid views over the Downs and Solent, set peacefully in the hills above Totland Bay. The large garden leads onto a short walk to the beach. Yarmouth and Freshwater are within 2 miles with golf, tennis etc. The West Wight is famous for its good country walks and beaches.

Vera Mc Mullan
Tel/Fax: 01983 753189

B&B from £27.50pp, Rooms 1 single, 1 twin, 1 double, 1 family, some en-suite, Restricted smoking, Children welcome, No pets, Open all year except Christmas & New Year.

Cottage GLENEAGLES, Lower Green, St Helens, Isle of Wight
Email carolpearce@onetel.net.uk
Website www.tuckedup.com/gleneagles.html

Map Ref 10

Gleneagles is a delightful cottage with a wonderful position-overlooking St Helens village green, just 300 yards from Bembridge harbour with its marina and lovely beaches. Restaurants, pub, shops nearby. The cottage is small but beautiful, originally the village chemist, now totally rebuilt to an exceptional standard, pretty furnishings throughout. Downstairs: well-fitted kitchen and open-plan dining/sitting room, French doors to sunny patio, BBQ. Spiral staircase leads to two bedrooms: one with futon/bunk bed, the other with romantic 4-poster.

1 cottage, sleeps up to 4, Price per week £175 to £550, No smoking, Children over 6, Pets by prior arrangement, Available April to October.

Contact: Carol Pearce, Lantern Court, Ducie Avenue, Bembridge, Isle of Wight PO35 5RT
Tel: 01983 872285
Fax: 01983 875725

"Most impressive" said Bertie "What have we got on the list today?"
"Oh, Rhudolan and Conwy" said Belle "Then on to Caenarvon".

BELLE & BERTIE IN WALES

HEREFORDSHIRE & WORCESTERSHIRE

Nestled between the Malvern Hills to the east and Wales to the West, Herefordshire is a quiet rural county dominated by fields and hedgerows. The river Wye meanders peaceably through the picturesque towns of Ross-on-Wye and Symonds Yat, while pockets of stunning countryside – such as CS Lewis's Golden Valley on the Welsh border – remain delightfully remote and virtually unvisited. Also resplendent on the River Wye stands the ancient cathedral city of Hereford, once capital of the Saxon kingdom of Mercia. Although largely reconstructed and certainly not the prettiest of English cathedrals, Hereford does famously house two ancient treasures: the 13th century Mappi Mundi and the chained library of some 1500 volumes. Particularly fine examples of the county's renowned black and white architecture can also be found around Hereford, most notably in the handsome market town of Ledbury and the picturesque village of Eardisland.

Also in Ledbury, and certainly worth a visit for the friendly atmosphere alone, Eastnor Castle stands surrounded by its famous arboretum and lake. Having undergone extensive restoration in the last 50 years, this 19th century fairytale castle now looks as dramatic inside as it does out.

Drama also abounds in and around the15th century fortified manor house of Hampton Court, near Leominster, with its 1000 acres of grounds and gardens which include canals, pavilions, a waterfall, a sunken garden, a maze and a secret tunnel; while just a stone's throw away, Berrington Hall also glitters in Herefordshire's grand historic crown, not least because its rather plain, neo-classical exterior gives no clue to the lavish grandeur of the decor within.

Immediately adjoining Herefordshire and sharing at least in part its rural tradition, Worcestershire comprises the flatlands of the Severn Vale and the Vale of Evesham and is surrounded by hills – the Malverns to the west and the ever-popular Cotswolds to the south. The city of Worcester features a fine cathedral, first begun as far back as 1084, while the celebrated village of Broadway in the Northern Cotswolds has famously inspired writers, artists and composers – from JM Barrie to Worcestershire's own Edward Elgar. Great Malvern, with its dramatic backdrop of the Malvern Hills, was once painted by Turner – while the Vale of Evesham in the county's south-eastern corner is a magnet for photographers in spring when its myriad of fruit trees are in full bloom.

Like Herefordshire, Worcestershire also has some fine country homes, perhaps none more grand than Hanbury Hall near Droitwich. In its beautiful setting of parkland, this elegant William and Mary style mansion retains a lived in feel and houses unique collections of porcelain and murals. The formal 18th century gardens include a bowling green, a particularly pleasant Orangery and a working mushroom house.

Near the village of Hagley, the Palladian-style Hagley Hall also cannot fail to impress, with its grand 18th century furniture and especially fine Italian plasterwork; while in slightly more reverend style tranquil Hartlebury Castle near Kidderminster, home to the Bishops of Worcester for over a thousand years, features stunningly proportioned state rooms, fine episcopal portraits and a fascinating museum following the inhabitants of this historic county back to Roman times.

HEREFORDSHIRE & WORCESTERSHIRE

Mrs Jayne Webster, Number 18
Tel: 01885 488 845
Map Ref 1 *see page 140*
Chrix & Jenny Juckes, The Old Rectory
Tel: 01981 240498
Map Ref 2 *see page 140*
Mrs Carol Hart, The Bowens Country House
Tel: 01432 860430
Map Ref 3 *see page 140*
Mrs Audrey Mayson, Old Rectory
Tel: 01981 590 218
Map Ref 4 *see page 141*
Jennie Layton, Grafton Villa
Tel: 01432 268689
Map Ref 5 *see page 141*
Catherine & Marguerite Fothergill, Highfield
Tel: 01568 613216
Map Ref 6 *see page 141*
Rose & Leslie Wiles, Lower Bache House
Te: 01568 750304
Map Ref 7 *see page 142*
Elizabeth Thomas,Woonton Court Farm
Tel: 01568 750232
Map Ref 8 *see page 142*
Mrs Jean Bengry, The Vauld Farm
Tel: 01568 797898
Map Ref 9 *see page 142*
10 Mrs Heather Gammond, Rudhall Farm
Tel: 01989 780240
Map Ref 10 *see page 144*
Topsy Beves, Tarn
Tel: 01299 402243
Map Ref 11 *see page 144*
Jenny Mason, The Steps
Tel: 01527 892678
Map Ref 12 *see page 144*
Mrs Sheila Blankstone,
St. Elisabeth's Cottage
Tel: 01562 883883
Map Ref 13 *see page 145*
Elizabeth Thomas,
Mill House Flat
Tel: 01568 750232
Map Ref 8 *see page 145*

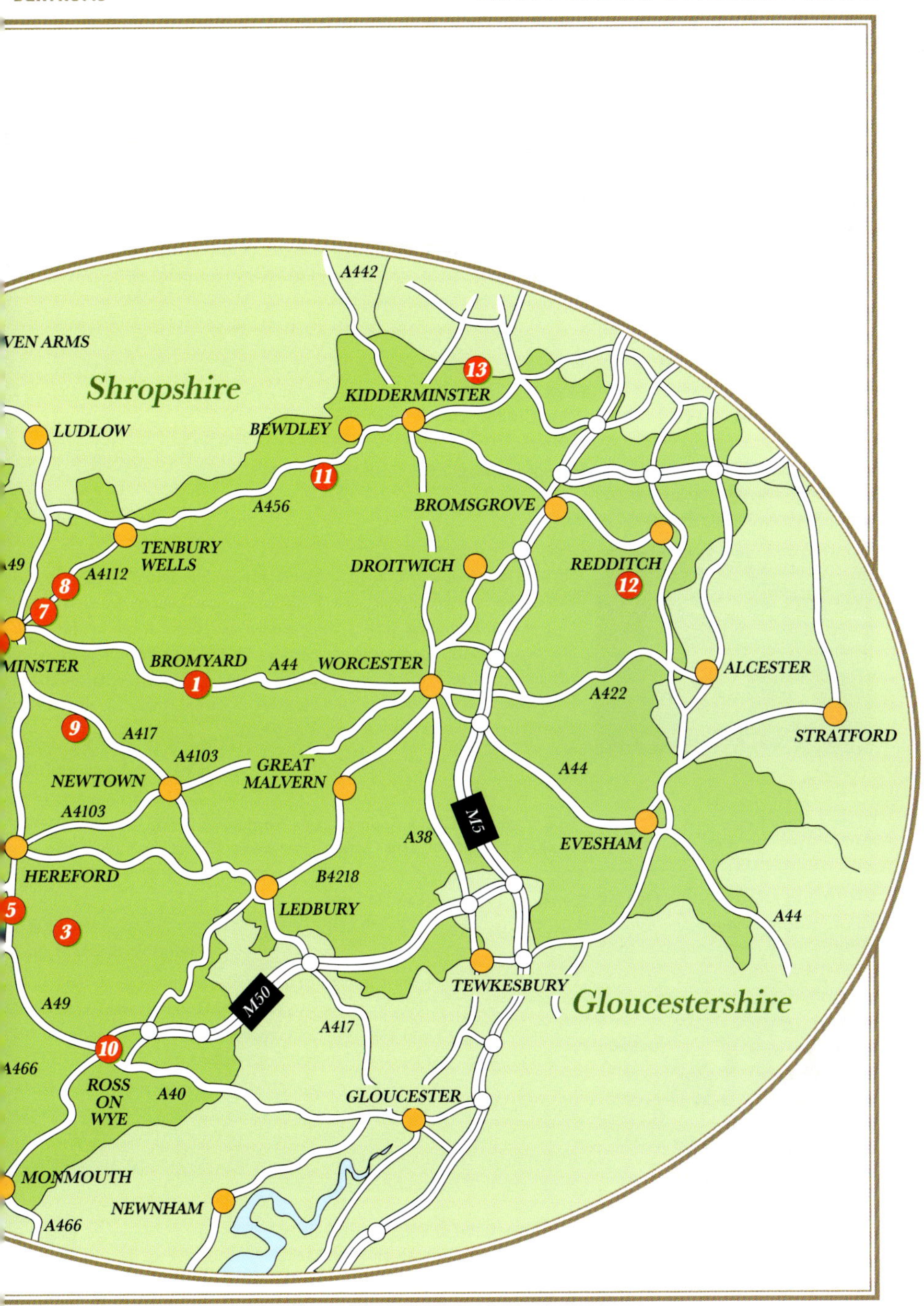
A442
13
KIDDERMINSTER
BEWDLEY
11
A456
BROMSGROVE
TENBURY
WELLS
A4112
8
7
DROITWICH
REDDITCH
12
MINSTER
BROMYARD
1
A44
WORCESTER
ALCESTER
A422
STRATFORD
9
A417
A4103
GREAT
MALVERN
NEWTOWN
A44
A4103
M5
A38
EVESHAM
HEREFORD
B4218
LEDBURY
5
3
A44
M50
TEWKESBURY
Gloucestershire
A49
A417
10
A466
ROSS
ON
WYE
A40
GLOUCESTER
MONMOUTH
NEWNHAM
A466
Shropshire
LUDLOW
VEN ARMS

NUMBER 18, 18 Broad Street, Bromyard, Herefordshire HR7 4BT

Map Ref 1
Nearest Road A44

Number 18 is situated in the heart of the historic market town of Bromyard. The 17th century timber framed building, with a Georgian facade has been carefully restored to reflect its fine character. Antique furnishings, a hospitality tray and television in each room ensure that guests receive a warm welcome. Breakfasts are served at our oak dining table and feature local and home made produce. Special dietary needs can be catered for. Numerous pubs and restaurants are within easy reach of the front door.

Mrs Jayne Webster
Tel: 01885 488 845

B&B from £25pp, Rooms 1 twin, 1 family, shared bathroom, No smoking or pets, Children over 7, Open all year.

THE OLD RECTORY, Ewyas Harold, Herefordshire HR2 0EY
Email jenny.juckes@btopenworld.com
Website www.golden-valley.co.uk/rectory

Map Ref 2
Nearest Road A465

Situated in the Golden Valley equidistant between Hereford, Abergavenny and Hay-on-Wye, the Old Rectory is a delightful Georgian country house set in its own secluded grounds, with a lovely garden and views across to the Black Mountains. Rooms are spacious and elegant with a feel of comfortable antiquity - open fires in winter, open French windows in summer! Walks can start from the garden gate, and the village pub serving excellent evening meals is a short stroll. Central heating, comfy beds, no smoking please.

Chrix & Jenny Juckes
Tel/Fax: 01981 240498

B&B from £23-£25pp, Rooms 1 en-suite double, 2 twin (1 en-suite), No smoking, children or pets, Open all year except Christmas & New Year.

THE BOWENS COUNTRY HOUSE, Fownhope, Herefordshire HR1 4PS
Email Thebowenshotel@aol.com
Website www.Thebowenshotel.co.uk

Map Ref 3
Nearest Road B4224, M50

Peacefully situated opposite the church on the edge of the village on the B4224 in the Wye Valley AONB, midway between Hereford and Ross-on-Wye. Ideal for touring, walking, and exploring the Welsh Borders, Malverns, Cotswolds, Brecon Beacons and the wooded countryside of Herefordshire. Tastefully restored 17th century country house set in 2 acres of gardens. Comfortable, well appointed bedrooms, all fully en-suite each with TV, telephone, central heating and tea/coffee facilities. Oak beamed lounge with inglenook fireplace. Superb home-cooked meals, including vegetarian dishes, using local/home produce. Bargain breaks available. ETB and AA 4 Diamonds.

Mrs Carol Hart
Tel/Fax: 01432 860430

B&B from £25-£32.50pp, Dinner available D'Hote £15, Rooms 1 single, 6 twin/double, 3 family, all en-suite, Children welcome, Pets by arrangement, Open all year.

OLD RECTORY, Byford, Hereford, Herefordshire HR4 7LD
Email info@cm.ltd.com
Website www.smoothhound.co.uk/hotels/oldrectory2.html
Map Ref 4
Nearest Road A438

Byford is a hamlet in beautiful rural Herefordshire close to the River Wye on the Wye Valley walk. Our home is Georgian, elegant and spacious. The dining room has three ceiling to floor windows, pine shutters and doors. A magnificent cedar tree dominates the garden and herbaceous borders. Bedrooms are large with views of parkland and hills, they have sofas, books, TV, tea/coffee and lovely en-suite facilities. Visit delightful villages, churches, gardens and mountains galore we are delighted to recommend village pubs and restaurants.

Mrs Audrey Mayson
Tel: 01981 590 218
Fax: 01981 590 499

B&B from £25-£30pp, Dinner available on request £15, Rooms 2 double, 1 twin, all en-suite, No smoking, Children over 10, Pets outside only, Open March to October.

GRAFTON VILLA, Grafton, Hereford, Herefordshire HR2 8ED
Email jennielayton@ereal.net
Website www.graftonvilla.co.uk
Map Ref 5
Nearest Road A49

A much loved and cherished farmhouse, decorated with flair using designer fabrics and treasured antiques. Surrounded by acres of lawns and herbaceous borders overlooking wonderful countryside. Peaceful, spacious en-suite bedrooms enjoying panoramic views, four poster, brass beds. Award Winning Breakfasts featuring local, fresh and home produce. Great centre for Wye Valley. Hereford Cathedral, Mappa Mundi, amazing gardens, historic castles and glorious walks. Situated two miles south of Hereford city, drive leads off A49, 300 yards past Grafton Inn. Brochure available. Holiday cottage suitable for disabled guest sleeps 4/5.

Jennie Layton
Tel: 01432 268689

B&B from £23-£26pp, Rooms 1 double, 1 twin, 1 family, all en-suite, No smoking or pets, Children welcome, Open January to November.

HIGHFIELD, Newtown, Ivington Road, Leominster, Herefordshire HR6 8QD
Email info@stay-at-highfield.co.uk
Website www.stay-at-highfield.co.uk
Map Ref 6
Nearest Road A44, A49

This attractive Edwardian house offers a comfortable relaxing stay in pleasant rural surroundings. All three bedrooms have tea/coffee trays, radio-alarm clocks, and own bathroom facilities (one being en-suite). Meals are lovingly prepared from fresh local (when-ever possible) ingredients and to suit all tastes. There is a television lounge available, and another sitting room with local information literature. Located close to Leominster and handy for the Black and White Village Trail. Good walking and golfing nearby. ETB classification 4 Diamonds.

Catherine & Marguerite Fothergill
Tel: 01568 613216

B&B from £20-£26pp, Dinner £13.50, Rooms 1 double, 2 twin, 1 en-suite, 2 private bathroom, No smoking, children or pets, Open March to November.

Full page photo opposite

LOWER BACHE HOUSE, kimbolton, near Leominster, Herefordshire HR6 0ER
Email leslie.wiles@care4free.net

Map Ref 7
Nearest Road A4112

This award winning 17th century country house, set in delightful cottage gardens and fourteen acres of private nature reserve, nestling in a tiny tranquil valley, provides self contained suites each with its own private sitting room. Water colours, original prints, plants, books and ornaments create an atmosphere of quality and comfort. A renowned cuisine, using locally produced organic meat and vegetables complete the hallmarks of peace, privacy and fine food of this charming country retreat. An opportunity to savour rural England at its very best.

Rose & Leslie Wiles
Te: 01568 750304

B&B from £33.50pp, Dinner from £16.50, Rooms 4, 3 room suites, No smoking or pets, Children over 8, Open all year.

WOONTON COURT FARM, Leysters, Leominster, Herefordshire HR6 0HL
Email thomas.woostoncourt@farmersweekly.net
Website www.woontoncourt.co.uk

Map Ref 8
Nearest Road A49, A4112

Tudor farm house on family farm, North Herefordshire, well placed for Leominster, Ludlow, Hereford, Tenbury Wells. Excellent for visiting National Trust Properties, lovely garden and woodlands. Farm walks. Local produce. Comfortable bedrooms, en-suite with tea/coffee making facilities. Sitting room with wood burning stove, available all day. Rural tranquility. Enjoy the stars. Ample parking off road.

Elizabeth Thomas
Tel/Fax: 01568 750232

B&B from £22-£26pp, Light Supper £7.50, Rooms 1 single, 1 double, 1 twin, 1 family, en-suite, Children & pets welcome, Open all year except Christmas.

THE VAULD FARM, The Vauld, Marden, Herefordshire HR1 3HA

Map Ref 9
Nearest Road A49, A417

The Vauld Farm offers spacious comfortable en-suite rooms with tea/coffee facilities and TV. Built in 1510 the former farmhouse has a wealth of exposed beams and original flagstone floors. Hearty breakfasts and evening meals are served at the large farmhouse table in the dining room with open log fireplace. Located in a peaceful rural hamlet, situated 8 miles from Hereford city. Ideal for discovering the delights of the county. Ample safe parking in courtyard with duck pond and gardens.

Mrs Jean Bengry
Tel: 01568 797898

B&B from £27.50-£30pp, Dinner £20, Rooms 3 double, 2 twin, all en-suite, Restricted smoking, Children over 12, No pets, Open all year.

RUDHALL FARM, Ross-on-Wye, Herefordshire HR9 7TL

Map Ref 10
Nearest Road B4221

Rudhall is an elegant, early Georgian farmhouse with extensive views in a picturesque valley with millstream and lake, offering something special where guests' comfort is of prime importance. Ideal base for exploring the beautiful Wye Valley, Forest of Dean and beyond. Welcoming hospitality starts with a tea tray in the sitting room or large terraced garden. Aga cooked breakfasts (diets catered for) using local produce. Bedrooms of character with co-ordinated fabrics and every 21st century facility. Highly recommended by guests.

Mrs Heather Gammond
Tel: 01989 780240

B&B from £27.50pp, Rooms 2 double, guests bathroom, No smoking or pets, Open all year except Christmas & New Year.

TARN, Long Bank, Bewdley, Worcestershire DY12 2QT

Map Ref 11
Nearest Road A456

Attractive country house with library. Set in 17 acres of gardens and fields, with spectacular views, and by an ancient coppice. All bedrooms have basins and there are two shower-rooms and one bathroom. Excellent breakfasts with home baked rolls. Conveniently situated for Worcestershire way walk (car service), Wyre Forest, River Severn, Midland Safari Park, Severn Valley Steam Railway, gardens, stately homes and golf. Ample parking space.

Topsy Beves
Tel: 01299 402243

B&B from £21-£25pp, Rooms 2 single, 2 twin, No smoking, Children welcome, Pets by prior arrangement, Open February to November.

THE STEPS, 6 High Street, Feckenham, Worcestershire B96 6HS
Email jenny@thesteps.co.uk
Website www.thesteps.co.uk

Map Ref 12
Nearest Road B4090, A38

The Steps, set in a lovely village but still convenient for local towns and motorways, is a quiet retreat for business people, families and guests visiting the many places of interest in the area. All rooms are decorated to a high standard and the lovely sitting room offers a peaceful spot for reading or watching your favourite TV programmes, and is warmed by log fires in winter. Breakfast is served overlooking the delightful walled garden where the collection of family pets will keep you entertained.

Jenny Mason
Tel: 01527 892678

B&B from £20-£25pp, Dinner £10, Rooms 1 single, 1 en-suite, 1 twin, No smoking, Children & Pets welcome, Open all year.

ST. ELISABETH'S COTTAGE, Woodman Lane, Clent, Stourbridge, Worcestershire DY9 9PX

Map Ref 13
Nearest Road A491

Beautiful country cottage in tranquil setting with 6 acres of landscaped garden plus outdoor heated swimming pool. Lovely country walks. Accommodation includes TV in all rooms plus coffee and tea making facilities. Resident's lounge available. Plenty of pubs and restaurants nearby. Easy access to M5, M6, M42 and M40. 25 minutes from NEC and Birmingham Airport. Destinations within easy reach: Symphony Hall and Convention Centre in Birmingham, Black Country Museum, Dudley, Stourbridge Crystal Factories, Severn Valley Railway.

Mrs Sheila Blankstone
Tel: 01562 883883
Fax: 01562 885034

B&B from £30pp, Rooms 1 twin, 2 double, all en-suite, No smoking, Pets welcome, Open all year.

MILL HOUSE FLAT, Leyster, Leominster, Herefordshire
Email thomas.woontoncourt@farmersweekly.net
Website www.woontoncourt.co.uk

Map Ref 8

A former cider house converted to a high standard of comfort. Sleeps 3/4. Central heated accommodation, large double room, small bedroom single for two children, kitchen with electric cooker, microwave, fridge, colour TV and linen provided. Electricity included, pay phone, washing machine/dryer. Patio garden parking. Freedom to walk on farm. Nature trail. Farm produce. Short breaks, extra accommodation in farmhouse nearby. ETC 3 Stars, Commended.

1 flat, sleeps 3-4, Price per week from £180 low season, from £280 high season, Short breaks available from £95, No smoking or pets, Children welcome, Available all year.

Contact: Elizabeth Thomas, Woonton Court Farm, Leysters, Leominster, Herefordshire HR6 0HL
Tel/Fax: 01568 750232

"If I go back any further I'll be in the water!" said Belle
"That's it" said Bertie "You and most of Rhuddlan Castle - thank you!"

BELLE & BERTIE IN WALES

KENT

Kent is fondly referred to as The Garden of England and from its lush countryside, open rolling hills, hop fields and orchards it is certainly easy to see why. Situated in the far south-eastern corner of England, Kent offers miles of distinctive historical coastline, charming coastal towns, picturesque inland villages and a legacy of historic oast houses, castles, stately homes and gardens. Significant towns in Kent include the well known ports of Dover and Folkestone, historic Margate on the Isle of Thanet – where St Augustine landed in 596 – and of course Canterbury, home to the magnificent cathedral. It was indeed to this very cathedral that one the most important medieval pilgrimages in Europe was made after the martyrdom of Archbishop Thomas Becket in 1170, famously immortalised by Geoffrey Chaucer in The Canterbury Tales.

In true 'Garden of England' style, Kent offers the horticulturally inclined visitor a wealth of historic houses and gardens to enthuse over – infact there are so many you may need to plan your itinerary carefully in advance.

Chartwell near Westerham, overlooking the magnificent Weald of Kent, makes for a particularly interesting and historic starting point. Residence of Sir Winston Churchill from 1924, he famously said of his adored home: 'I love this place – a day away from Chartwell is a day wasted' – a sentiment horoughly appreciated by many visitors to his charming house and garden. Memorabilia ertaining to Sir Winston and Lady Churchill bound in the house – while in the grounds isitors can see garden walls built by Churchill imself, the pond where he fed his golden orfe laily and the garden studio where he loved to aint, complete with original easel and paint ox within.

Historic Maidstone – in the very heart of Kent – makes a pleasant base for visitors and rom here many of the county's most prized ttractions can be explored, including Leeds Castle set in the middle of a natural lake and lescribed by some as 'the loveliest castle in the world'. Another delightful highlight of the rea includes Boughton Monchelsera Place, a attlemented manor house dating from round the 16th century. Internal rchitecture varies from Tudor through to Georgian and includes a particularly andsome Jacobean staircase – while the mpressive grounds afford fine views, the nedieval church of St Peter and its splendid ose gardens and ancient lynch gate.

Garden lovers will delight in the romance of Scotney Castle Garden, with its 14th century moated castle backdrop and profusion of rhododendrons, kalmia, azaleas and wisteria; while Yalding Organic Gardens, a nearby and altogether more modern project, features fourteen newly created gardens reflecting mankind's experience of gardening over the centuries.

A short drive to Edenbridge unveils yet another of Kent's historic jewels in the form of Hever Castle – a grand Tudor manor house and childhood home of Anne Boleyn. Although the house contains some interesting Tudor items, it is actually the grounds of the castle that are quite breathtaking by their design. Entirely created between 1904 and 1908 by American millionaire William Waldorf, they have only now matured to their formal glory to include award-winning rose gardens, a traditional yew maze, a four acre walled garden and a 110 metre herbaceous border.

For a peaceful finale, Beech Court Gardens near Ashford promises to soothe the soul and lift the spirits with its tranquil gardens and famous birdsong. Magnificent trees, spacious lawns, cascading roses and viburnum walks make this a wonderful place to visit at any time of the year – although knowledgeable locals profess the colours in autumn to be quite out of this world.

KENT

Bernard Broad, The Coach House
Tel: 01233 820583
Map Ref 1 *see page 150*

Phillada Pym, Barnfield
Tel: 01233 712421
Map Ref 2 *see page 150*

Mrs Lilly Wilton, Bulltown Farmhouse
Tel: 01233 813505
Map Ref 4 *see page 150*

Brenda & Michael Harrison,
Hopes Grove Cottage
Tel: 01233 850423
Map Ref 3 *see page 152*

Ian & Jennifer Chapman, Thanington Hotel
Tel: 01227 453227
Map Ref 5 *see page 152*

Mrs Jubber, Cathedral Gate Hotel
Tel: 01227 464381
Map Ref 5 *see page 152*

Mrs Williams, Clare Ellen Guest House
Tel: 01227 760205
Map Ref 5 *see page 153*

Roger & Susan Linch, Upper Ansdore
Tel: 01227 700672
Map Ref 6 *see page 153*

Gavin Oakley, Wallett's Court Country House Hotel, Restaurant & Spa
Tel: 01304 852424
Map Ref 8 *see page 153*

Prudence & Peter Latham, Tenterden House
Tel: 01227 751593
Map Ref 9 *see page 154*

Markham & Susan Chesterfield, Frith Farm House
Tel: 01795 890701
Map Ref 10 *see page 154*

Mrs Jo Lindsay, Jordans
Tel: 01732 810379
Map Ref 12 *see page 154*

Anne Turner, Leavers Oast
Tel: 01732 850924
Map Ref 11 *see page 156*

Pamela & Rodney Mumford, Merzie Meadows
Tel: 01622 820 500
Map Ref 13 *see page 156*

Mrs Mary Dakin, The Old Parsonage
Tel: 01892 750773
Map Ref 14 *see page*

Angela Jane Godbold, Danehurst House
Tel: 01892 527739
Map Ref 15 *see page 157*

Anneke Leemhuis, Number Ten
Tel: 01892 522450
Map Ref 16 *see page 157*

Essex
SOUTHEND ON SEA
SHEERNESS
ESTER
A249
GILLINGHAM
HAM
MARGATE
HERNE BAY
WHITSTABLE
BROADSTAIRS
A2
FAVERSHAM
A299
A253
A28
RAMSGATE
M2
9
10
A2
5
TONE
CANTERBURY
SANDWICH
M20
6
2
A2
A256
DEAL
A274
ASHFORD
4
1
8
BIDDENDEN
3
DOVER
HIGH HALDEN
NBROOK
A2070
FOLKESTONE
A229
TENTERDEN
NEW ROMNEY
A28
RYE
A259
A259
HASTINGS

THE COACH HOUSE, Oakmead Farm, near Ashford, Kent TN26 3DU

Map Ref
Nearest Road A2

Guests are warmly welcomed at The Coach House, a comfortable family home set well back from the road in 5 acres of gardens and paddocks; there is secluded courtyard parking. Breakfast of your choice is cooked using fresh local produce and served in the dining room or conservatory which guests can also use as a sitting room. One mile from the village, central for ferries, tunnel, Eurostar. Canterbury, Leeds, Castle and Sissinghurst are some of the tourist attractions within easy reach. Dutch spoken. Closed November to February.

Bernard Broad
Tel/Fax: 01233 820583

B&B from £20pp, Rooms 1 double, 1 twin, 1 family, all en-suite/private facilities, Children welcome, No pets, Open March to October.

BARNFIELD, Charing, Ashford, Kent TN27 0BN
Email phillada@pym2.co.uk

Map Ref
Nearest Road A20

Charming and romantic 15th century farmhouse in superb location, in old English garden, overlooking a lake and surround by farmland. Most bedrooms have their own washbasin. All rooms have tea/coffee facilities. Bathroom, with 6 foot bath, and 2 separate loos are shared. Breakfast from 5.30am for Cross Channel travellers. 20 minutes to Tunnel. 40 minutes to Dover. Handy for Leeds Castle, Sissinghurst, Canterbury and Bluewater. Hourly trains to London. Ample parking. Washing and drying facilities. Cycle storage.

Phillada Pym
Tel/Fax: 01233 712421

B&B from £28-£30pp, Rooms 3 single, 2 double, 1 twin, No smoking or pets, Children welcome, Open all year except Christmas.

BULLTOWN FARMHOUSE, Bulltown Lane, West Brabourne, Ashford, Kent TN25 5NB
Email wiltons@bulltown.fsnet.co.uk

Map Ref 4
Nearest Road A20, M20

Bulltown Farmhouse is an attractively restored 15th century timber framed Kentish farmhouse surrounded by cottage garden. It is situated on the south western side of the North Downs so is ideal for walking. Each room is heavily beamed with interesting features of medieval windows, fireplaces and are tastefully decorated. The views are unspoilt. Only homemade or local produce used. Conveniently situated for ports, or the Cathedral city of Canterbury and other places of historic interest or gardens. A warm welcome will await you.

Full page photo opposite

Mrs Lilly Wilton
Tel: 01233 813505
Fax: 01227 709544

B&B from £22.50-£25pp, Rooms 1 double, 1 twin, 1 family, all en-suite, No smoking or pets, Children welcome, Open all year.

HOPES GROVE COTTAGE, High Halden, near Ashford, Kent TN26 3LY
Email Brenda@hopesgrovecottage.org.uk
Website www.hopesgrovecotttage.org.uk

Map Ref 3
Nearest Road A28, M20

Hopes Grove Cottage is a charming 17th century listed cottage in the village of High Halden between Ashford and Tenterden (A28). Ideally located for Ashford International Station (Eurostar or London). Channel Tunnel Terminal. Dover ports and Castle, Sissinghurst and Leeds Castle, Canterbury Cathedral. Many tourist attractions. Local Inn within walking distance. Accommodation is en-suite with family room comprising double and single bed, TV, tea/coffee facility. Good size single room and access to separate bathroom. Guests lounge, patio, spacious garden. Substantial reduction for children.

Brenda & Michael Harrison
Tel: 01233 850423
Fax: 01233 850851

B&B from £20-£25pp, Rooms 1 single, 1 family, both en-suite/private bathroom, No smoking, Children & pets welcome, Open all year except Christmas & New Year.

THANINGTON HOTEL, 140 Wincheap, Canterbury, Kent CT1 3RY
Email thanington@lineone.net
Website www.thanington-hotel.co.uk

Map Ref 5
Nearest Road A28

Spacious Georgian Bed and Breakfast hotel offering high quality accommodation for the discerning traveller. 14 en-suite bedrooms including ground floor rooms, 2 family rooms and superior rooms with 4 posters or antique bedsteads. Games room with snooker table, bar and private car parking. Pretty enclosed courtyard garden overlooking the indoor heated swimming pool. An oasis in a bustling city and an ideal base for visiting the gardens and castles of Kent. AA, RAC and ETB 5 Diamonds and Gold Award. Credit cards accepted.

Ian & Jennifer Chapman
Tel: 01227 453227
Fax: 01227 453225

B&B from £73 per room, Rooms 9 double, 3 twin, 2 family, all en-suite, Restricted smoking, Children & pets welcome, Open all year.

CATHEDRAL GATE HOTEL, 36 Burgate, Canterbury, Kent CT1 2HA
Email cgate@cgate.demon.co.uk
Website www.cathgate.co.uk

Map Ref 5
Nearest Road A2, M2

A family run medieval hotel next to the main gateway to Canterbury Cathedral. With massive beams, sloping floors and winding corridors and a warm welcome. Our comfortable rooms have TV, tea/coffee facilities and direct dial telephones, some are en-suite. Residents licence, bar and lounge. Continental breakfast included, full English breakfast extra from February onwards. Credit cards accepted.

Mrs Jubber
Tel: 01227 464381
Fax: 01227 462800

B&B from £24-£88pr, Dinner from £8, Rooms 6 single, 9 double, 7 twin, 5 family, some en-suite, Children welcome, Pets by arrangement, Open all year.

CLARE ELLEN GUEST HOUSE, 9 Victoria Road, Canterbury, Kent CT1 3SG
Email loraine.williams@clareellenguesthouse.co.uk
Website www.clareellenguesthouse.co.uk

Map Ref 5
Nearest Road A28, A2

A warm welcome and Bed and Breakfast in style. Large quiet elegant en-suite rooms all with colour TV, clock/radio, ceiling fans, hairdryers and tea/coffee facilities. Vegetarians and special diets catered for on request. Ironing centre and trouser press for guest's convenience. Numerous restaurants close by. Six minutes walk to the city centre and coach station, four minutes to Canterbury East station. Close proximity to the cricket ground and University. Private car park and garage available. Credit cards accepted.

Mrs Loraine Williams
Tel: 01227 760205
Fax: 01227 784482

B&B from £25-£28pp, Rooms 1 single, 3 double, 2 twin, 2 family, all en-suite, Children welcome, No pets, Open all year.

UPPER ANSDORE, Duckpit Lane, Petham, Canterbury, Kent CT4 5QB
Email roger@ansdore.fsnet.co.uk
Website www.smoothhound.co.uk/hotels/upperans.html

Map Ref 6
Nearest Road B2068

Medieval house 600 year old. You are assured of a warm welcome, and a full English breakfast with our own free range eggs, etc. Excellent location for walking, cycling and exploring the surrounding areas. Lyminge Forest and Kent Trust Nature Reserver both one mile. Access to the North Downs Way four miles. All bedrooms have en-suite with tea/coffee facilities. There are exposed timbers in all rooms, and guests are supplied with their own keys. Credit cards accepted.

Roger & Susan Linch
Tel: 01227 700672
Fax: 01227 700840

B&B from £45-£48pr (double room), Rooms 3 double, 1 twin, 1 family, all en-suite, No smoking, Children over 5, Pets welcome, Open all year except Christmas & New Year.

WALLETT'S COURT COUNTRY HOUSE HOTEL, Westcliff, St Margaret's-at-Cliffe, Dover, Kent CT15 6EW
Email stay@wallettscourt.com
Website www.wallettscourt.com

Map Ref 8
Nearest Road A258, A2, A20

Relaxed and secluded, yet only 3 miles from Dover in the Heart of White Cliffs Country, this 17th century manor house hotel with restaurant and spa is simply beautiful. Luxurious bedrooms have antique four-poster beds, vaulted beamed ceilings and some rooms afford distant views of the English Channel. The restaurant noteworthy in its own right is mentioned in many major food guides and serves some of the finest cuisine in Kent. The Spa, a haven of relaxation, houses an indoor pool, sauna, steam room and Jacuzzi. Credit cards accepted.

Gavin Oakley
Tel: 01304 852424
Fax: 01304 853430

B&B from £45-£75pp, Dinner £35, Rooms 12 double, 3 twin, 1 family, all en-suite, Restricted smoking, Children welcome, No pets, Open all year except Christmas & New Year.

TENTERDEN HOUSE, 209 The Street, Boughton, Faversham, Kent ME13 9BL
Email platham@tesco.net

Map Ref 9
Nearest Road M2

The renovated gardener's cottage of this listed Tudor house, provides two en-suite bedrooms (one double, one twin) which can be used separately or together for families or friends. Situated in the village, close to Canterbury, the ferry ports and Euro Tunnel, it makes an ideal base for day trips to France and for touring rural and historic Kent. Off-road parking is provided, tea/coffee facilities and TV. Full English breakfast is served in the main house and a choice of excellent pub or restaurant food is within easy walking distance.

Prudence & Peter Latham
Tel: 01227 751593

B&B from £20pp, Rooms 1 twin, 1 double, both en-suite, Children welcome, No pets, Open all year except Christmas.

FRITH FARM HOUSE, Otterden, Faversham, Kent ME13 0DD
Email enquiries@frithfarmhouse.co.uk
Website www.frithfarmhouse.co.uk

Map Ref 10

Frith Farm is situated on the North Downs in an area of outstanding natural beauty. The house, an elegant Georgian building, is reached by a sweeping drive and surrounded by well looked after lawns and gardens. The interior is decorated with flair and great individuality using fine fabrics and antiques. A delightful and relaxing place to stay. One bedroom has 4 poster and all have en-suite shower, tea/coffee making facilities, and TV. There is an indoor swimming pool. Horse riding, golf, Pilgrims and North Downs Way are all nearby. Frith is a short drive from Canterbury, Dover and Leeds Castle. A warm welcome is assured.

Markham & Susan Chesterfield
Tel: 01795 890701
Fax: 01795 890009

B&B from £32pp-£35p, Rooms 1 twin 2 double, all en-suite, No smoking, Children over 10, Open all year.

JORDANS, Sheet Hill, Plaxtol, Sevenoaks, Kent TN15 0PU

Map Ref 12
Nearest Road A227, A25, M20, M25

Beautiful picture postcard 15th century Tudor house, awarded a historic building of Kent plague. Shown on two television programs. Plaxtol is a picturesque village amongst orchards and parkland. Rooms are beautifully furnished. Jordans has massive oak beams inglenooks, leaded windows. The garden is enchanting with roses, delphiniums, flowering shrubs and trees. Within easy reach of Ightham Mote, Leeds Castle, Hever Castle, Penshurst, Chartwell and Knole. Mrs Lindsay is a qualified tourist guide. London 35 minutes by train. There is easy access to airports Heathrow and Gatwick.

Mrs Jo Lindsay
Tel/Fax: 01732 810379

B&B from £33-£36pp (double), £42-£50 (single), Rooms 1 single, 2 double/twins, most en-suite, No smoking or pets, Children over 12, Open mid January to mid December.

Full page photo opposite

LEAVERS OAST, Stanford Lane, Hadlow, Kent TN11 0JN
Email denis@leavers-oast.freeserve.co.uk

Map Ref 11
Nearest Road A26

A warm friendly welcome and imaginative cooking is to be found in this beautiful 19th century Oast. The en-suite bedroom and two rounded bedrooms all provide very attractive and comfortable accommodation with TV and coffee/tea making facilities. The house is furnished with interesting antiques and the lovely garden overlooks open country. An ideal base for visiting Leeds, Hever and Scotney Castles, while Knole, Chartwell and Sissinghurst are close by. It is not surprising that many guests extend their stay or return to Leavers Oast.

Anne Turner
Tel/Fax: 01732 850924

B&B from £29-£32.50pp, Dinner £22, Rooms 2 double (1 en-suite), 1 twin, No smoking or pets, Children over 12, Open all year.

MERZIE MEADOWS, Hunton Road, Marden, near Tonbridge, Kent TN12 9SL
Website www.smoothhound.co.uk/hotels/merzie.html

Map Ref 13
Nearest Road M20, A229, B2079, A21

Unique country home set in lovely rural surroundings near to Leeds and Sissinghurst Castles many historic houses and gardens to visit nearby, convenient also for London, Dover, Canterbury. Two well appointed double en-suite bedrooms. Guests wing can also be used as triple, both bedrooms provide space, privacy and comfort overlooking extensive landscaped grounds with conservation areas. Many good eating places locally. Recommended by Which? AA Premier Selected, 5 Diamonds. Ideal for longer stays. Red Diamonds.

Pamela & Rodney Mumford
Tel/Fax: 01622 820 500

B&B from £27.50-£30pp, Rooms 2 double en-suite, No smoking or pets, Children over 15, Open mid February to mid December.

THE OLD PARSONAGE, Church Lane, Frant, Tunbridge Wells, Kent TN3 9DX
Email oldparson@aol.com
Website www.theoldparsonagehotel.co.uk

Map Ref 14
Nearest Road A267

The Old Parsonage is a magnificent Georgian house in a quiet, pretty village providing superior accommodation, luxurious en-suite bedrooms including two 4 posters, antique-furnished reception rooms and a spacious sunny conservatory, where guests may relax in armchair comfort with afternoon tea, overlooking the ballustraded terrace and secluded walled garden. For evening meals the village pub restaurants are 2 mins walk away. Short drive to many historic houses and gardens. SEETB award winner 'Bed & Breakfast of the Year', AA Premier selected. ETB Deluxe.

Mrs Mary Dakin
Tel: 01892 750773
Fax: 01892 750773

B&B from £39pp, Rooms 1 twin, 2 double, all en-suite, restricted smoking, Pets by arrangement, Open all year.

DANEHURST HOUSE, 41 Lower Green Road, Rusthall, Tunbridge Wells, Kent TN4 8TW
Email info@danehurst.net

Map Ref 15
Nearest Road A21, A264

Charming, gabled Victorian house in a village setting. Tastefully furnish rooms. Excellent quality large beds, en-suite facilities that are equipped with a wealth of thoughtful extras. There is a baby grand piano, in the drawing room and the Victorian style conservatory is a delightful setting for breakfast be it full English, fish, cold meats or continental. The lovely garden has a waterfall and Koi carp swim happily in the pond. While indoors style and flair in both decor and furnishings enhance the houses intrinsic charm. Credit cards accepted.

Angela Jane Godbold
Tel: 01892 527739
Fax: 01892 514804

B&B from £45-£85pp, Rooms 1 single, 3 double, 2 twin, all en-suite, No smoking or pets, Children over 8, Open all year except February and last week in August.

NUMBER TEN, Modest Corner, Southborough, Tunbridge Wells, Kent TN4 0LS
Email modestanneke@lineone.net

Map Ref 16
Nearest Road A26, A21, M25

You will experience a warm welcome in this very comfortable, tastefully decorated B&B, situated on the outer edge of Tunbridge Wells in a little hamlet away from noisy traffic. Ideally placed for visiting the south east with its many historic attractions such as Hever Castle, Sissinghurst and Chartwell. Easy access to M25 and Tonbridge Station, with trains to London every 20 minutes. Beautiful walks straight from the house. Once you have been you will want to come again. 3 Diamonds.

Anneke Leemhuis
Tel: 01892 522450

B&B from £25-£35pp, Rooms 1 double en-suite, 2 twin, No smoking, Children & pets welcome, Open all year except Christmas & New Year.

"What a view" said Belle, "Conwy Castle and another spectacular Telford bridge"

BELLE & BERTIE IN WALES

LANCASHIRE

Lancashire was once best known as an industrial county, particularly famous for its coal and cotton and home to the historic city of Lancaster – flourishing trading port and, at one time, central to the world slave market.

There is, however, a lot more to Lancashire than industrial hubs as its splendid countryside proves beyond any doubt. To the east of the county towards the Pennines lies Lancashire's Hill Country – a unique combination of rural moorland and woodland dotted with picturesque towns and villages and providing excellent walking terrain. To the west, a splendid coastline featuring ever-changing land and seascapes includes the resort towns of Blackpool, Lytham and Fleetwood, all boasting their own historic character and charm. The delightful River Wyre also features some attractive villages along its banks, Poulton-le-Fylde being particularly of note with its cobbled streets, medieval stocks and fine historic churches.

Although the towns to the south of the county can be described as mainly industrial, they are not without their highlights. Set amid beautiful countryside, Preston is the administrative capital of Lancashire and enjoys a rich history dating back to the Doomsday Book of 1080. Interesting architecture within the town includes the Grade 1 listed Harris Museum and Art Gallery – a magnificent Greek Revival building that dominates the town centre; and the Parish Church of St John with its stunning heraldic stained glass. Slightly outwith Preston, near the village Houghton is Houghton Tower – home to the 14th Baronet and described as one of the most dramatic looking houses in northern England. Three houses have occupied this captivating hill site since 1100, the present house being re-built by Thomas Houghton between 1560-1565. Also stunning by design and situated nearby is Samlesbury Hall, a black and white timbered house built in 1325 and set in particularly attractive grounds.

For visitors interested in ecclesiastical architecture, Blackburn Cathedral is built on an historic Saxon site and features the recently re-built Lantern Tower – the building's 'crowing glory' incorporating 56 symbolic panels of stained glass; while two significant country homes can also be found situated close to Blackburn: Martholme – part of a medieval manor house with 17th century additions near the village of Great Harwood; and Gawthorpe Hall – first built in 1600 and restored by Sir Charles Barry in the 1850s.

Situated to the north-west of the county, the city of Lancaster dates back to Roman times and features some particularly fine Georgian architecture. Lancaster Castle is also imposingly situated here, incorporating Hadrian's Tower, a courtroom and some particularly gruesome instruments of torture. Immediately next to castle is the equally fine Priory Church founded in 1094 but extensively remodelled later in the Middle Ages. The 17th century Judge's Lodgings can also be found on nearby China Street.

Last but certainly not least for visitors travelling north in the county is the village of Camforth and, more specifically, a nearby stately home boasting one of the most beautiful situations in the British Isles. Leighton Hall – home to the Reynolds family and featuring an impressive neo-gothic façade – enjoys fine furnishings within, impressive grounds without and the quite, quite stunning panorama of the Lakeland Fells as a backdrop.

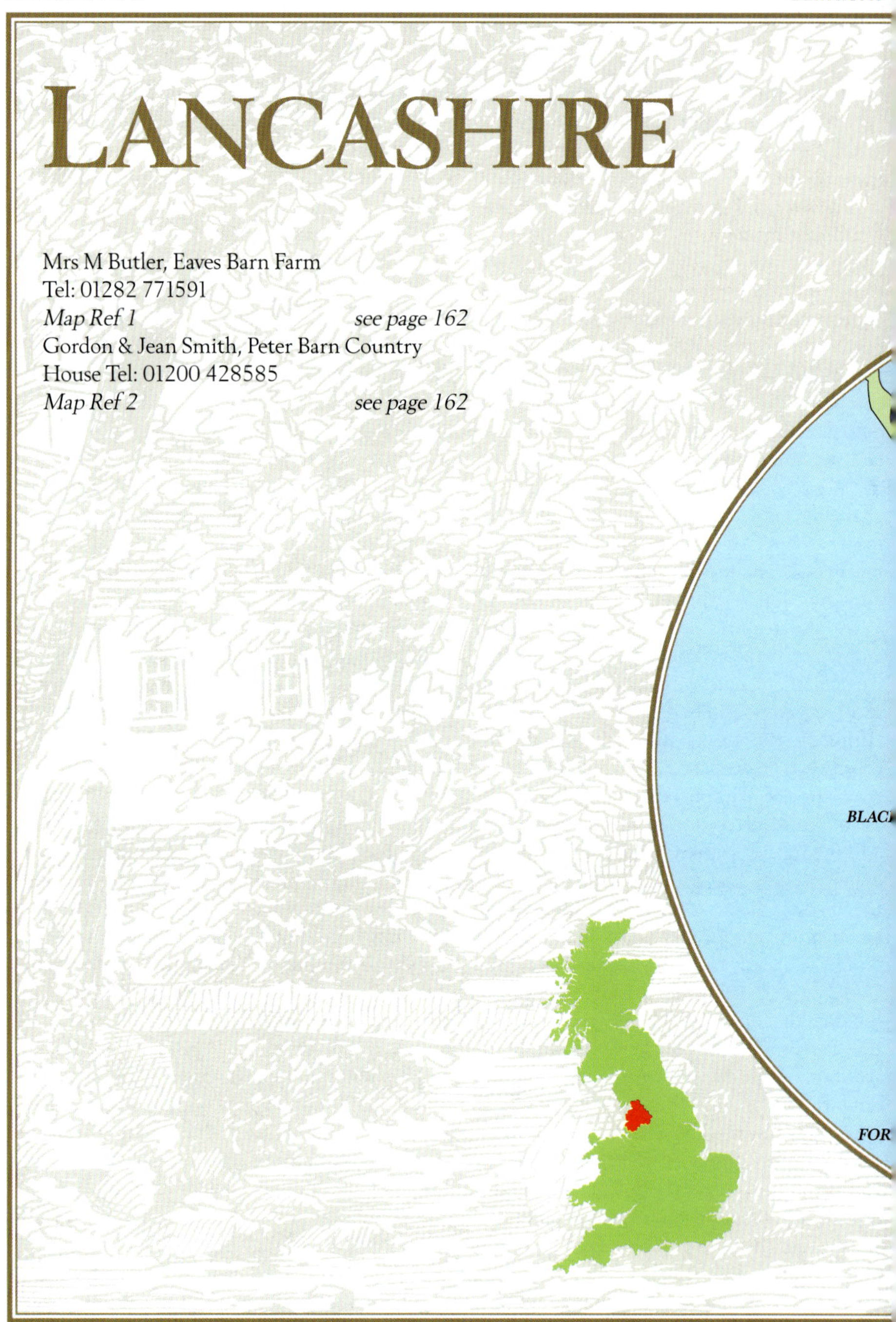

LANCASHIRE

Mrs M Butler, Eaves Barn Farm
Tel: 01282 771591
Map Ref 1 *see page 162*

Gordon & Jean Smith, Peter Barn Country
House Tel: 01200 428585
Map Ref 2 *see page 162*

Cumbria
Yorkshire
KIRKBY LONSDALE
A6
CARNFORTH
INGLETON
CLAPHAM
A65
MORECAMBE
LANCASTER
HEYSHAM
SETTLE
LONG PRESTON
A65
A59
SKIPTON
WOOD
A588
SLAIDBURN
B6478
GISBURN
GARSTANG
A59
BARNOLDSWICK
A6068
A586
M6
POULTON LE FYLDE
CLITHEROE
COLNE
WHALLEY
M65
M55
A671
A59
BURNLEY
A584
PRESTON
A677
BLACKBURN
ACCRINGTON
A59
A565
RAWTENSTALL
TODMORDEN
DARWEN
BACUP
LEYLAND
RAMSBOTTOM
A58
A570
A59
CHORLEY
M66
A666
ROCHDALE
RMSKIRK
BOLTON
SKELMERSDALE
M6
M61
BURY
M58
WIGAN
A6

EAVES BARN FARM, Hapton, Burnley, Lancashire BB12 7LP
Email mavis@eavesbarnfarm.co.uk
Website www.eavesbarnfarm.co.uk

Map Ref 1
Nearest Road M5, A679

Full page photo opposite

Eaves Barn is a working farm with a spacious cottage attached to the main house offering luxurious facilities. The elegant guests lounge has a log open fire and is traditionally furnished including antiques. Individually designed bedrooms with colour TV, en-suite facilities. A full English breakfast is served in the Victorian style conservatory. 'Best Bed & Breakfast' in Lancashire 1992. Situated within easy reach of the Ribble Valley and Fylde Coast, Lake District, Yorkshire Dales and the Lancashire hills. Burnley, Blackburn, Preston and Manchester Airport can be reached using the motorway network.

Mrs M Butler
Tel: 01282 771591
Fax: 01282 771591

B&B from £25pp, Rooms 1 single, 1 twin, 1 double, all en-suite, Children welcome over 12, No pets, Open all year except Christmas.

PETER BARN COUNTRY HOUSE, Cross Lane, Waddington, Clitheroe, Lancashire BB7 3JH
Email jean@peterbarn.fsnet.co.uk

Map Ref 2
Nearest Road A59, M6 J31

Award winning Lancashire hospitality is offered in our charmingly restored stone built Tithe Barn on the edge of the Forest of Bowland. Oak beams, squashy sofas and log fires on chillier evenings in guests sitting room with wonderful views of our beautiful Ribble Valley. Three tastefully furnished bedrooms with all comforts. An acre of impressive gardens with stream and ponds. Jean's home made muesli and marmalade is legendary. Excellent walking, good eating nearby, easy reach of the M6, coast and Lake District. Queen Mother's Award (Environmental); ETC 4 Diamonds, Highly Recommended; Sunday Observer Top 20 B&Bs in Great Britain.

Gordon & Jean Smith
Tel: 01200 428585

B&B from £25pp, Rooms 1 twin, 2 double, all en-suite, No smoking or pets, Open all year.

Please mention

A GREAT PLACE TO STAY

when enquiring about accommodation

Leicestershire, Nottinghamshire & Rutland

Set in the heart of England, Leicestershire is a county of beautiful waterways, secluded valleys and pleasant woodland. To the east around Melton Mowbray, rolling farmland, picturesque villages and fine gothic architecture abound – while to the west the once coal-dominated towns of Coalville and Moira present unique character and an interesting insight into their industrial pasts. As a result of the rapid industrial growth of the 19th century, the lively city of Leicester acquired a wonderful legacy of fine Victorian architecture – although the origins of the county's capital actually date back to Roman times. Highlights of this pleasant city include Belgrave Hall & Gardens on Church Road – a period house with decoration ranging from 1750 to 1900 and situated within formal Victorian gardens; The Guildhall – a magnificent timber-framed medieval building first used by the Corpus Christi Guild and now a performance venue; and Newarke Houses Museum, tracing 500 years of Leicestershire history by way of reconstructed domestic displays and street scenes.

Slightly south of Leicester, near the village of Lutterworth, Stanford Hall presents a fine example of a country home from the William and Mary period. The grand interiors include a splendid pink and gold Ballroom with an impressive coved ceiling – while the grounds delight with peaceful walks along the River Avon.

Heading north, horticultural enthusiasts should certainly stop at Wartnaby Gardens in Melton Mowbray – if only to wonder at the sheer variety of plants alone. Made up of a series of small gardens, Wartnaby features a white garden, a sunken garden, a purple border of shrubs and roses, old-fashioned roses, herbaceous borders, primulas, ferns, astilbes and several varieties of trees. Added to this are numerous greenhouses and a beautiful Grecian pattern beech hedge. And if that's not enough, the splendid Belvoir Castle – commanding magnificent views over the Vale of Belvoir on the western boundary of the county – boasts impressive Statue Gardens and magnificent floral displays.

Adjoining Leicestershire to the North, the county of Nottinghamshire is perhaps best known for Sherwood Forrest and its most famous legendary resident Robin Hood. There is, however, a lot more than a good story to attract the visitor to this predominantly rural area of middle England, as the tranquil green landscape, redbrick cottages, ancient woodland and riverside villages clearly testify. The Saxon city of Nottingham can be found to the south of the county and, rather interestingly, stands upon a maze of man-made sandstone caves dating back to medieval times. Notable buildings in and around the city include Wollaton Hall, an extravagant Tudor mansion built in 1568 and now housing the Nottingham Natural History Museum; Holme Pierrepont Hall – a late medieval manor house set in thirty acres of park and gardens; and the magnificent Gothic masterpiece that is Southwell Minster. Literature lovers may also be interested in visiting the birthplace of DH Lawrence, Nottingham's most controversial author, at 8a Victoria Street, Eastwood.

More northerly highlights in the county include classical Papplewick Hall with its 18th century woodland garden; the delightful Georgian country retreat of Norwood Park; and Hodsock Priory Gardens near Worksop – particularly pleasant woodland grounds featuring a myriad of flowering plants and bulbs. If you can, visit in spring to enjoy the unforgettable carpet of snowdrops.

LEICESTERSHIRE, NOTTINGHAMSHIRE & RUTLAND

Sue Goodwin, Hillside House
Tel: 01664 566312
Map Ref 1 *see page 168*

Pamela Holden, The Grange
Tel: 01664 560775
Map Ref 1 *see page 168*

Mrs Betty Hinchley, Titchfield Guest House
Tel: 01623 810921/810356
Map Ref 2 *see page 168*

Michael & Sheila Spratt, Greenwood Lodge City Guesthouse
Tel: 0115 9621206
Map Ref 3 *see page 169*

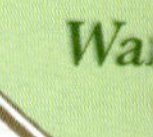

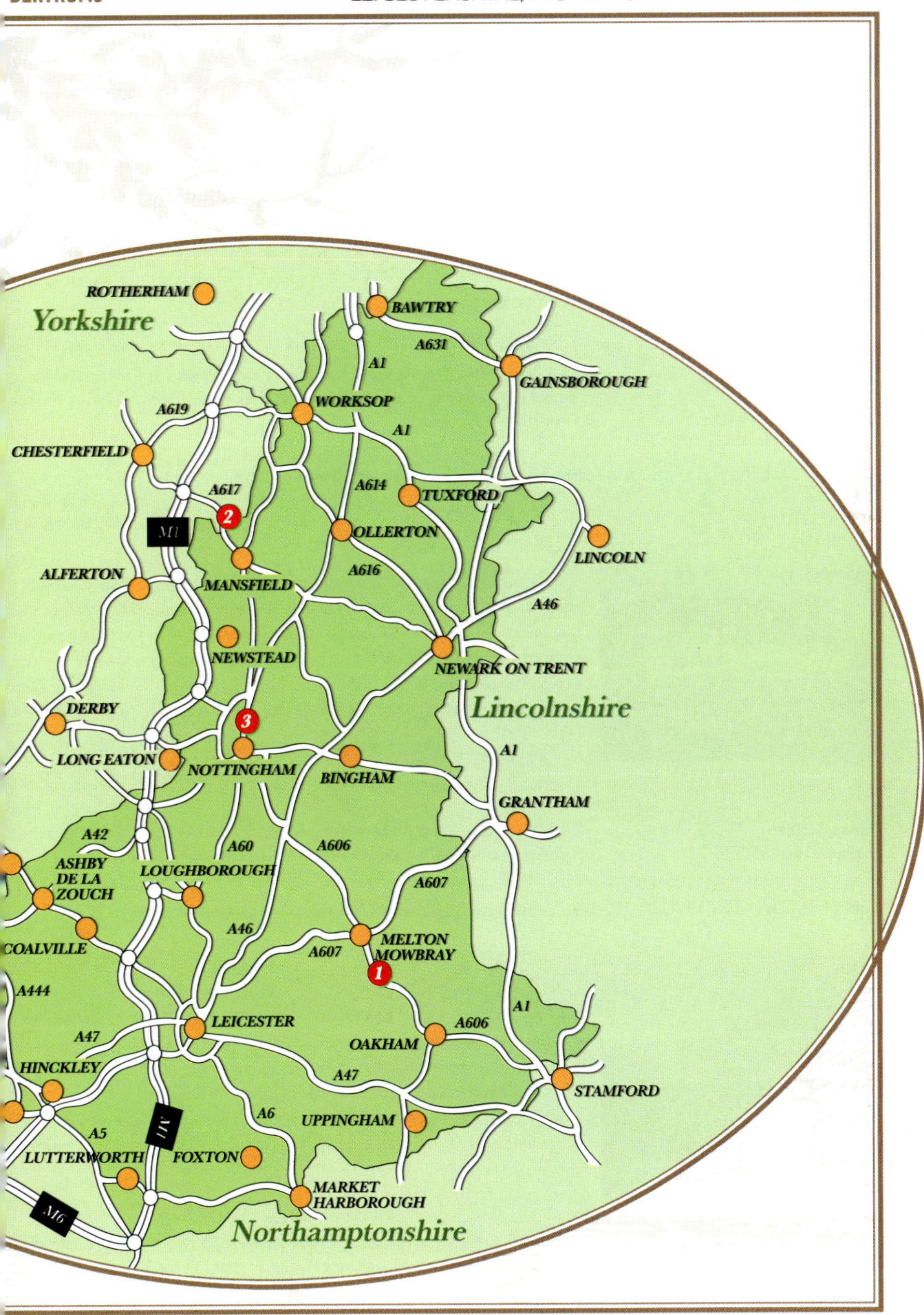
ROTHERHAM
Yorkshire
BAWTRY
A631
A1
GAINSBOROUGH
A619
WORKSOP
A1
CHESTERFIELD
A617
A614
TUXFORD
2
M1
OLLERTON
LINCOLN
ALFERTON
MANSFIELD
A616
A46
NEWSTEAD
NEWARK ON TRENT
DERBY
Lincolnshire
3
LONG EATON
NOTTINGHAM
BINGHAM
A1
GRANTHAM
A42
A60
A606
ASHBY
DE LA
ZOUCH
LOUGHBOROUGH
A607
A46
MELTON
MOWBRAY
COALVILLE
A607
1
A444
A1
LEICESTER
A606
A47
OAKHAM
HINCKLEY
A47
STAMFORD
A6
UPPINGHAM
A5
M1
LUTTERWORTH
FOXTON
MARKET
HARBOROUGH
M6
Northamptonshire

HILLSIDE HOUSE, 27 Melton Road, Burton Lazars, Melton Mowbray, Leicestershire LE14 2UR
Email hillhs27@aol.com
Website www.hillside-house.co.uk

Map Ref 1
Nearest Road A606

Looking out over rolling countryside this comfortable converted old farm building offer one double room en-suite, one twin room en-suite, one twin with exclusive private bathroom. Rooms have tea/coffee facilities, hair dryers and what you would expect to find in a well appointed house. Off road parking. Tourist rating 4 Diamonds. 10% reduction for 3 nights stay (except special occasions). Markets Tuesdays and Saturdays. Belvoir Castle, Rutland Water, Geoff Hamiltons Gardens, Burghley House close by.

Sue Goodwin
Tel: 01664 566312
Fax: 01664 501819

B&B from £19-£22pp, Rooms 1 double, 2 twin, all en-suite/private facilities, Restricted smoking, Children over 10, No pets, Open all year except Christmas & New Year.

THE GRANGE, New Road, Burton Lazars, Melton Mowbray, Leicestershire LE14 2UU

Map Ref 1
Nearest Road A606, M1, A1

This beautiful country house set in formal gardens of two acres with sweeping lawns and outstanding views surrounds you with elegance and comfort. All bedrooms are en-suite and furnished to a high standard with TV, telephone and tea/coffee facilities. The spacious drawing room has an open log burning fire down. We are 1 ½ Melton Mowbray. 7 miles Oakham. 14 miles Leicester. Rutland Water, Belvoir Castle, Belton House and Burghley House are all close to us.

Pamela Holden
Tel/Fax: 01664 560775

B&B from £25-£35pp, Rooms 1 single, 2 double, 1 twin, 1 family, all en-suite, Restricted smoking, Children welcome, No pets, Open all year.

TITCHFIELD GUEST HOUSE, 300-302 Chesterfield Road North, Mansfield, Nottinghamshire NG19 7QU

Map Ref 2
Nearest Road A617

Titchfield is two houses converted into one family run guest house offering eight comfortable rooms, a lounge with TV, a kitchen for making hot drinks etc, a bathroom and showers, it also has an adjoining garage. It is near to Mansfield which is a busy market town, Sherwood Forest and the Peak District are easily accessible. We are very handy for touring this lovely area and onward travel. A warm and friendly welcome is assured at all time, you will feel very wanted. Credit cards accepted.

Mrs Betty Hinchley
Tel: 01623 810921/810356
Fax: 01623 810386

B&B from £18-£19pp, Rooms 4 single, 1 double, 2 twin, 1 family, Restricted smoking, Children & pets welcome, Open all year except Christmas & New Year.

GREENWOOD LODGE CITY GUESTHOUSE, Third Avenue, Sherwood Rise, Nottingham, NG7 6JH
Email coolspratt@aol.com
Website www.greenwoodlodgecityguesthouse.co.uk
Map Ref 3
Nearest Road A60

Greenwood Lodge City Guest House is less than a mile from the centre of Nottingham. Just off the A60 Mansfield Road, situated in a quiet area and is the home of Sheila and Michael Spratt who offer superior accommodation, all en-suite with hospitality tray, trouser press, TV, hair dryer and fine four poster. Magnificent conservatory dining room in elegant gardens. Ample off-street parking. Five Diamonds with Gold Award. Within short distance of Newstead Abbey, Chatsworth House, Sherwood Forest, Belvoir Castle. ETC 4 Diamonds and Gold Award.

Michael & Sheila Spratt
Tel: 0115 9621206
Fax: 0115 9621206

B&B from £30pp, Rooms 1 single, 1 twin, 4 double, four poster beds, all en-suite, No smoking, Children welcome, Open all year.

"Why" asked the guide "Is there only one clockwise staircase out of eight?"
"No idea" said Bertie "For the left handed soldiers, to have room for their sword arm"
And the guide demonstrated with his stick

BELLE & BERTIE IN WALES

LINCOLNSHIRE

Slightly off the beaten track but certainly well worth discovering, Lincolnshire stretches from the bay known as The Wash to as far as the Humber on England's eastern seaboard. The diverse topography of the county features the rolling hills and deep-sided valleys of The Wolds to the north and the flat agricultural Fens to the south – and there are some interesting salt marshes and fine beaches to be found along its coastal plains, too.

Unspoilt towns such as Stamford to the south of the county ooze Olde Englande charm with cobbled streets, fine medieval architecture and picturesque red roofs – and make for particularly pleasant places to enjoy a leisurely lunch. Just one mile from charming Stamford lies Burghley House, an immensely grand late Elizabethan mansion featuring parklands designed by Capability Brown and a particularly notable sculpture garden. Within the house can be found 18 magnificent state rooms, including the quite remarkable Heaven Room – painted by Antonio Verrio in the 17th century and featuring floor-to-ceiling gods and goddesses languishing among the columns.

Travelling north, the red-brick town of Grantham is also worth a visit, if only to admire the lofty spire of the 13th century church of St Wulfram's. Although 85-metres high, the impressive spire falls three metres short of Lincolnshire's highest, that of St Botolph's in the county's historic port of Boston on The Wash.

Close to Grantham, the village of Belton boasts one of England's crowning achievements of Restoration country house architecture in the shape of the impeccable Belton House. Built in 1685-88 for Sir John Brownlow and altered by James Wyatt in the 1770s, the house is renowned for its fine plasterwork ceilings and wood carvings attributed to the famous Dutch carver Grinling Gibbons. The pleasant 400-hectare parklands feature lakeside walks, an impressive church with family monuments and formal gardens with orangery.

Continuing north in the county, the university town of Lincoln abounds with interesting Tudor architecture, very steep medieval streets and is home to one of the finest Gothic cathedrals in Europe. Lincoln Castle, built just four years prior to the cathedral by William The Conqueror in 1068, is also of outstanding historical interest. Visitors can enjoy fine views from the battlements and an informative exhibition, including Lincoln's copy of the Magna Carta.

Slightly outwith the busy hub of Lincoln sits Doddinton Hall, a stunning Smythson mansion with particularly stunning grounds in spring and summer. Horticulturists will revel in the superb mix of formal box-edged parterres, meticulously planted borders and wild gardens, while within the 15th century Hall interior buffs can enthuse over elegant Georgian decor and the superb collections of porcelain, paintings and furniture that represent 400 years of unbroken family occupation.

LINCOLNSHIRE

Mrs Lesley Honnor, Pipwell Manor
Tel: 01406 423119
Map Ref 1 *see page 174*

Mrs C Harrison, Baumber Park
Tel: 01507 578235
Map Ref 2 *see page 174*

Judy Bankes Price, Greenfield Farm
Tel: 01507 578457
Map Ref 3 *see page 174*

Richard & Judith Hand, West View Cottages
Tel: 01507 327209
Map Ref 4 *see page 175*

BRIGG
CLEETHORPES
WALTHAM
A15
CAISTOR
A159
A631
MARKET RASEN
A16
A1031
LOUTH
A15
A46
B1202
MABLETHORPE
A158
WRAGBY
A16
LINCOLN
A52
HORNCASTLE
PARTNEY
A155
SKEGNESS
WADDINGTON
A15
A17
CONINGSBY
A52
A153
A16
A1
A17
SLEAFORD
BOSTON
HUNSTANTON
A52
A16
GRANTHAM
DONINGTON
A17
A15
LONG SUTTON
A1
SPALDING
HOLBEACH
Norfolk
BOURNE
A17
WISBECH
MARKET DEEPING
STAMFORD

PIPWELL MANOR, Saracens Head, Holbeach, Lincolnshire PE12 8AL
Email honnor@pipwellmanor.freeserve.co.uk
Website www.SmoothHound.co.uk/hotels/pipwell.html

Map Ref 1
Nearest Road A17

This Georgian house was built around 1740 and is a Grade II listed building. It has been tastefully restored and redecorated in the appropriate style and retains many of its original features. All 4 bedrooms are attractive and well furnished and have tea/coffee making facilities. Parking is available and guests are welcomed with home made cakes and tea. Pipwell Manor stands amid gardens and paddocks in a small village just off the A17 in the Lincolnshire Fens. A lovely place to stay. AA 4 Diamonds, 'Which' Good B&B Guide, 'Country Living'. 'Which Good Hotel Guide'.

Mrs Lesley Honnor
Tel/Fax: 01406 423119

B&B from £24pp, Rooms 2 double, 1 twin, 1 single, all with en-suite or private facilities, No smoking or pets, Open all year except Christmas & New Year.

BAUMBER PARK, Baumber, near Horncastle, Lincolnshire LN9 5NE
Website uk.geocities.com/baumberpark/thehouse

Map Ref 2
Nearest Road A158

Spacious, elegant farmhouse of character in a quiet parkland setting on a mixed farm. Large gardens, wildlife pond, grass tennis court. Fine bedrooms with lovely views, period furniture, log fires and books. Close to the Lincolnshire Wolds, this rolling countryside is little known and quite unspoilt. Bridleways and lanes ideal for walking, cycling or riding: stabling for horses available. Woodhall Spa's championship golf courses nearby. Aviation heritage, historic Lincoln, interesting market towns and many antiques shops. Peace, relaxation and a warm welcome. ETC 4 Diamonds.

Mrs C Harrison
Tel: 01507 578235
Fax: 01507 578417

B&B from £22.50-£27.50pp, Dinner by prior arrangement £12, Rooms 1 single, 1 double en-suite, 1 twin with private shower room, Restricted smoking, Children welcome, Open all year except Christmas & New Year.

GREENFIELD FARM, Mill Lane/Cow Lane, Minting, Horncastle, Lincolnshire LN9 5PJ
Email greenfieldfarm@farming.co.uk

Map Ref 3
Nearest Road A158

Enjoy a quiet stay in our lovely spacious home, surrounded by extensive grounds and dominated by a wonderful wildlife pond. Centrally placed and easy to find, Lincoln Cathedral is 15 minutes away and the sleepy Lincolnshire Wolds 5 minutes. We are close to the aviation trails, antique centres and Cadwell Park. The bedrooms have modern en-suite shower rooms with heated towel rails, tea/coffee making facilities and wonderful views. A typical farmhouse breakfast is served, you must try the Lincolnshire sausages and homemade marmalade. Plenty of parking, traditional pub one mile. AA 4 Diamonds.

Judy Bankes Price
Tel/Fax: 01507 578457
Mobile: 07768 368829

B&B from £23pp, Rooms 2 double, 1 twin, all en-suite, No smoking or dogs, Children over 10, Open mid January to mid December.

WEST VIEW COTTAGES, South Cockrington, Louth, Lincolnshire
Email richard@nicholson55.freeserve.co.uk

Map Ref 4

Beautifully converted single storey farm buildings. Tastefully decorated to a high standard. Ideally located in a quiet village. Linen, duvets, blankets and towels provided. Electricity and heating included in price. Electric cooker, microwave, fridge, laundry room, colour TV, video, hair dryer, cot, high chair, patio, garden furniture and barbecue. Parking for four cars. Market town of Louth is 4 miles away. Suitable walking, cycling and bird watching are close by.

3 cottages, sleep 2-4, Price per week from £190 low season, £250 high season, Children & pets welcome, Available all year.

Contact: Richard & Judith Hand, West View, South West Lane, South Cockerington, Louth, Lincolnshire LN11 7ED
Tel: 01507 327209

" What with portculises and arrow slit windows and murder holes for pouring down boiling pitch, I don't think I'd have had a go at Conwy" said Bertie. "Nor me" said Belle.

BELLE & BERTIE IN WALES

NORFOLK

This predominantly flat county on the east coast of England is perhaps best known for its historic sea-faring towns such as King's Lynn and Great Yarmouth and the Norfolk Broads – a delightful series of criss-crossing waterways comprising rivers, ancient flooded peat diggings, lakes and meres – long popular for boating holidays. The salt marshes of west Norfolk along The Wash provide superb bird-watching opportunities, while the stunning coastline of the north features clean, award-winning beaches and a string of small coastal villages that retain an ambience of old.

Norfolk also enjoys a rich history, as its many magnificent castles, historic houses and over 700 medieval churches can testify. In the Middle Ages the prosperous county town of Norwich was bigger than London and today boasts a splendid Norman castle keep, below which arguably lies one of England's most complete medieval cities. These days Norwich is home to the university of East Anglia and makes for a particularly pleasant place to visit with some interesting architecture both in and out of town. Elm Hill provides a fine example of street restoration, retaining its medieval charm and atmosphere, while Dragon Hall in King Street has been described as 'one of the most exciting 15th century buildings in Europe'. Just 600 yards from the town centre on Earlham Road, the 19th century Plantation Garden comprises a gothic fountain, lawns, Italianate terrace and woodland walkways to provide the perfect complement to urban living.

On the outskirts of Norwich sits the magnificent Blickling Hall – a Jacobean masterpiece of symmetry and elegance famed for its extraordinary long gallery, fine library and notable collections of paintings and tapestries. Felbrigg Hall too, near the village of Felbrigg and also close to Norwich, has been described as one of East Anglia's finest 17th century houses, the wonderful walled gardens featuring a dovecote and delightful orchards.

Travelling west in the county, the historic town of Kings Lynn – situated on the estuary of the Great River Ouse – is also well worth an afternoon's stroll. One of England's chief ports in the Middle Ages, Kings Lynn retains the last remnants of the Hanseatic League that flourished during medieval times – and to some extent the intriguing atmosphere of the bustling port lingers in the nooks and crannies of the old town.

The influence that once existed in King's Lynn is particularly evident outwith the town, exemplified by some truly remarkable country retreats. Although only partly intact, Castle Acre Priory clearly displays the wealth of a bygone era, featuring highly elaborate decoration on its still standing west church front and splendid prior's lodgings and chapel. Oxburgh Hall, built in 1492, provides a fine example of a medieval manor house complete with moat; while Houghton House is quite simply breathtaking in its stature and regarded as one of the finest examples of Palladian architecture in England.

No visit to Norfolk would be complete, of course, without paying homage to that most famous country retreat of all – Sandringham House. It is here that the Queen and her family enjoy the splendour of north-west Norfolk and the elegant proportions of this elegant home, still maintained in the style of King Edward VII and Queen Alexandra. All the ground floor rooms used by the Royal family are open to the public and contain a fascinating array of treasured ornaments, portraits and family photographs – while the charming gardens promote an aura of calm and allows the imagination to wonder at the many Royal discussions that may well have taken place here over the years.

NORFOLK

Mrs Richardson, The Old Pump House
Tel: 01263 733789
Map Ref 1 *see page 180*

David & Annie Bartlett, Bartles Lodge
Tel: 01362 637177
Map Ref 2 *see page 180*

Mrs Jenny Bell, Peacock House
Tel: 01362 860371
Map Ref 3 *see page 180*

Paul & Yolanda Davey, Strenneth
Tel: 01379 688182
Map Ref 4 *see page 182*

Mary & Jeremy Brettingham-Smith, Glebe Farmhouse
Tel: 01328 730133
Map Ref 5 *see page 182*

Alan & Muriel Webster, Tower Cottage
Tel: 01493 394053
Map Ref 6 *see page 182*

Colin & Lesley Rudd, The Moat House
Tel: 01508 570149
Map Ref 7 *see page 183*

Amanda Case, Lower Farm
Tel: 01485 520240
Map Ref 8 *see page 183*

John & Hermione Birkbeck, Litcham Hall
Tel: 01328 701389
Map Ref 9 *see page 183*

Phil & Ray Coe, Brooksbank
Tel: 01603 720420
Map Ref 10 *see page 184*

Mrs Marion Ford, Old Bottle House
Tel: 01842 878012
Map Ref 11 *see page 184*

Jennifer Bloom, Kimberley Home farm
Tel: 01953 603137
Map Ref 12 *see page 184*

WELLS NEXT THE SEA
CLEY NEXT THE SEA
SHERINGHAM
CROMER
A149
A148
HOLT
FAKENHAM
A148
NORTH WALSHAM
AYLSHAM
SMALLBURGH
A1067
A149
HEMSBY
EAST DEREHAM
A47
NORWICH
ACLE
CAISTER ON SEA
A47
SWAFFHAM
WYMONDHAM
A47
GREAT YARMOUTH
A134
WATTON
A1065
ATTLEBOROUGH
A11
A140
BUNGAY
LOWESTOFT
BECCLES
THETFORD
DISS
A11
A134
HALESWORTH
A143
Suffolk
A1120
1
2
3
4
5
6
7
8
9
10
11
12

Full page photo opposite

THE OLD PUMP HOUSE, 2 Holman Road, Aylsham, Norfolk NR11 6BY

Map Ref 1
Nearest Road A140

This comfortable 1750's house faces the thatched pump and has six bedrooms, four en-suite (including one four poster), with colour TV and tea/coffee facilities. English breakfast is served in the pine shuttered red room overlooking the peaceful garden. Aylsham is ideal for visiting the Broads, the coast, Norwich, National Trust houses, steam railways and unspoilt countryside. Well behaved children are welcome. Bed and breakfast from £20 to £30. Non smoking. Off road parking. ETC 4 Diamonds. Credit cards accepted.

Mrs Richardson
Tel/Fax: 01263 733789

B&B from £20-£30pp, Dinner by prior arrangement £15, Rooms 1 single, 3 double, 1 twin, 1 family, most en-suite, No smoking, Children welcome, Pets by prior arrangement, Open all year except Christmas & New Year.

BARTLES LODGE, Church Street, Elsing, Dereham, Norfolk NR20 3EA

Map Ref 2
Nearest Road A1067, A47

If you would like a peaceful, tranquil stay in the heart of Norfolk's most beautiful countryside, yet only a short drive to some of England's finest beaches, then Bartles Lodge could be the place for you. All rooms are tastefully decorated in country style, and have full en-suite facilities etc. Overlooking 12 acres of landscaped meadows with its own private fishing lakes. The local village inn is nearby for evening meals. Why not telephone David or Annie so that we can tell you about our lovely home.

David & Annie Bartlett
Tel: 01362 637177

B&B from £23pp, Rooms 4 double, 3 twin, Open all year.

PEACOCK HOUSE, Peacock Lane, Old Beetley, Dereham, Norfolk NR20 4DG
Email PeackH@aol.com
Website www.smoothhound.co.uk/hotels/peacockh.html

Map Ref 3
Nearest Road A47, B1146

Peacock House is a lovely old farmhouse, peacefully situated. All guest rooms are en-suite, beautifully furnished in traditional country style; each have colour televisions and hospitality trays. Guests have their own attractive sitting room and are welcome to enjoy the garden. Croquet is available. Norwich with its cathedral, castle and speciality shops, the spectacular Norfolk beaches, Sandringham, National Trust houses and other places of interest, are all within easy reach. Off road parking, no smoking, well-behaved pets and children welcome. ETC 4 Diamonds - Gold Award 2002.

Mrs Jenny Bell
Tel: 01362 860371

B&B from £22.50-£24pp, Rooms 1 double, 1 twin, 1 family, all en-suite, No smoking, Children & pets welcome, Open all year.

PUMP HOUSE
& BREAKFAST

STRENNETH, Airfield Road, Fersfield, Diss, Norfolk IP22 2BP
Email pdavey@strenneth.co.uk
Website www.strenneth.co.uk

Map Ref 4
Nearest Road A1066, A11, A14

Strenneth is a family run business, situated in unspoiled countryside just 10 minutes drive from the market town of Diss and Bressingham Gardens. The 17th century building has exposed beams, and has been fully renovated with a single storey courtyard wing with off road parking and plenty of walks nearby. The seven bedrooms, including a Four Poster are tastefully arranged with period furniture. All have colour TV, hospitality trays, central heating and en-suite facilities. The establishment is smoke free and the guest lounge has a log fire on cold winter evenings. There is an extensive breakfast menu using local produce.

Paul & Yolanda Davey
Tel: 01379 688182
Fax: 01379 688260

B&B from £25pp, Rooms 1 single, 2 twin, 4 double, all en-suite, No smoking, Children and Pets welcome, Open all year.

GLEBE FARMHOUSE, Wells Road, North Creake, Fakenham, Norfolk NR21 9LG
Email jb@eastnortheast.co.uk

Map Ref 5
Nearest Road A148

Our quiet and colourful Grade II Listed farmhouse is a relaxed family home on the edge of the village. We have two B&B rooms, one en-suite, one attic room with shower/w.c. next door, both with tea/coffee facilities. Organic eggs and homemade bread for breakfast. Vegetarians welcome. Fresh flowers and cotton sheets. Cot and child's bed available. Many excellent pubs and restaurants nearby. Also fine houses and gardens to visit. Varied beaches and many other activities for everybody.

Mary & Jeremy Brettingham-Smith
Tel: 01328 730133
Fax: 01328 730444

B&B from £25pp, Rooms 1 double en-suite, 1 double, No smoking or pets, Children welcome, Open all year except Christmas & New Year.

TOWER COTTAGE, Black Street, Winterton-on-Sea, Great Yarmouth, Norfolk NR29 4AP
Email towercott@aladdinscave.net
Website www.towercottage.co.uk

Map Ref 6
Nearest Road B1159

Enjoy a warm welcome at this lovely old cottage, opposite the imposing flint church, in a pretty village. Beamed, en-suite, ground floor bedrooms in a converted barn, overlooking the garden. One room has a sitting area, each has its own entrance, TV and tea making in all rooms. Excellent breakfast with homemade preserves served amongst the grapevines in the conservatory in summer. Car park. Good pub food, unspoilt sandy beach, dunes and nature reserve, a short stroll. Norfolk Broads 2 miles. Norwich 19 miles.

Alan & Muriel Webster
Tel: 01493 394053

B&B from £20-£24pp, Rooms 2 en-suite double, 1 twin with private bathroom, No smoking or pets, Children over 8, Open all year.

THE MOAT HOUSE, Rectory Lane, Hethel, Norfolk NR14 8HD
Email colles@hethelmoat.freeserve.co.uk

Map Ref 7
Nearest Road A11

An elegant Georgian house ideally located for visiting Norwich and the Norfolk area. The luxurious indoor swimming pool is available all year. Credit cards accepted.

Colin & Lesley Rudd
Tel/Fax: 01508 570149

B&B from £37.50-£45pp (single supplement), Dinner £22, Rooms 1 single, 1 double, No smoking, children or pets, Open all year except Christmas & New Year.

LOWER FARM, Harpley, King's Lynn, Norfolk PE31 6TU

Map Ref 8
Nearest Road A148

Lower Farm, is set in beautiful surroundings with 2 acres of gardens, three spacious double rooms, two en-suite and one with private bathroom. All rooms have fridges, TV and tea/coffee facilities. Good pub. Village Sandringham and Houghton Hall are minutes away also the village of Burnham Market. Good golf courses and sailing on the coast. Also good walking. Stabling is available for horses. Dogs in cars or stables. This is a very beautiful part of Norfolk to visit.

Amanda Case
Tel/Fax: 01485 520240

B&B from £20-£28pp, Rooms 3 double, all en-suite/private facilities, No smoking, Children over 12, Open all year.

LITCHAM HALL, Litcham, King's Lynn, Norfolk PE32 2QQ
Email j.birkbeck@amserve.com
Website www.bbgl.co.uk

Map Ref 9
Nearest Road B1145, A1065, A47

Fine listed Georgian house built in 1781 on edge of pretty village in central Norfolk. 30 minutes from lovely north Norfolk coast. 3 acre garden sometimes opened for charity. Use of pool by arrangement. Beautifully furnished guests sitting room, TV. Easy reach of Sandringham, Blickling, Holkham, Houghton, Norwich, in fact anywhere in Norfolk. Old country house atmosphere.

John & Hermione Birkbeck
Tel: 01328 701389
Fax: 01328 701164

B&B from £25-£32.50pp, Dinner by arrangement £20, Rooms 3 twin (2 private bathroom), Pets welcome, Open all year except Christmas & New Year.

BROOKSBANK, 1 Lower Street, Salhouse, Norwich, Norfolk NR13 6RW
Email ray@brooksbank8.freeserve.co.uk

Map Ref 10

Brooksbank House is next door to a quiet public house, where meals are obtainable, centred in the broadland village of Salhouse. TV lounge for guests use only. Extensive breakfast menu. 2 double on first floor and 1 twin bedded ground floor en-suite rooms. Satellite colour TV, hospitality trays in all rooms. Ample car parking at rear. Outside heated swimming pool in summer only. Salhouse is situated 2 miles from Wroxham and 6 miles from Norwich. Also adjoining self catering cottage with TV. Please telephone for brochure.

Phil & Ray Coe
Tel: 01603 720420

B&B from £18pp, Rooms 1 twin, 2 double, all en-suite, No smoking, Children welcome, No pets, Open all year.

OLD BOTTLE HOUSE, Cranwich, Mundford, Thetford, Norfolk IP26 5JL

Map Ref 11
Nearest Road A134

A warm welcome is assured at the Old Bottle House. This is a 300 year old former coaching inn, which has a lovely garden and rural views. The house is set in a wonderful position on the edge of Thetford Forest. The spacious colour co-ordinated bedrooms have tea/coffee making facilities, and colour TV. Delicious meals are served in the dining room which has an inglenook fireplace. There is a pleasant seating area on the galleried landing where guests may relax after a busy day.

Mrs Marion Ford
Tel: 01842 878012

B&B from £22.50-£25pp, Dinner £14, Rooms 1 double/family, 2 twin, No smoking, Children over 5, No pets, Open all year except Christmas & New Year.

KIMBERLEY HOME FARM, Wymondham, Norfolk NR18 0RW

Map Ref 12
Nearest Road A11, A47

This beautifully furnished farmhouse with large garden and hard tennis court is one and a half miles from the market town of Wymondham and nine miles from Norwich. This fascinating part of East Anglia has the Norfolk and Suffolk coastline about an hours drive, with the Norfolk Broads half an hour. The pleasant double and twin bedrooms are on the first floor with a large bathroom and a charming family suite on the second. Full English breakfasts are served in this farmhouse and excellent dinners may be had by advance arrangement.

Jennifer Bloom
Tel: 01953 603137
Fax: 01953 604836

B&B from £27.50-£32.50pp, Dinner by arrangement £17.50, Rooms 1 double, 1 twin, 1 family with private bathroom, 1 private bathroom, Children welcome, No pets, Open March to October.

NORTHUMBRIA, CLEVELAND & COUNTY DURHAM

Lying to the North East of England and enjoying a fine coastline and a particularly wild interior, Northumberland is a county steeped in bloody history of Scots/English battles and featuring some particularly splendid castles, walls and fortifications as a result. Hadrian's Wall – the greatest single engineering project ever undertaken by the Roman Empire – runs through Northumberland to the south, while the 400 square mile Northumberland National Park stretches north through remote hill country to the Cheviot Hills and the Scottish Border beyond. A wealth of prehistoric settlements, castles, towers, bastles and kilns, the Park is a fascinating testimony to the many peoples who have influenced this county and represents one of England's truly unspoilt heritage areas.

As well as fascinating interior, Northumberland also boasts a dramatic and historic coastline. Holy Island – or Lindisfarne as it was once known – was where St Aidan founded a monastery in 635 and which became quickly recognised as a major centre of learning and Christianity. Reached by a tidal causeway, the island is popular with tourists who flock to see the remains of Lindisfarne Priory and Lindisfarne Castle – originally built in 1550 and restored in 1903. Slightly south, the rocky outcrops of the Farne Islands, where St Cuthbert lived and died, can also be found off the coast. There is a tiny chapel dedicated to him on the Inner Farne, now managed by the National Trust.

The Northumberland coastal road makes for a particularly pleasant drive through quaint seaside villages and market towns, many of which are unsurprisingly dominated by castles. Although many are ruined – a particularly fine example being that at Warkworth – others have been converted into extremely grand country homes. The site of Bamburgh Castle has been a royal centre since AD 547 and, although the keep dates back to Norman times, the remainder has been twice extensively restored, first in the 1750s and subsequently in the 20th century. It is now the quite stunning home of the Armstrong family, enjoying exquisite interiors and unsurpassed views from its ramparts. Restoration has also transformed the more southerly castle of Alnwick from a major stronghold in the 14th century into an elegant and comfortable family home, still lived in today by the Duke of Northumberland. The castle enjoys a magnificent setting within Capability Brown landscaped grounds, also currently undergoing significant restoration to return them to their former 18th century splendour.

Continuing south near the town of Morpeth, Cragside represents one of the most modern and surprising houses of its era. Built in the 1880's by 1st Lord Armstrong, this unique home featured hot and cold running water, central heating, telephones, a Turkish bath suite and – most remarkably – it was the first house in the world to be lit by hydro-electricity. Also set in particularly interesting grounds Cragside is a must-see for any visitor.

Nearby County Durham includes some of the most beautiful parts of the northern Pennines and, of course, Durham – the most spectacular cathedral town in Britain. Stunningly situated on a peninsula surrounded by the River Wear, Durham Cathedral was built as a shrine to St Cuthbert and dates almost entirely from the 12th century. It is one of the most complete and spectacular examples of Norman architecture in Britain and, whether viewed up close or from the superb vantage point of the outer bank, it is a spellbinding sight. Also of interest in this surprisingly small town is the university – the third oldest in England – and Durham Castle, also situated on the cathedral peninsula.

Just north of Durham, the particularly notable Beamish Open-Air Museum is symbolic of the county's coal-mining past. Visitors can go underground and explore mine heads, a working farm, cottages, a school and shops. Slightly further north and also worth a detour while in the area, Washington Old Hall is the 12th century house of the Washington family and contains many George Washington commemoratives. The Hall can be found in the Tyne & Wear village named after the famous family.

South-west of Durham, the attractive market town of Barnard Castle makes a good base for exploring the northern Pennines and the beautiful surrounding countryside. The sprawling ruins of Barnrad Castle itself can be explored here, built by the Baliol family and thought to date back to the 12th century; while equally grand in scale and entirely intact, nearby Raby Castle has been described as one of the most impressive lived-in castles in England. Surrounded by a moat, Raby's romantic medieval exterior is perfectly complemented by a truly sumptuous interior – making it the ultimate fairytale castle for any visitor.

NORTHUMBRIA, CLEVELAND & COUNTY DURHAM

Mr & Mrs.B Staff, Holmhead Guest House
Tel: 016977 47402
Map Ref 1 *see page 191*
Delia Slack, Ash House
Tel: 01740 654654
Map Ref 2 *see page 191*
Joan & David Darntal, Idsley House
Tel: 01388 814237
Map Ref 3 *see page 191*
Lynne Anderson,
The Coach House at Crookham
Tel: 01890 820293/01289 309738
Map Ref 4 *see page 192*
Mrs E A Courage, Rye Hill Farm
Tel: 01434 673259
Map Ref 5 *see page 192*
Simon & Katie Stewart, The Hermitage
Tel: 01434 681248
Map Ref 6 *see page 192*
Stephen & Celia Gay, Shieldhall
Tel: 01830 540 387
Map Ref 7 *see page 193*
Mrs Furness,Cuddy's Hall Holiday Cottage
Tel: 016977 48160
Map Ref 8 *see page 193*

BERWICK UPON TWEED
HOLY ISLAND
FARNE ISLANDS
BELFORD
BAMBURGH
SEAHOUSES
WOOLER
A697
A1
ALNWICK
ALNMOUTH
WARKWORTH
AMBLE
ROTHBURY
A1
A1068
OTTERBURN
ASHINGTON
NEWBIGGIN
MORPETH
A696
BLYTH
CRAMLINGTON
PONTELAND
WHITLEY BAY
NEWCASTLE UPON TYNE
TYNEMOUTH
CORBRIDGE
SOUTH SHIELDS
HEXHAM
GATESHEAD
A68
WASHINGTON
SUNDERLAND
CHESTER LE STREET
BLANCHLAND
CONSETT
STANHOPE
A68
DURHAM
CROOK
PETERLEE
A19
A689
HARTLEPOOL
BISHOP AUCKLAND
REDCAR
MIDDLETON
BARNARD CASTLE
STOCKTON
BOWES
DARLINGTON
MIDDLESBOROUGH

HOLMHEAD GUEST HOUSE, on Thirlwall Castle Farm, Hadrians Wall, Greenhead, via Brampton, CA8 7HY
Email holmhead@hadrianswall.freeserve.co.uk
Website www.bandbhadrianswall.com

Map Ref 1
Nearest Road A69, M6 jct 43

Full page photo opposite

Enjoy fine food and hospitality with a personal touch, in a smoke free atmosphere. This lovely old farmhouse is built with Hadrians wall stones, near the most spectacular remains. Four cosy bedrooms with shower/wc en-suite. Quality home cooking using fresh produce, guests dine together at candlelit table dinner party style. Speciality list of organically grown/produced wines featuring world award winners. Small cocktail bar and TV, books, maps and guides in lounge. Your host is a former Northumbria Tour Guide and is an expert on Hadrians Wall. Special breaks arranged. Self catering and camping barn available.

Brian & Pauline Staff
Tel/Fax: 016977 47402

B&B from £29pp, Dinner from £20, Rooms 2 twin 1 double, 1 family, all en-suite, No smoking, Children welcome, No pets, Open all year except Christmas & New Year.

ASH HOUSE, 24 The Green, Cornforth, County Durham DL17 9JH
Email delden@btopenworld.com

Map Ref 2
Nearest Road A1M, A177, A688, A167

Ash House is a beautifully appointed period house, combining a delicate mixture of homeliness and Victorian flair. Elegant rooms, individually and tastefully decorated, combining antique furnishings, beautiful fabrics, carved four posters and modern fittings. Spacious, graceful and filled with character, Ash House offers a warm welcome to both the road weary traveller and those wishing merely to unwind in the quiet elegance of this charming home on the village green. Private parking. Well placed between York and Edinburgh. Adjacent A1M motorway. Excellent value.

Delia Slack
Tel: 01740 654654
Mobile: 07711 133547

B&B from £20-£30pp, Rooms 1 double, 1 twin, 1 family, Restricted smoking, Children & pets welcome, Open all year except Christmas & New Year.

IDSLEY HOUSE, 4 Green Lane, Spennymoor, County Durham DL16 6HD

Map Ref 3
Nearest Road A167, A688

Joan and David Dartnall welcome you to their home which they opened to guests in 1980. Idsley House has 5 spacious rooms all furnished to a high standard. Breakfast is served in the conservatory overlooking mature garden. Excellent English breakfast assured or something lighter for a smaller appetite. Vegetarian/diabetic catered for or any other diets by arrangements. Guests have access at all times. Guests are welcome on day of arrival after 4 O'clock. We both belong to Durham, Spennymoor area and have lots of local knowledge. Davids special interest Geneology and willing to assist if interested. A warm Northern welcome assured.

Joan & David Darntall
Tel: 01388 814237

B&B from £24-£34pp, Rooms 1 single, 1 double, 2 twin, 1 family, all en-suite, Children over 10, Pets welcome, Open all year except Christmas & New Year.

THE COACH HOUSE AT CROOKHAM, Cornhill on Tweed, Northumberland TD12 4TD
Email stay@coachhousecrookham.com
Website www.coachhousecrookham.com

Map Ref 4
Nearest Road A697

Ideally situated for exploring Northumberland's National Trust coastline. The Coach House is one hour's drive on excellent roads from Edinburgh or Newcastle. Built about 1680 the brick and stone buildings around a courtyard have been converted into spacious bedrooms. They are accessible to wheelchair bound guests. The food is fresh and varied reflecting modern ideas on healthy eating with some Mediterranean influence. Where possible, local produce is used. Breakfast satisfies all tastes with fruits, homemade cereals and porridge plus a cooked breakfast using top quality ingredients.

Lynne Anderson
Tel: 01289 309738 or 01890 820293
Fax: 01890 820284

B&B from £27pp, Dinner £19.50, Rooms 1 single, 5 en-suite twin, 2 en suite double, Restricted smoking, Children & pets welcome by arrangement, Open Easter - October 31st.

RYE HILL FARM, Slaley, Hexham, Northumberland NE47 0AH
Email info@ryehillfarm.co.uk
Website www.ryehillfarm.co.uk

Map Ref 5
Nearest Road B6306

Rye Hill Farm offers you the freedom to enjoy the pleasures of Northumberland throughout the year whilst living comfortably in the pleasant family atmosphere of a cosy farmhouse adapted especially to receive holidaymakers. Bedrooms are all en-suite, centrally heated and have large bath towels. A full English breakfast and an optional 3 course evening meal are served in the dining room which has an open log fire and a table licence. Pay phone and tourist information in the reception lounge. Guests are invited to use the games room and look around the farm. Credit cards accepted.

Mrs E A Courage
Tel: 01434 673259
Fax: 01434 673259

B&B from £22.50pp, Dinner from £14, Rooms 3 double, 2 family, 1 twin, Pets welcome by arrangement, Open all year.

THE HERMITAGE, Swinburne, Hexham, Northumberland NE48 4DG
Email katie.stewart@themeet.co.uk

Map Ref 6
Nearest Road A6079

The Hermitage is an elegant and comfortable house. Furnished with antiques and old family pictures. The rooms are spacious and beautifully decorated. There is a large well kept garden, terrace to sit out on in the evenings and a tennis court. All bedrooms have tea and coffee making facilities. The drawing room has an open fire, lit on cooler evenings and a television. There is total peace and quiet. Very convenient for the Roman Wall and Northumberland castles and mansions. Ample parking.

Simon & Katie Stewart
Tel: 01434 681248
Fax: 01434 681110

B&B from £35pp,(£10 single supplement), Rooms 1 single, 2 twin, 1 double, all en-suite/private, Restricted smoking, Children over 10, Pets restricted, Open March to October.

SHIELDHALL, Wallington, Morpeth, Northumberland NE61 4AQ
Email Robinson.Gay@btinternet.com
Website www.shiedhallguesthouse.co.uk

Map Ref 7
Nearest Road A696, B6342

Within acres of beautifully matured gardens and overlooking the National Trust's Wallington Estate, this charmingly restored 18th century farm stead, centres around an attractive courtyard onto which each beautifully furnished guest suite opens. Each room is en-suite with TV, coffee, etc. Stephen's family are cabinet makers and antique restorers and there is much evidence of their artistry. A secret licensed bar opens before dinner where guests may meet to discuss travellers tales. Dinners are of local and seasonal produce, complimented by Celia's excellent English cooking. Credit cards accepted.

Stephen & Celia Gay
Tel: 01830 540 387
Fax: 01830 540 490

B&B from £22-£35pp, Rooms 2 double, 2 twin, all en-suite, No smoking, Children over 12, Open all year except Christmas & New Year.

CUDDY'S HALL HOLIDAY COTTAGE, Bailey, Newcastleton, Roxburghshire
Email joannafurness@btopenworld.com
Website www.cuddys-hall.co.uk

Map Ref 8

Cumbrian/Scottish borders. Traditional family cottage, well maintained and equipped throughout. Set amidst beautiful forest and winding streams (part of Kielder Forest Park) abundant with wildlife. Superb forest walks/cycle routes, start right at the door. Private garden, patio and barbecue/lockable shed for cycles, fishing tackle etc. On the 'Reivers Cycle Route'. Bed linen, duvets, towels, electricity, central heating and a welcome food pack inclusive. Good base to explore - Hadrians Wall, the Lakes and Scotland. Pony trekking, fishing and golf nearby. Short breaks available.

1 cottage, sleeps up to 5, Price per week £200 to £300 (at peak times), No smoking, Children welcome over 7, No pets, Available all year.

Contact: Mrs Joanna Furness, No. 2 Cuddy's Hall, Bailey, Newcastleton, Roxburghshire TD9 0TP
Tel/Fax: 016977 48160

OXFORDSHIRE

While green rolling countryside, a meandering River Thames, the chalk Chilterns and the scenic limestone Cotswolds make up the pleasant topography of Oxfordshire, there is no doubt that it is the celebrated academic centre of Oxford itself that affords this county its world renown.

Britain's oldest university town, Oxford is awash with magnificent honey-coloured colleges, grand architecture and lofty spires – and positively exudes academic history and tradition. Lovers of architecture will revel in the grand design of Christ Church College, first founded in 1525, and revere at Christ Church Cathedral – Oxford's Anglican cathedral since the reign of King Henry VIII and the smallest to be found in the country. Sir Christopher Wren designed the upper part of the Tudor-based Tom Tower in 1682 – the bell of which (Great Tom) chimes 101 times each evening at 9.05pm, the time the original 101 students attending the college were called to retire.

New College Chapel features some superb 14th century stained glass and gardens containing a section of Oxford's original medieval wall; while Divinity School, with its magnificent vaulted ceilings, is renowned as a masterpiece of 15th century architecture.

Magdalen College is perhaps the richest of all the Oxford colleges and the beautiful grounds, which include a deer park, fine river walks and pristine lawns, featured in the recent film Shadowlands – the story of the life of CS Lewis. Famous Magdalen undergraduates include Oscar Wilde, Sir John Betjeman and Dudley Moore.

Fascinating though Oxford is, there is plenty more to see in this pretty county as a short drive north to the village of Woodstock will testify. Although featuring some fine architecture in its own right, the village is best known for the vast baroque fantasy that is Blenheim Palace. Birthplace of Winston Churchill, Blenheim was gifted to John Churchill, Duke of Marlborough, by Queen Anne and dates back to the early 18th century. Its vast 800-hectare grounds also reflect the evolution of grand design with much of the vast parkland landscaped by none other than Capability Brown.

To the far north of the county, the 'nursery rhyme' village of Banbury (Ride A Cock Horse) has some fine homes and gardens nearby. Built in 1300, Brougton Castle stands – mainly intact - on an island complete with three acre moat. Enlarged in 1550 and 1600, the house also boasts magnificent plaster ceilings, panelling and fireplaces – and if roses are your particular favourite, the gardens are a veritable feast for the eyes.

Rose enthusiasts will also enjoy Alkerton's Brook Cottage – a four acre hillside garden also incorporating water features, clematis and co-ordinated borders; while Sulgrove Manor - the ancestoral seat of George Washington in the nearby village of Sulgrove – also features grandly designed gardens dating back to Shakespearian times.

Perhaps no visit to Oxfordshire could be complete without a journey south to Henley-on-Thames – home since 1839 to the Royal Regatta where the oarsman of Oxford and Cambridge universities battle it out each July amid a sea of picnics, Pimms and a certain degree of pomposity. The spectacle is well worth participating in and will also bring you conveniently close to one of Oxfordshire's prize historic homes. Fawley Court, designed by Chrisopher Wren and built for Colonel W Freeman in 1684, now houses a museum containing rare documents, military memorabilia and a well-preserved collection of historical sabres. The real glory of the house, however, lies in its exquisite design and internal décor – a testament to the talent of Grinling Gibbons and James Wyatt – and the delightful gardens engineered by landscaping genius Lancelot 'Capability' Brown.

OXFORDSHIRE

Stephen & Mary-pen Wills, Swallows Barn
Tel: 01295 738325
Map Ref 1 *see page 199*
Mrs Penny Howden, Slater's Farm
Tel: 01491 628675
Map Ref 2 *see page 199*
Mrs Pavlovice & Mrs Trkulja, Pine Castle
Hotel Tel: 01865 241497
Map Ref 3 *see page 199*
Parvesh & Narinder Bhella, Green Gables
Tel: 01865 725870
Map Ref 3 *see page 200*
Mary Anne Florey, Rectory Farm
Tel: 01865 300207
Map Ref 5 *see page 200*

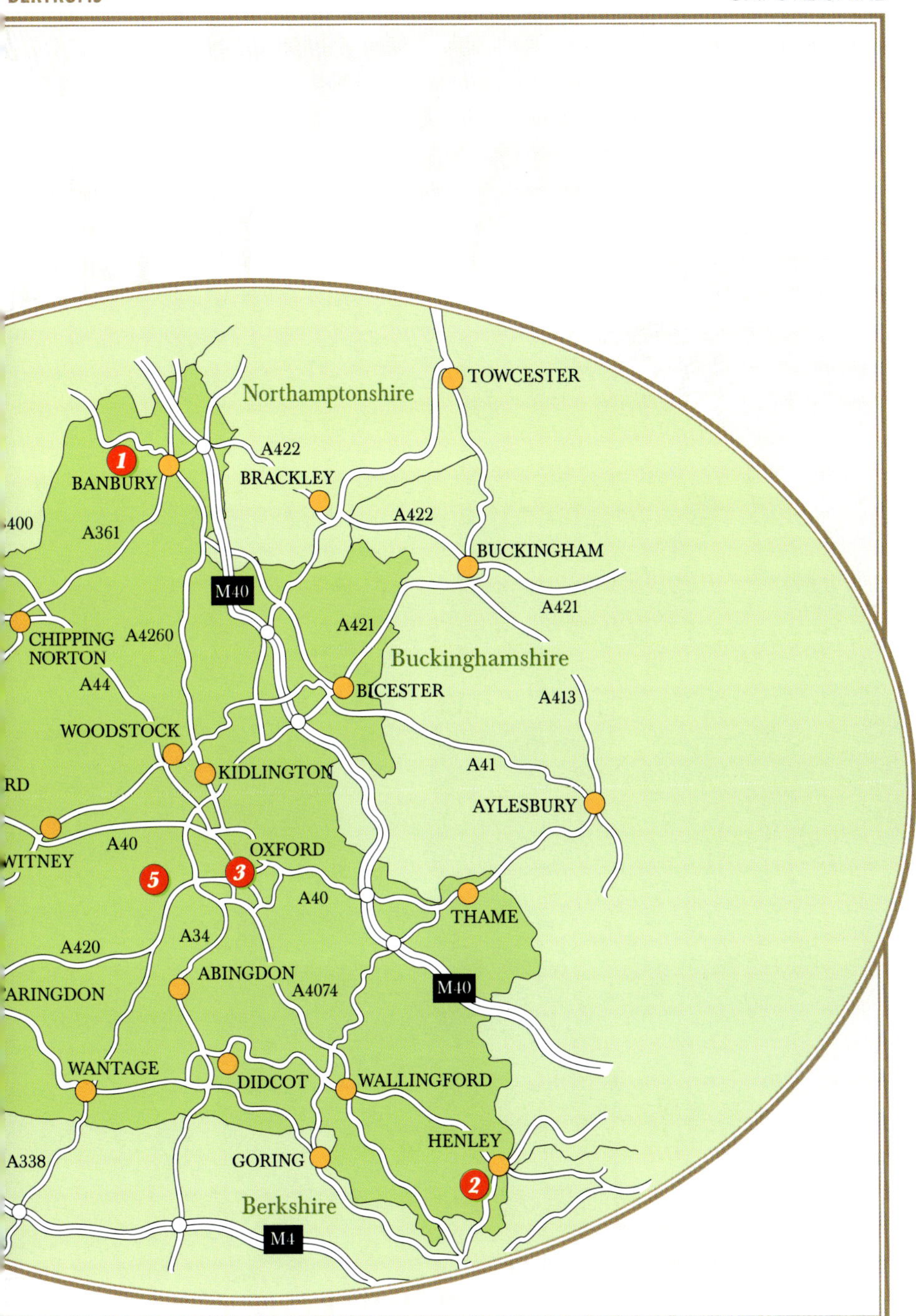
Northamptonshire
TOWCESTER
A422
BANBURY
BRACKLEY
A422
A361
BUCKINGHAM
M40
A421
A421
CHIPPING NORTON
A4260
Buckinghamshire
A44
BICESTER
A413
WOODSTOCK
KIDLINGTON
A41
AYLESBURY
A40
OXFORD
A40
THAME
A420
A34
ABINGDON
A4074
M40
WANTAGE
DIDCOT
WALLINGFORD
HENLEY
A338
GORING
Berkshire
M4

SWALLOWS BARN, Shutford Road, Balscote, Banbury, Oxfordshire OX15 6JJ
Email swallowsbarn.freeserve.co.uk

Map Ref 1

Full page photo opposite

Swallows still dart among the eves where once a farm barn stood in this idyllic Cotswold village. Our spacious 'honey' stone house has been blended into the rural scene - the old stone wall a back drop to the waterfall and charming tiered garden. The guest room is very large, sunny and comfortable with elegant chintz furnishing, country antiques, sofa, tea and TV. We can accommodate extra family. Breakfast is at the Georgian dining table or on the terrace. Walks abound and Oxford, Stratford on Avon and Warwick are an easy drive.

Stephen & Mary-pen Wills
Tel: 01295 738325
Fax: 01295 738314

B&B from £30pp, Rooms 1 en-suite twin/double, 1 family, Restricted smoking, Children welcome, Pets by arrangement, Open February to December.

SLATER'S FARM, Peppard Common, Henley on Thames, Oxfordshire RG9 5JL

Map Ref 2
Nearest Road B481

A warm and friendly home, Slater's Farm is a quietly situated, attractive Georgian country house with an acre of lovely garden including a tennis court, which guests are welcome to use. All the bedrooms are attractively furnished for the comfort of guests. Traditional pubs within a few hundred yards serve good evening meals. Lovely walks through unspoilt countryside. The Chilterns, Windsor, Oxford, Cotswolds all within easy driving distance. Heathrow is less than an hour away. French and German are spoken.

Mrs Penny Howden
Tel/Fax: 01491 628675

B&B from £25pp, Dinner £15, Rooms 1 double, 2 twin, most private, No smoking or pets, Children welcome, Open all year except Christmas & New Year.

PINE CASTLE HOTEL, 290-292 Iffley Road, Oxford, Oxfordshire OX4 4AE
Email stay@pinecastle.co.uk
Website www.oxfordcity.co.uk/hotels/pinecastle

Map Ref 3

The comfortable rooms are well-furnished and have en-suite bathrooms, colour televisions, direct-dial telephones, hair dryers and a selection of reading material. All bedrooms are non-smoking, as is the breakfast room but smokers are welcome to use the lounge were there is also a small bar. Well situated midway between Ring Road and city centre and served by an excellent local bus service. River walk close by.

Mrs Pavlovice & Mrs Trkulja
Tel: 01865 241497
Fax: 01865 727230

B&B from £32.50pp, Rooms 2 twin, 5 double, 1 family, all en-suite, Restricted smoking, Children welcome, No pets, Open all year.

GREEN GABLES, 326 Abingdon Road, Oxford, Oxfordshire OX1 4TE
Email green.gables@virgin.net

Map Ref 3

Green Gables is a characterful, detached Edwardian house, secluded from the road by trees and 1 mile from city centre on frequent bus route. Bright, spacious rooms, many en-suite. Ample parking.

Parvesh & Narinder Bhella
Tel: 01865 725870
Fax: 01865 723115

B&B from £24pp, Rooms 1 single, 2 twin, 4 double, 2 family, No pets, Open all year except Christmas and New Year.

RECTORY FARM, Northmoor, near Witney, Oxfordshire OX29 5SX
Email PJ.Florey@farmline.com
Website www.oxtowns.co.uk/rectoryfarm

Map Ref 5
Nearest Road A415

A pot of tea, homemade shortbread, along with a warm welcome and a peaceful, comfortable stay await you at Rectory Farm. A 16th century farmhouse retaining old charm alongside modern comforts. Both rooms have en-suite facilities, central heating and hot drinks tray.Guests' own sitting room with woodburning stove. We are conveniently situated for Oxford (10 miles), the Cotswolds, Blenheim Palace and the Thames path. Self catering also available. Why not treat yourself. Pick up the phone and give us a call!

Mary Anne Florey
Tel: 01865 300207
Fax: 01865 300559

B&B from £26-£36pp, Rooms 1 double, 1 twin, both en-suite, No smoking, children or pets, Open all year except Christmas & New Year.

Full page photo opposite

"Castle View" said Belle "Yes, if you lean out of the bedroom window you probably could just see Caenarvon Castle"

Belle & Bertie in Wales

SHROPSHIRE

Shropshire is a geographically large county situated between Birmingham to the east and the Welsh borders to the west. Its mainly rural topography includes flat northerly upland, rolling midland hills and the ancient limestone escarpments of Wenlock Edge, the Long Mynd and the Stiperstones to the south. Interesting medieval towns and villages punctuate this pleasant landscape and, far from the madding crowd, it proves a perfect county in which to relax and enjoy the sights.

Situated upon the River Severn to the south of the county, Shrewsbury is the attractive capital of Shropshire and also claims to be the finest Tudor town in Britain. It's many half-timbered buildings and winding streets certainly give the place a charming ambience and a tour of the town and its many nuances is highly recommended. Notable buildings include Shrewsbury Abbey, a mighty red sandstone structure that has served as a parish church since the 12th century; and Shrewsbury Castle, originally built in Norman times and now housing The Shropshire Regimental Museum. Imposing Attingham Park – another jewel in Shrewsbury's crown – can be found slightly north of the town amid 500 acres of lush parkland. A fine example of a Georgian country home, the house contains splendid paintings and furniture.

South of Shrewsbury, Ludlow also features impressive Georgian architecture as well as a rambling ruined castle dating back to the 11th century. Nearby Clun castle is from the same period and enjoys an outstanding rural setting.

Travelling west in the county, the village of Ironbridge boasts both a beautiful situation and a proud history as the birthplace of the industrial revolution. It was here in 1709 that the first iron was produced and a series of interesting museums within the town rate it as a World Heritage site. Also of note in Ironbridge is Buildwas Abbey – the extensive remains of a Cistercian structure built in 1135 against a backdrop of trees beside the River Severn.

Slightly north near the village of Shifnal, another magnificent country home – Weston Park – can be found set in impressive parkland landscaped by the celebrated Lancelot Capability Brown. Built in 1671, this vast, elegant home offers a warm welcome and a particularly superb collection of paintings.

Continuing north to Market Drayton, the wonderful gardens of Hodnet Hall can be strolled around and savoured, whatever the season. Although dating back originally to the 11th century, the gardens were seriously developed in 1921 to include fine woodland walks and impressive formal displays. Also on the border of Shropshire and Staffordshire and three miles from Market Drayton, Oakley Hall provides a fine example of a Queen Anne mansion. Set in 100 acres of rolling parkland, the Hall represents a fine balance of formal architecture amid wild surroundings that so aptly sum up this inspiring county.

SHROPSHIRE

Miriam Ellison, New House Farm
Tel: 01588 638314
Map Ref 1 *see page 206*

Maureen Sanders, Cottage Farm
Tel: 01588 660555
Map Ref 2 *see page 206*

Mrs Beryl Maxwell, Shortgrove
Tel: 01584 711418
Map Ref 4 *see page 206*

Mrs Pauline Williamson, Mickley House
Tel: 01630 638505
Map Ref 5 *see page 208*

Pam Morrissey, Top Farm House
Tel: 01691 682582
Map Ref 6 *see page 208*

Mrs M Jones, Ashfield Farmhouse
Tel: 01691 653589
Map Ref 7 *see page 208*

Mike & Gill Mitchell, The White House
Tel: 01743 860414
Map Ref 8 *see page 209*

Mrs Barbara Barnes, Foxleigh House
Tel: 01939 233528
Map Ref 9 *see page 209*

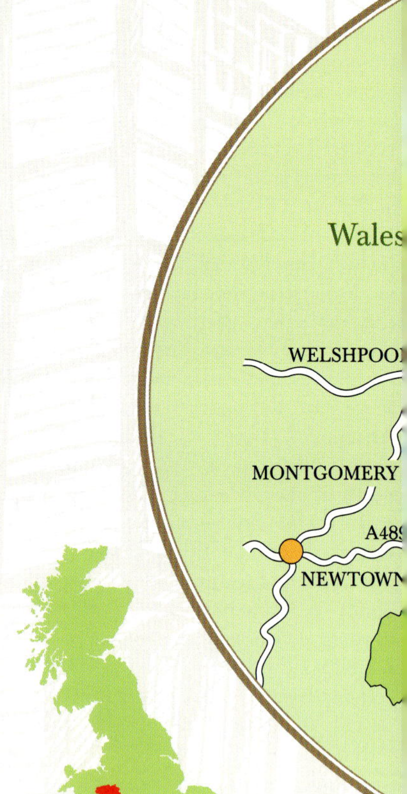

WHITCHURCH
ELLESMERE
A495
MARKET
DRAYTON
A51
STONE
SWESTRY
5
HODNET
Staffordshire
A5
WEM
9
LYS
A49
A41
M6
6
A53
NEWPORT
A518
STAFFORD
A442
A518
SHREWSBURY
A485
TELFORD
A5
8
IRONBRIDGE
CANNOCK
488
M54
A49
A458
MUCH
WENLOCK
A442
B4378
WOLVERHAMPTON
CHURCH
STRETTON
BRIDGNORTH
DUDLEY
A489
B4368
CRAVEN
ARMS
A442
LUDLOW
KIDDERMINSTER
A456
4

NEW HOUSE FARM, Clun, Shropshire SY7 8NJ
Email sarah@bishopscastle.co.uk
Website www.new-house-clun.co.uk

Map Ref 1

Rural bliss in unspoilt countryside - quiet roads - ideal for walking. Offa's Dyke, Shropshire Way, Kerry Ridgeway from the door step. The farm includes an Iron Age Hill Fort, Caer-din-Ring alternatively sit and enjoy a good book and relax in a large country garden. Two very spacious bedrooms with outstanding views, period furnished with TV, coffee/tea tray and many thoughtful extras. Full English breakfast and for evening dinner, help and advice is given for the various restaurants and pubs in the area.

Miriam Ellison
Tel: 01588 638314

B&B from £27.50-£28pp, Rooms 1 twin, 1 family, both en-suite/private bathroom, No smoking Children over 10, Open Easter to end of October.

COTTAGE FARM, Clunton, near Craven Arms, Shropshire SY7 0HZ

Map Ref 2
Nearest Road A49, B4368

Clunton is a small village on the B4368 between Ludlow and Clun in the beautiful Clun Valley with superb landscapes and numerous footpaths. Cottage Farm, which dates back 400 years has many exposed timbers and stone walls which along with roaring log fires in winter help to create a wonderful ambience. There are three bedrooms each with tea/coffee making facilities and each decorated in true country style. 2 double bedrooms (one with en-suite facilities). One single bedroom with shared bathroom.

Maureen Sanders
Tel: 01588 660555

B&B from £22.50-£25pp, Dinner £12.50, Rooms 1 single, 2 double (1 en-suite), No smoking or pets, Children over 12, Open all year except Christmas.

SHORTGROVE, Brimfield Common, Ludlow, Shropshire SY8 4NZ

Map Ref 4
Nearest Road A49

Shortgrove is a Grade II Listed Elizabethan timber framed house with gardens and grounds of three and a half acres on a gated common 5 miles south of Ludlow in absolute peace and quiet, One and a half miles from A49. The whole house is exceptional inside and out with every comfort to make a stay here memorable. Food is to an extremely high standard Beryl is a cookery tutor. Nearby are castles, National Trust houses, many antiques shops, Hereford with its Cathedral and mappa Mundi, beautiful Ludlow much mentioned in the national press black and white villages, Hay on Wye for book buffs, Mortimer Forest walking and riding. Brochure.

Full page photo opposite

Mrs Beryl Maxwell
Tel: 01584 711418

B&B from £32pp, Rooms 1 en-suite twin, 1 private double, No smoking, children or pets, Open Easter to October.

MICKLEY HOUSE, Faulsgreen, Tern Hill, Market Drayton, Shropshire TF6 5AP
Email mickleyhouse@hotmail.com

Map Ref 5
Nearest Road A41, A53

Relax and enjoy the peaceful atmosphere and home comforts of Mickley House, set in 1 acre of beautifully landscaped gardens. Stroll through rose and clematis covered pergola to water features. Central for Shrewsbury, Ironbridge, Chester, Wollerton Old Hall, Dorothy Clive and Bridgemere. The house retains some of its Victorian origins, oak beams and interesting fireplaces. All bedrooms en-suite. Two ground floor, one with kingsize Louis XV style bed. Upstairs one twin with balcony overlooking the garden, one small cosy double. Fridges, hospitality trays, colour TV. Business guests welcome. 2 miles off A41.

Mrs Pauline Williamson
Tel/Fax: 01630 638505

B&B from £23-£35pp, Rooms 1 single, 1 double, 1 twin, all en-suite, No smoking, children or pets, Open all year except Christmas & New Year.

TOP FARM HOUSE, Knockin, near Oswestry, Shropshire SY10 8HN
Email p.a.m@knockin.freeserve.co.uk
Website www.topfarmknockin.co.uk

Map Ref 6
Nearest Road A5

Lovely back and white 16th century house offering old fashioned hospitality with every modern convenience. All rooms en-suite with tea and coffee making facilities, trouser press, colour TV, hairdryers, comfortable chair and room to move around. Hearty breakfasts are served in elegant dining room overlooking the garden. Attractive guests drawing room with grand piano. Situated in attractive village of Knockin, pub in walking distance. Convenient for Wales, Chester, Shrewsbury, Oswestry, Chirk and Powis Castle close by. Great atmosphere, friendly hosts.

Pam Morrissey
Tel: 01691 682582
Fax: 01691 682070

B&B from £24pp, Rooms 1 twin, 1 double, 1 family, all en-suite, Children over 12, Pets welcome, Open all year.

ASHFIELD FARMHOUSE, Maesbury, Oswestry, Shropshire SY10 8JH
Email ashfield@ashfieldfarmhouse.co.uk
Website www.ashfieldfarmhouse.co.uk

Map Ref 7
Nearest Road A5, A483

Honeysuckle and scarlet creepers ramble this lovely 16th century coach-house and Georgian farmhouse nestling in Welsh Borderlands. Only 1 mile from Oswestry, A5 and A483. Scented gardens, lovely views, excellent hospitality, period decor and oak furnishing and lovely fabrics. Oak staircase, marble fireplace and ships stove. Exceptionally pretty, comfortable en-suite rooms, cottagey yet spacious and fully equipped. Fresh flowers and olde worlde charm fill the dining and drawing rooms. Ample parking. Chester, Llangollen, Shrewsbury, Ironbridge and South Shropshire closeby. Castles, lakes and hidden valleys of North Wales on our doorstep. Business people very welcome. Brochure available. ETC 4 Diamonds, Silver Award.

Mrs M Jones
Tel: 01691 653589
Fax: 01691 653589

B&B from £22.50pp, Rooms 3 double/single/twin/family, 2 interconnecting family rooms, 2 en-suite, 1 private bath/shower room, Restricted smoking, Children welcome, Pets by arrangement, Open all year.

THE WHITE HOUSE, Hanwood, Shrewsbury, Shropshire SY5 8LP
Email mgm@whitehousehanwood.freeserve.co.uk
Website www.whitehousehanwood.freeserve.co.uk

Map Ref 8
Nearest Road A488, A5

We offer peace and quiet in our delightful 16th century half-timbered guest house with two acre gardens and river. Shrewsbury, Ironbridge, Ludlow and Wales are all nearby as well as the Long Mynd for walking. We have guests' sitting room and our bedrooms have Victorian brass beds, tea and coffee facilities, etc. Our chickens and our bees provide the eggs and the honey for breakfast and we are licensed (to restore the spirit after a journey!). Euros welcome.

Mike & Gill Mitchell
Tel: 01743 860414

B&B from £27.50pp, Rooms 1 single, 1 twin, 4 double, most en-suite, No smoking or pets, Children over 12, Open all year.

FOXLEIGH HOUSE, Foxleigh Drive, Wem, near Shrewsbury, Shropshire SY4 5BP
Email Foxleigh01@aol.com

Map Ref 9
Nearest Road A49, B5476

Foxleigh House a home of character in the heart of Wem. Relax in the spacious rooms, delightfully furnished in the style of a more leisured age with modern comforts. Foxleigh offers bed and breakfast in a large twin bedded room with private bathroom, and a family suite of three rooms (sleeps 5-6) with private bathroom. All rooms have colour TV and tea/coffee trays. Wem is a small market town and is an ideal touring centre for Shropshire, Cheshire and Wales. Beautiful gardens and National Trust properties abound and Hawkstone Golf Club and famous park and follies are four miles away. Brochure. ETB 2 Crown Commended, AA 4-Q.

B&B from £20-£24, Dinner £11.50 by arrangement, Rooms 1 twin, 1 family suite (sleeps 5-6), both with private bathroom, Children over 8, Open all year except Christmas.

Mrs Barbara Barnes
Tel/Fax: 01939 233528

SOMERSET

Originally part of the ancient kingdom of Wessex, Somerset is a largely agricultural county offering miles of unspoilt countryside, fine beaches and low-lying mountain ridges. Diverse walking can also be found within the county from the rolling southern lowlands to the limestone Mendip Hills in the north featuring dramatic gorges and caves thought to be inhabited since prehistoric times. The sandstone ridge of the Quantocks to the west delights with winding lanes and wooded dells, while villages such as Crowcombe – still featuring ancient cottages built of stone and cob – make for interesting places to stroll around and stop for lunch.

Wells is perhaps Somerset's most interesting town and also England's smallest cathedral city. Built between 1108 and 1508, this beautiful cathedral incorporates several Gothic styles, most significantly the statuary West Front built between 1230 and 1250 and painstakingly restored in 1986. Exquisite stained glass and embroideries can be seen within the cathedral, along with a fascinating mechanical clock situated high in the north transept and dating back to 1392. To the delight of visitors it features jousting knights upon the hour and on each quarter hour in summer. Just beyond the cathedral is the imposing Bishops' Palace, a fortified, moated medieval residence which dates back to the 13th century and is today the home of the Bishop of Bath and Wells. The palace features beautiful gardens and an arboretum.

In the eclectic town of Glastonbury the ancient abbey and scenic Tor make for popular haunts with visitors, and for those who enjoy a good legend as well as a beautiful garden, Chalice Well & Gardens are a must. Nestling around one of Britain's oldest holy wells, it is reputed that Joseph of Arimethea visited here bearing the Chalice of the Last Supper, and King Arthur too on his quest for the Holy Grail. Whether you believe the myths or not, this garden with its iron-rich waters and stunning array of plants is a haven of peace and tranquillity and an inspiring place to while away an afternoon.

Moving south, Hestercombe Gardens near Taunton is also breathtaking in both its design and history. Spanning three centuries the grounds boast lakes, temples and woodland and magnificent formal gardens designed by Sir Edwin Lutyens and planted by Gertrude Jekyll. Completed in 1906 and incorporating pools, terraces and an orangery, Hestercombe is thought to be the finest legacy of their famous partnership. Incidentally, the gardens of Barrington Court in nearby Illminster, which feature an unusual series of walled rooms, are also thought to be strongly influenced by Gertrude Jekyll.

Within an easy drive of Taunton lies another jewel in Somerset's crown in the form of Montacute House. This magnificent Elizabethan residence – built to an H-shaped ground plan – is home to many fine Renaissance artefacts and set in particularly impressive formal gardens – the grandeur of which was captured to perfection in the award-winning film Sense and Sensibility starring Kate Blanchet and Alan Rickman.

SOMERSET

Diana Brewer, Wood Advent Farm
Tel: 01984 640920
Map Ref 1 *see page 215*

Mr & Mrs Grattan, Park Farm House
Tel: 01749 343673
Map Ref 2 *see page 215*

Susie & Martin Dearden, Pennard House
Tel: 01749 860266
Map Ref 3 *see page 215*

Caro Ayre, Greenham Hall
Tel: 01823 672603
Map Ref 4 *see page 216*

Mrs H Millard, Double-Gate Farm
Tel: 01458 832217
Map Ref 5 *see page 216*

Mrs Pat English, Riverside Grange
Tel: 01749 890761
Map Ref 6 *see page 216*

Mrs Wendy Thompson, Stoneleigh House
Tel: 01749 870668
Map Ref 7 *see page219*

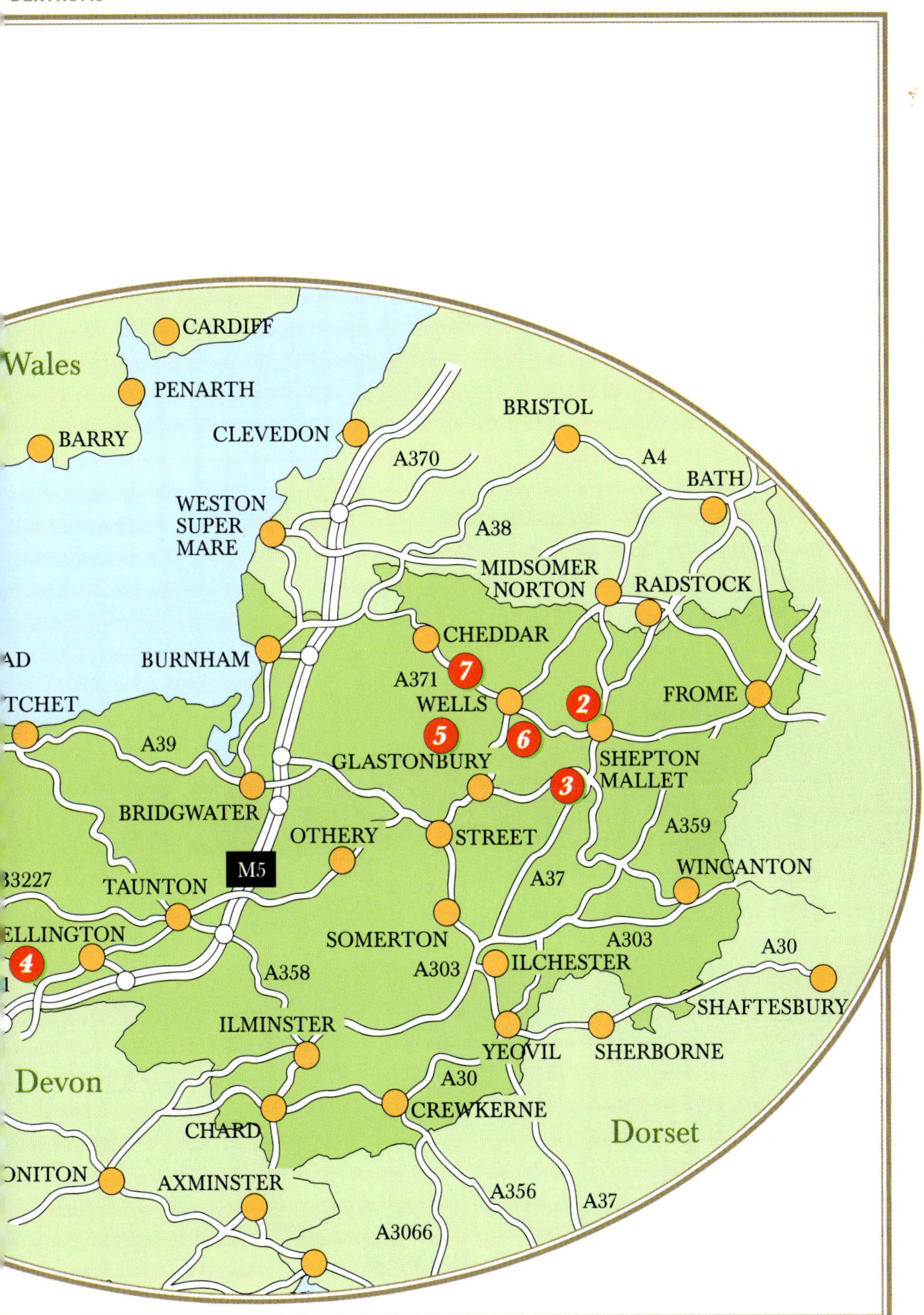
Wales
CARDIFF
PENARTH
BARRY
CLEVEDON
BRISTOL
A370
A4
BATH
WESTON SUPER MARE
A38
MIDSOMER NORTON
RADSTOCK
CHEDDAR
BURNHAM
A371
WELLS
FROME
SHEPTON MALLET
A39
GLASTONBURY
BRIDGWATER
OTHERY
STREET
A359
M5
A37
WINCANTON
TAUNTON
SOMERTON
A303
A30
A358
ILCHESTER
SHAFTESBURY
ILMINSTER
YEOVIL
SHERBORNE
Devon
CREWKERNE
CHARD
Dorset
AXMINSTER
A356
A3066
7
2
5
6
3
4

WOOD ADVENT FARM, Roadwater, Exmoor, Somerset TA23 0RR
Email info@woodadventfarm.co.uk
Website www.woodadventfarm.co.uk

Map Ref 1
Nearest Road M5, A39

Tucked away in Exmoor truly off the beaten track, off the beaten track, offering discerning guests quality en-suite accommodation in stunning countryside. Two large reception rooms with log fires and central heating, dining room where delicious Exmoor dishes are served with good wines and our own spring water, or just relax in the gardens and take afternoon tea and homemade cake by the heated swimming pool. Fantastic base for visiting the West Country, we look forward too welcoming you. Credit cards accepted.

Full page photo opposite

Diana Brewer
Tel/Fax: 01984 640920

B&B from £22.50-£27.50pp, Dinner £16.50, Rooms 3 double, 2 twin, all en-suite, Restricted smoking, Children over 10, No pets, Open all year.

PARK FARM HOUSE, Forum Lane, Bowlish, Shepton Mallet, Somerset BA4 5JL
Email john.marjorie@ukonline.co.uk

Map Ref 2
Nearest Road A371

Park Farm House is a 17th century house in a conversation area with a large peaceful garden. There is a off-road parking. Convenient for Bath, Wells, Bristol, Cheddar Gorge, Wookey Hole, Clarke's Village and Haynes Motor Museum. Our accommodation consists of a twin bedroom with en-suite bathroom. A double bedroom and twin bedroom with private bathroom and sitting room - ideal for families. There are many good pubs and restaurants.

Mr & Mrs Grattan
Tel: 01749 343673
Fax: 01749 345279

B&B from £18.50pp, Rooms 1 double, 2 twin, all en-suite, Children welcome, No pets, Open all year.

PENNARD HOUSE, East Pennard, Shepton Mallet, Somerset BA4 6TP
Email susie.d@ukonline.co.uk

Map Ref 3
Nearest Road A37

A beautiful Georgian house situated on the last south facing slope of the Mendip Hills, in secluded gardens, surrounded by meadows, woodlands and cider orchards. Grass tennis court and Victorian spring-fed swimming pool. Furnished in antique furniture. Television and tea/coffee making facilities available. The house is ideally situated for visiting Glastonbury, Wells, Bath and the historic houses and gardens of Hadspen, Stourhead, Longleat, Montacute and many others.

Susie & Martin Dearden
Tel/Fax: 01749 860266

B&B from £30pp, Rooms 1 single, 2 twin (1 en-suite, 1 private bathroom), 1 double en-suite, Restricted smoking, Children welcome, No pets, Open all year except Christmas & New Year.

GREENHAM HALL, Greenham, Wellington, Somerset TA21 0JJ
Email greenhamhall@btopenworld.com
Website www.greenhamhall.co.uk

Map Ref 4
Nearest Road A38, M5

A warm welcome awaits you in our spacious Victorian turreted house. The informal atmosphere and the quiet rural location are perfect for a peaceful break. A garden lover's paradise. There is something for everyone, from countryside walking, to visiting a wide range of gardens, historic houses, and museums, or the active can try horse riding, golf, fishing or cycling. Excellent food at nearby pubs. Ten minutes drive from M5, perfect location for breaking the journey to Cornwall and the Eden Project. Credit cards accepted.

Caro Ayre
Tel: 01823 672603
Fax: 01823 672307

B&B from £25-£35pp, Rooms 4 double, 2 twin, 1 family, most en-suite, Open all year.

DOUBLE-GATE FARM, Godney, Wells, Somerset BA5 1RX
Email doublegatefarm@aol.com
Website www.doublegatefarm.com

Map Ref 5
Nearest Road A39, M5

Double-Gate Farm nestles on the banks of the River Sheppey, on the Somerset levels. An award winning B&B. All bedrooms are en-suite, attractively decorated and thoughtfully equipped. Breakfast is taken in the farmhouse dining room or in the garden. An extensive menu offers local and home grown produce accompanied with freshly home made bread. Family pets include "Jasper-Pilchards", "Laid back Jack" and "Miss Jessops". Centrally situated, Double-Gate makes an ideal base for exploring this very pretty and interesting county. Credit cards accepted.

Mrs H Millard
Tel: 01458 832217
Fax: 01458 835612

B&B from £27.50-£30pp, Rooms 3 double, 2 twin, 1 family, all en-suite, No smoking or pets, Children welcome, Open all year except Christmas & New Year.

RIVERSIDE GRANGE, Tanyard Lane, North Wootton, near Wells, Somerset BA4 4AE
Email riversidegrange@hotmail.com

Map Ref 6
Nearest Road A37

Riverside Grange is a charming converted tannery quietly situated on the river edge overlooking orchards set in an area of outstanding natural beauty. The rooms are tastefully furnished to a high standard and include tea and coffee making facilities and colour televisions. North Wootton is a short drive from both Wells and Glastonbury, and the famous factory shopping outlet 'Clarks Village' in street. There is a village inn serving good food within a short walk. AA 5 Diamonds Premier selected.

Mrs Pat English
Tel: 01749 890761

B&B from £22.50pp, Rooms 1 twin, 1 double, 1 No smoking or pets, Open all year except Christmas & New Year.

STONELEIGH HOUSE, Westbury-sub-Mendip, near Wells, Somerset BA5 1HF
Email stoneleigh@dial.pipex.com
Website www.stoneleigh.dial.pipex.com

Map Ref 7
Nearest Road A371

A beautiful 18th century farmhouse (flagstone floors, beams, crooked walls) situated between Wells and Cheddar. Wonderful southerly views over unspoilt countryside to Glastonbury Tor from the bedrooms and guests lounge. The bedrooms are prettily furnished with country antiques, and the en-suite bath/shower rooms work properly! Round this off with a delicious breakfast. Wendy's decorative needlework, Tony's classic cars, the old forge, a cottagey garden and friendly cats. Large car park. Excellent pubs nearby.

Full page photo opposite

Mrs Wendy Thompson
Tel/Fax: 01749 870668

B&B from £26pp, Rooms 2 double, 1 twin, 2 en-suite, 1 private bathroom, Children over 10, No smoking, Open all year except Christmas.

"Well now" said Mrs Towers "You could go down to Cricieth on the coast here that was Welsh until Edward took it over, and then down here to Harlech"

BELLE & BERTIE IN WALES

SUFFOLK

The people of Suffolk pride themselves on their gentle pace of life and there is certainly a very rural, charming ambience to this historically rich county. Medieval wool towns and quaint villages punctuate the mainly flat landscape of woodland, rivers and meadows – inspirational to so many painters, including Constable, Gainsborough and Munnings. To the east, Suffolk enjoys forty five miles of mainly conserved coastline offering ample walking and bird watching, as well as some charming seaside villages.

The county town of Ipswich has changed little over the years and features much history and character – The Ancient House (dated 1670, with older parts) is renowned for its exquisite hammer-beam roof and is just one gem among a wealth of timber-framed buildings. Twelve medieval churches offer testimony to the importance of the town as it developed in the Middle Ages; while the magnificent Tudor manor, Christchurch Mansion, provides a fine example of lavish country living. Set in a sixty five acre park, Christchurch features Dutch-style gables and enormous interiors which include notable works by Constable and Gainsborough. Shrubland Park Gardens, just six miles north of Ipswich, are also well worth a visit. Designed by Charles Barry, they provide one of the finest examples of Italianate gardens in the country.

Travelling west, the medieval village of Lavenham boasts some marvellously crooked half-timbered houses, a fine church and, most significantly, The Guildhall of Corpus Christi which dominates the market place. This magnificent 16th century building houses displays of local history and features a walled garden with a dye plant area – a testament to the village's heyday as a cloth manufacturer.

Another village of particular note in the area is Long Melford, so named because it claims to have the longest High Street in England. An impressive 15th century church is to be found here as well as two fine stately homes. Built in 1578, Melford Hall is a turreted brick Tudor mansion situated in the heart of the village – and just one mile north stands Kentwell Hall, another fine house of the same period. Extended in the 16th century to become 'the epitome of an Elizabethan home', Kentwell is set amid tranquil moated gardens which include a handsome avenue of lime trees and a camera obscura.

The attractive riverside town of Bury St Edmunds to the north-west of the county enjoys a distinctive Georgian feel and a particularly rich historic past. The ruined abbey, built on the shrine of the martyred Saxon King Edmund, was at one time the most famous pilgrimage centre in the country and, situated amid award-winning gardens, it is still a popular location with visitors today. Other significant religious buildings in the town include St Mary's Church with its ancient curfew bell and St Edmondsbury Cathedral, an impressive 16th century structure featuring elegant later additions. In the town centre, Moyse's Hall dates back to Norman times and is thought to be one of Suffolk's oldest domestic buildings. It houses a wonderfully eccentric collection of local history and artefacts, alongside rare archaeological exhibits. The Athenaeum, which opened as an Assembly House in 1714, has also enjoyed a rich history of rendezvous, discussion and recital – indeed it was here that Charles Dickens gave public readings from his books. And within the more rural environs of Bury St Edmonds, Hengrave House with its magnificent Oriel Window and Frieze; Wyken Hall Gardens and the huge Rotunda that is Ickworth House, feature among the many delights.

SUFFOLK

Mrs Bobbie Watchorn, Earsham Park Farm
Tel: 01986 892180
Map Ref 1 *see page 225*

Mark & Kay Dewsbury, Manorhouse
Tel: 01359 270960
Map Ref 2 *see page 225*

Mrs Meg Parker, Old Vicarage
Tel: 01206 337248
Map Ref 3 *see page 225*

Michael & Sue Harvey, Gables Farm
Tel: 01379 586355
Map Ref 4 *see page 226*

Mrs Rosemary Willis, Priory House
Tel: 01379 586254
Map Ref 5 *see page 226*

Bridget & Robin Oaten, The Hatch
Tel: 01284 830226
Map Ref 6 *see page 226*

Mrs Hackett-Jones, Pipps Ford
Tel: 01449 760208
Map Ref 7 *see page 228*

Elizabeth Dixon, Church Farm
Tel: 01728 660101
Map Ref 8 *see page 228*

Anna & John Garwood, Poplar Hall
Tel: 01502 578549
Map Ref 9 *see page 228*

Michael & Sally Ball, The Old Rectory
Tel: 01728 746524
Map Ref 10 *see page 229*

Mrs Elizabeth Hickson, Grange Farm B&B
Tel: 01986 798388
Map Ref 11 *see page 229*

Mrs Penfold, Guildhall
Tel: 01728 628057
Map Ref 12 *see page 229*

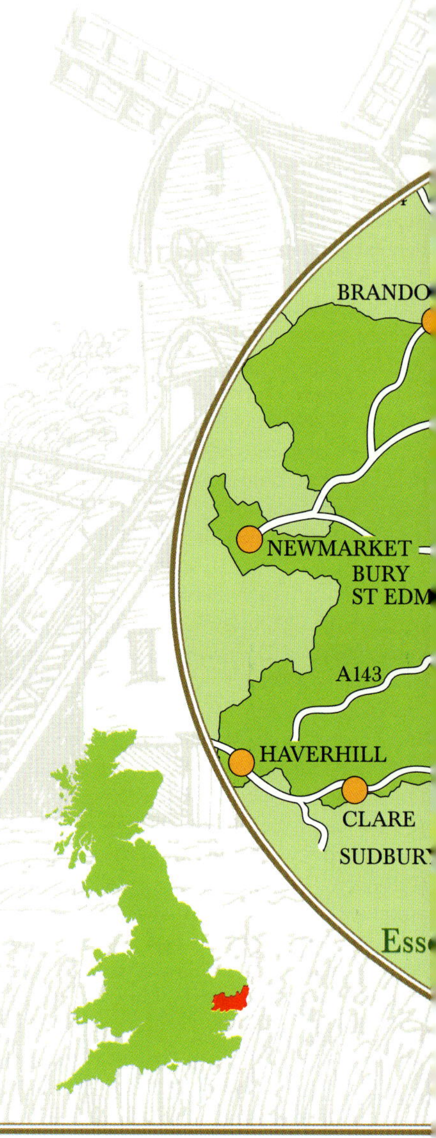

GREAT YARMOUTH
ORD
ATTLEBOROUGH
A11
A146
Norfolk
A140
BUNGAY
A143
LOWESTOFT
HETFORD
1
BECCLES
A1066
DISS
A143
A144
A145
KESSINGLAND
SCOLE
5
4
9
A143
SOUTHWOLD
HALESWORTH
A140
8
12
11
SAXMUNDHAM
WMARKET
A1120
LEISTON
7
A12
10
ALDEBURGH
A1141
A14
HADLEIGH
WOODBRIDGE
IPSWICH
3
A12
A137
FELIXSTOWE
HARWICH

EARSHAM PARK FARM, Harleston Road, Earsham, Bungay, Suffolk NR35 2AQ
Email bobbie@earsham-parkfarm.co.uk
Website www.earsham-parkfarm.co.uk

Map Ref 1
Nearest Road A143

Full page photo opposite

Standing on a hill overlooking the Waveney Valley this Victorian farmhouse has a relaxed and informal atmosphere. Each of the 3 spacious and light en-suite bedrooms has superb decor and furnishings. Enhanced by white embroidered linen, thick fluffy towels and extensive facilities. Breakfast is taken in the sunny dining room with its unique stencilled floor. Produce from the farms free-range animals is complimented by home baked bread and many other dishes. ETB 4 Diamonds and Silver Award Winning. A non-smoking establishment. Credit cards accepted.

Mrs Bobbie Watchorn
Tel/Fax: 01986 892180

B&B from £24-£38pp, Dinner £18, Rooms 2 double, 1 twin, all en-suite, No smoking, Children & pets welcome, Open all year.

MANORHOUSE, The Green, Beyton, Bury St Edmunds, Suffolk IP30 9AF
Email manorhouse@beyton.com
Website www.beyton.com

Map Ref 2
Nearest Road A14

Welcoming and relaxed, this award winning 15th century timbered longhouse, set in large gardens, overlooks village green. Furnished with antiques, oak beams, inglenooks and fresh flowers. Large, luxurious en-suite rooms with king-size or twin beds and sofa's. Tea-making facilities, TVs, fridge-freezer and laundry for guests. Excellent choice of breakfasts at individual tables. Good local inns to walk to. Ideally located 4 miles east of Bury St Edmunds and 35 minutes from Cambridge.

Mark & Kay Dewsbury
Tel: 01359 270960

B&B from £25-£30pp, Rooms 2 double, 2 twin, all en-suite, No smoking, children or pets, Open all year except Christmas & New Year.

OLD VICARAGE, Higham, near Colchester, Suffolk CO7 6JY
Email oldvic.com@bushinternet.com

Map Ref 3
Nearest Road A12

This charming detached 16th century house is situated in a beautiful Suffolk village. The fields of the Old Vic go down to the river Brets and Stour. There are boats on the river, swimming pool and tennis court. There is much to do visiting the famous villages Lavenham, Sudbury showing many Gasinburgh pictures. Sea in half an hour drive away. The house has 3 bedrooms with TV, tea making facilities and there is a fine drawing room overlooking the garden for guests.

Mrs Meg Parker
Tel: 01206 337248

B&B from £27-£30pp, Rooms 1 twin, 1 double, 1 family, 2 en-suite, Restricted smoking, Children & pets welcome, Open all year.

GABLES FARM, Earsham Street, Wingfield, Diss, Suffolk IP21 5RH
Email sue.harvey@lineone.net

Map Ref
Nearest Road B1118, A14

Gables Farm is a 16th Century timbered farmhouse set in moated gardens Wingfield is a quiet village in the heart of East Anglia, convenient for Norwich Bury St Edmunds and coast and many places of interest. Ideal for cycling and walking, fishing two miles away. Two double and one twin bedrooms (all en suite) and having colour TV and hospitality tray. Full English breakfast with free range eggs and local produce (where possible). Leaflet on request.

Michael & Sue Harvey
Tel/Fax: 01379 586355

B&B from £20pp, Rooms 1 twin, 2 double, all en-suite, No smoking, Children welcome, Restricted pets, Open all year except Christmas & New Year.

PRIORY HOUSE, Priory Road, Fressingfield, Eye, Suffolk IP21 5PH
Email Prioryhousebb@aol.com

Map Ref 5
Nearest Road B1118, A140

A warm welcome awaits visitors to this lovely 16th century farmhouse, set in an acre of secluded lawns and gardens. The comfortable bedrooms have tea/coffee facilities, and 2 rooms have private bathroom. Centrally heated. The house has a wealth of exposed beams, and is furnished with antique furniture. There is a guests lounge and pleasant dining room. Fressingfield is ideal for a peaceful relaxing holiday and as touring base for Norwich, Bury St Edmunds, the Broads, coast, historic buildings and gardens. Excellent food available in the village, 8 minutes walk. Colour brochure on request.

Mrs Rosemary Willis
Tel: 01379 586254

B&B from £27pp, Rooms 1 twin, 2 double, private bathrooms, Restricted smoking, Children over 10, Pets by arrangement, Open all year except Christmas & New Year.

THE HATCH, Pilgrims Lane, Cross Green, Hartest, Suffolk IP29 4ED
Email theoatens@tiscali.co.uk

Map Ref 6
Nearest Road B1066

The Hatch is a gorgeous thatched timber-framed listed 15th century house situated just outside the attractive 'High Suffolk' village of Hartest. Surrounded by farmland the house is comfortably furnished with fine fabrics and antiques. Guests have the use of the delightful drawing and sitting rooms, both having wonderful Inglenook fireplaces with log fires for cooler evenings. There is a lovely garden for guests to enjoy. Hartest is an ideal centre for visiting West Suffolk, Cambridge and Ely. Many attractive houses and gardens to visit. Great antique hunting area. ETB, AA 5 Diamonds, Gold Award.

Bridget & Robin Oaten
Tel: 01284 830226

B&B from £30pp, Rooms 1 twin, 1 double, No smoking, Children over 9, Open all year.

Full page photo opposite

PIPPS FORD, Needham Market, near Ipswich, Suffolk IP6 8LJ
Email b&b@pippsford.co.uk
Website www.pippsford.co.uk

Map Ref 7
Nearest Road A14, A140

Pipps Ford is the perfect place for a quiet holiday. Centrally placed in Suffolk, it is handy for the A14, A140 and A12. All bedrooms are en-suite. Evening meals are imaginative and good value. Pipps Ford specialises in small, bespoke conferences, and celebratory parties. Winner, Les Routiers Award of Excellence for B&B of the Year 2001. Credit cards accepted.

Mrs Hackett-Jones
Tel: 01449 760208
Fax: 01449 760561

B&B from £23.50pp, Dinner £22.50, Rooms 2 single, 4 double, 3 twin, all en-suite, Restricted smoking, Children over 5, Pets welcome, Open all year except Christmas & New Year.

CHURCH FARM, Yoxford Road, Sibton, Saxmundham, Suffolk IP17 2LX
Email dixons@church-farmhouse.demon.co.uk
Website www.church-farmhouse.demon.co.uk

Map Ref 8
Nearest Road A1120, A12

Surrounded by glorious countryside, our spacious 17th century house is the perfect setting to unwind. We are conveniently situated close to the Suffolk heritage coast mid-way between Southwold and Aldeburgh. Our bedrooms have colour TV, video, mini hi-fi, hairdryer and hospitality trays. They are spacious, light, beautifully furnished and exceptionally comfortable. Two doubles are en-suite, the twin with private bathroom. Relax in the elegant lounge and enjoy our lovely garden. Children over 6. Sorry, no smoking or pets.

Elizabeth Dixon
Tel: 01728 660101
Fax: 01728 660102

B&B from £55-£65pr, Rooms 2 double en-suite, 1 twin with private bathroom, No smoking or pets, Children over 6, Open all year except Christmas & New Year.

POPLAR HALL, Frostenden Corner, Frostenden, Southwold, Suffolk NR34 7JA
Website www.southwold.ws/poplar-hall

Map Ref 9
Nearest Road A12

Peaceful and quiet yet only 3½ miles from the lovely seaside town of Southwold. Poplar Hall is a 16th century thatched house in 1½ acre garden. Walks abound in the area, either coastal or country. Walberswick, Dunwich, Aldburgh, Snape are just a short distance. Poplar Hall offers luxury accommodation with TV, tea/coffee making facilities and vanity units in all rooms. Sitting, dining rooms are a pleasure to be in whilst enjoying our famed breakfast of fresh fruit, local fish, sausage, bacon and home made preserves. Also two cottages available in the grounds. ETC Four Diamonds.

Anna & John Garwood
Tel: 01502 578549

B&B from £24pp, Rooms 1 single, 2 double, 1 en-suite, No smoking, Children welcome, No pets.

THE OLD RECTORY, Campsea Ashe, Woodbridge, Suffolk IP13 0PU

Map Ref 10
Nearest Road A12

Peaceful Georgian rectory set in mature gardens. Relaxed and homely atmosphere. Log fires in drawing rooms and dining room. Spacious conservatory. Honesty bar. Fully licensed. All bedrooms en-suite with tea/coffee making facilities. Delicious home cooked food. Local home-made bread, variety of home-made marmalade, jam and local honey. Ideally situated for Snape, Woodbridge and coastal areas. Brochure available on request. Children welcome, television and games in drawing room.

Michael & Sally Ball
Tel/Fax: 01728 746524

B&B from £32.50pp, Dinner from £19.50 (Restaurant closed Sunday), Rooms 1 single, 2 twin, 4 double, all en-suite, Restricted smoking, Children & pets welcome, Open all year except Christmas.

GRANGE FARM B&B, Dennington, Woodbridge, Suffolk IP13 8BT

Map Ref 11
Nearest Road A1120, B1116

This is a charming home in a superb spot, the house dates from the 13th-14th century and the remains of a 12th century Moat and fish ponds surround the peaceful garden, which is full of bird life. There is an all weather tennis court for the energetic. In winter the Aga burns in the kitchen, a log fire in the sitting room. The bread and marmalade are homemade, the honey local. Look no further, close to Minsmere, Snape Maltings, Sutton Hoo and Framlingham Castle. Good pubs nearby.

Mrs Elizabeth Hickson
Tel: 01986 798388
Mobile: 07774 182835

B&B from £22pp, Rooms 3 single/double/twin, No smoking or pets, Children over 12, Open March to December.

GUILDHALL, Church Street, Worlingworth, Suffolk IP13 7NS

Map Ref 12
Nearest Road A1120

Guildhall is 16th century thatched and listed Grade II. Set in rural countryside ideal for bird watching, walking and painting. The Heritage coast is approx 30 minutes. Southwold, Minsmere, historic Framlingham, Eye, or Diss a short drive. Rooms are heavily beamed, beautifully furnished and centrally heated. Tea and coffee facilities. Separate TV guest lounge with inglenook. Full English breakfast (dinner by previous arrangement) served in a charming dining room or conservatory. Large mature gardens with summer house at your disposal.

Mrs Penfold
Tel/Fax: 01728 628057

B&B from £22-£24pp, Dinner by arrangement from £12, Rooms 2 double, 1 en-suite, 1 private facilities, No smoking, pets or children, Open mid March - 31st September.

SURREY

Positioned to the south-west of London, Surrey's slightly sprawling commuter towns eventually give way to the majestic North Downs where sloping grasslands intersperse with woodland to give fine rural vistas. The Thames and Wey wind their way through the county and it is on the first of these rivers, near the village of East Molesley, that the county's most prestigious country home, Hampton Court Palace, sits resplendent. Enjoying over 500 years of royal history, it was much favoured by King Henry VIII and indeed his State Rooms are among the most magnificent to be found within the palace. Sixty acres of immaculate riverside gardens surround this lavish building and highlights include the largest and oldest grapevine in Europe and the world famous maze. Also of world renown and situated in the nearby town of Richmond, The Royal Botanic Gardens at Kew cover 300 acres and feature immaculate lawns, brimming borders and an enormous 65ft Palm House housing a vast array of tropical plants.

Moving south in the county, Painshill Landscape Garden near Cobham is a lot less busy than Kew and quite breathtaking by design. Featuring a circuit walk with a series of emerging scenes, this 158-acre 18th century garden includes a 14-acre lake fed by an enormous water wheel, a Gothic temple, a ruined abbey, a Turkish tent and some quite magnificent Cedars of Lebanon. The conservation village of Cheam, also in the north of the county and famed for its pottery, makes for an interesting stop and in particular the Tudor country home of Whitehall, which tells the history of the area. An interesting medieval well can be found in the pleasant rear gardens.

To the east of Surrey and enjoying a pleasant parkland setting at the foot of the North Downs, Titsey Place represents one of the county's largest surviving historic estates. Although fist impressions are of a comfortable early 19th century retreat, this stunning mansion actually dates back some three hundred years earlier, although the grounds are typically Victorian by design.

The affluent town of Guildford, Surrey's administrative hub, lies on the high ridge of the North Downs to the west of the county and features some handsome buildings. A rather splendid Tudor town hall with 17th century façade dominates the High Street, while slightly to the south, a castle keep, thought to be built by William I, is set amid attractive landscaped gardens. The remains of Guildford Palace, dating back to the 12th century, can also be seen from the south-eastern corner of the gardens. Slightly north of the town centre on the top of Stag Hill sits Guildford Cathedral – an intriguing building which fuses Gothic austerity with 1960s minimalism.

Slightly south of Guildford, two more of Surrey's enigmatic beauty spots lie tucked away – certainly not to be missed if you happen to appreciate fine trees. The first is Ramster Gardens near Chiddingford, featuring twenty acres of wooded glades, impressive shrubs and superb walks. The second, Winkworth Arboretum near Godalming, incorporates beautiful hillside woodland, rare trees and two stunning lakes – one of which boasts a delightful 100-year-old boathouse. Visit in spring if you can when bluebells and azaleas abound – or autumn when the tree colours are quite magnificent.

SURREY

Carol Franklin-Adams, High Edser
Tel: 01483 278214
Map Ref 2 *see page 234*

Peter & Sandi Clark, The Old Parsonage
Tel: 01784 436706
Map Ref 3 *see page 234*

Adrian Grinsted, The Lawn Guest House
Tel: 01293 775751
Map Ref 4 *see page 234*

Elizabeth Carmichael, Deerfell
Tel: 01428 653409
Map Ref 5 *see page 235*

Mrs S.P Comer, Barn Cottage
Tel: 01306 611347
Map Ref 6 *see page 235*

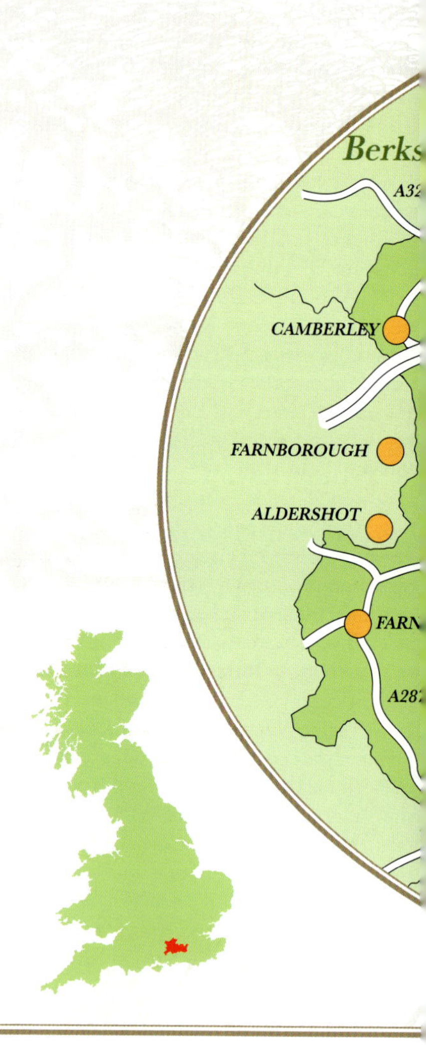

RICHMOND
STAINES
A316
London
A3
A308
A24
CROYDON
A232
BIGGIN
HILL
A3
EPSOM
A22
KING
A23
LEATHERHEAD
DORKING
GUILDFORD
OXTED
A25
A25 REIGATE
A25
6
A24
4
HORLEY
A22
B2126
London
Gatwick
Airport
2
ALMING
B2128
A23
A281
CRANLEIGH
CRAWLEY
A264
SLEMERE
A281
A29
A23
HORSHAM
5

HIGH EDSER, Shere Road, Ewhurst, Cranleigh, Surrey GU6 7PQ
Email franklinadams@highedser.demon.co.uk

Map Ref 2
Nearest Road A25, B2126, B2128

A 16th century farmhouse set in Area of Outstanding Natural Beauty. Good for walks, cycling and riding. Close to many National Trust properties. Wisley RHS Garden. Easy access to London, ten miles from Guildford, Dorking, Godalming and Horsham. Tea/coffee in rooms. Guests own small sitting room. Tennis court that can be used by guests. Plenty of off road parking.

Carol Franklin-Adams
Tel: 01483 278214
Fax: 01483 278200

B&B from £25-£35pp, Rooms 2 double, 1 twin, No smoking, Children & well behaved dogs welcome, Open all year except Christmas & New Year.

THE OLD PARSONAGE, Parsonage Road, Englefield Green, Surrey TW20 0JW
Email the.old.parsonage@talk21.com
Website www.theoldparsonage.com

Map Ref 3
Nearest Road A30, M25 J13

The Old Parsonage is a late Georgian house set in a pretty village on the edge of Windsor Great Park. Guest accommodation is traditionally furnished and overlooks the old fashioned gardens. Bedrooms are equipped with TV and tea/coffee making facilities. All meals are freshly prepared to order and wine is available. Local facilities include a health spa with beauty salon, swimming, golf and horse riding. Conveniently situated for Heathrow (20 minutes), M25, M4, Windsor Ascot, Wisley Gardens and Egham mainline station (Waterloo 25 minutes).

Peter & Sandi Clark
Tel: 01784 436706
Fax: 01784 436706

B&B from £25pp, Dinner from £15, Rooms 1 single, 1 twin, 3 double, 1 family, most en-suite, No smoking or pets, Children welcome, Open all year except Christmas.

THE LAWN GUEST HOUSE, 30 Massetts Road, Horley, Gatwick, Surrey RH6 7DF
Email info@lawnguesthouse.co.uk
Website www.lawnguesthouse.co.uk

Map Ref 4
Nearest Road A23, M23

Everything for the Gatwick Airport Traveller. English Tourist Council - 4 Diamonds and Silver Award. RAC - 4 Diamonds, Sparkling Diamond and Warm Welcome. Imposing Victorian house; Non smoking establishment. 5 minutes from Gatwick airport; 2 minutes walk Horley, with shops, restaurants, pubs and banks. Station 300 yards; London 40 minutes, Brighton 45 minutes. Bedrooms all en-suite; colour/text TV, hairdryers, tea/coffee/chocolate trays, d/d phones, radio alarm clocks. English breakfast or healthy alternative. Overnight parking. Long term parking/airport transfers by arrangement. Credit cards accepted.

Adrian Grinsted
Tel: 01293 775751
Fax: 01293 821803

B&B from £20-£27.50pp, Rooms 3 double, 3 twin, 6 family, all en-suite, No smoking, Children & pets welcome, Open all year.

DEERFELL, Blackdown Park, Fernden Lane, Haslemere, Surrey GU27 3BU
Email deerfell@tesco.net

Map Ref 5
Nearest Road A286, A283, A3

Deerfell lies secluded on the south west side of National Trust Blackdown Hill, with wonderful views towards the South Downs and open country. Rooms are peaceful and comfortable with en-suite bath/shower, tea/coffee making facilities and a television also third room with separate bath/shower. Guests have the use of a comfortable sitting room with open fire in cold weather. There is a relaxing sun room for guests use and breakfast is served in the attractive dining room. Many places of interest, London accessible from nearby Haslemere station only 4 miles away. Gatwick/Heathrow one hour.

Elizabeth Carmichael
Tel: 01428 653409
Fax: 01428 656106

B&B from £24-£28pp, Dinner £12.50, Rooms 3 double/twin, all en-suite/private bathrooms, No smoking or pets, Children over 6, Open mid December to mid January.

BARN COTTAGE, Church Road, Leigh, Reigate, Surrey RH2 8RF

Map Ref 6
Nearest Road A217, M25

Barn Cottage is a converted 17th century barn, furnished with antique, set in a large garden with tennis court and swimming pool. We have television and tea/coffee making facilities in both rooms. Leigh is a pretty village, The Plough Pub is 100 yards away. We provide transport to Gatwick (15 minutes) and Redhill Station (30 minutes to London or Brighton). Dorking famous for antiques is 5 miles away. National Trust properties nearby include Hever Castle and Chartwell (Churchill's House). Introduction to Walton Heath Golf Club, (two Championship 18 holes) is available.

Mrs S.P Comer
Tel: 01306 611347

B&B from £25-£35pp, Rooms 1 double en-suite, 1 twin, Restricted smoking, Children welcome, Open all year.

Please mention
A GREAT PLACE TO STAY
when enquiring about accommodation

SUSSEX

Situated to the south-east of England, the county of Sussex is commonly divided in two. East Sussex is by far the more popular choice with visitors, while West Sussex tends to harbour its picturesque pockets, historic towns and fine country homes in an altogether more understated manor.

Featuring fine countryside around the South Downs, some quite breathtaking chalk cliffs and the popular resort towns of Eastbourne and Brighton, it is easy to appreciate the draw of East Sussex however. Beautiful medieval villages such as Rye, Lewes and Winchelsea delight with their half-timbered buildings and twisting alleyways; while history abounds in nearby Hastings and Battle – scene of the great clash of 1066 and the last successful invasion of Britain. The extrovert hub of Brighton is also a magnet for visitors – indeed wealthy Londoners have been flocking here to enjoy the sea air since the 1750s, as the Regency architecture of the town stands testament to so splendidly. Brighton is also home to The Royal Pavilion – exotic former seaside residence of King George IV an absolute must for any visitor.

As to be expected in an area boasting much history, travel and wealth, East Sussex has an abundance of castles, grand country homes and fine gardens on offer – one of the finest of these being Firle Place near the village of

Lewes. Home to the Gage family for over 500 years, this stunningly situated house was remodelled on the French chateau style in the 18th century and houses some wonderful English and European works of art. Nearby Glynde Place offers a particularly fine – if somewhat austere – example of an Elizabethan manor house; while Lewes' imposing Norman castle affords magnificent views across the South Downs.

A short journey north rewards garden enthusiasts with the Lancelot Capability Brown masterpiece of Sheffield Park Garden – a tranquil 120-acre parkland featuring four lakes and some particularly rare shrubs and trees. Described as a garden for all seasons, it is awash with informal colour from spring through to autumn and even delights in the winter months with atmospheric mists and frosts. On a much smaller scale but also appealingly informal, Merriments Gardens in Hurst Green are also well worth a visit. Set in just four acres of Weald farmland, this naturalistic garden has been planted according to prevailing conditions and is literally bursting with colour and originality. Nearby Bodiam Castle, built in 1385 and a particularly fine example of medieval architecture, should also not be missed while in the area.

At the heart of the Roman town of Chichister – main town of West Sussex – stands the impressive Chichister Cathedral, hub of Christian worship for over 900 years and boasting some fine Norman carvings. Also of note within this pleasant town is the Fisbourne Roman Palace – site of an ancient Roman villa dating back to around AD75 and featuring one of the finest in-situ mosaics in Britian.

Not far from Chichester lie two of perhaps the grandest country homes in West Sussex. Petworth House, standing imposingly within 700 acres of parkland, includes a Carved Room containing some of Grinling Gibbons finest limewood carvings, over 70 paintings of the house by Turner and a notable private art collection amassed over 350 years; while no visit to this county could be complete without a visit to the charming Goodwood House, now as much renowned for the race course in the grounds as the beautifully elegant country home.

SUSSEX

Vicki Richards, Woodacre
Tel: 01243 814301
Map Ref 1 *see page 240*

Paul & Pauline Collins, Fox Hole Farm
Tel: 01424 772053
Map Ref 2 *see page 240*

Mr & Mrs Slater, Little Hemingfold Hotel
Tel: 01424 774338
Map Ref 2 *see page 240*

Geoffrey & Sally Earlam, Timbers Edge
Tel: 01444 461456
Map Ref 3 *see page 243*

Sandra Jolly, Judins
Tel: 01435 882455
Map Ref 4 *see page 243*

Mrs Mary Waller, Hatpins
Tel: 01243 572644
Map Ref 5 *see page 243*

Adam Smith, Ockenden Manor
Tel: 01444 416111
Map Ref 6 *see page 244*

Mrs Sonia Stock, South Cottage
Tel: 01273 846636
Map Ref 7 *see page 244*

Lady Taylor, Duckyls
Tel/Fax: 01342 811038
Map Ref 8 *see page 244*

Barbara Yorke, Filsham Farm House
Tel: 01424 433109
Map Ref 9 *see page 247*

Mike & Susie Skinner,
Clayton Wickham Farmhouse
Tel: 01273 845698
Map Ref 10 *see page 247*

Peter & Mary Spreckley,
Woodmans Green Farm
Tel: 01428 741250
Map Ref 13 *see page 247*

Alex & Annabelle Costaras, Amberfold
Tel: 01730 812385
Map Ref 12 *see page 248*

Caroline Angela, Redford Cottage
Tel: 01428 741242
Map Ref 11 *see page 248*

Ms Moss, River Park Farm
Tel: 01798 860799
Map Ref 14 *see page 248*

HINDHEAD
HASLEMERE
13
11
14
PET
A272
MIDHURST
12
B2141
A286
CHICHESTER
5
SELSEY

Sara Brinkhurst,
Little Orchard House
Tel: 01797 223831
Map Ref 15 *see page 249*

Ivor & Diana Green, White Lion Cottages
Tel: 01825 840288
Map Ref 16 *see page 249*

London Gatwick Airport
M23
EAST GRINSTEAD
ROYAL TUNBRIDGE WELLS
A264
A262
CRAWLEY
A22
CROWBOROUGH
A21
Kent
HORSHAM
A267
TENTERDEN
HAYWARDS HEATH
A265
A28
A21
UCKFIELD
HEATHFIELD
RYE
COWFOLD
BURGESS HILL
BATTLE
A259
A23
A281
A275
A22
A267
A271
A271
LEWES
A23
A27
HAILSHAM
A259
HASTINGS
A283
A259
BEXHILL
HOVE
WORTHING
BRIGHTON
NEWHAVEN
A259
EASTBOURNE
2
3
4
6
7
8
9
10
15
16

Full page photo opposite

WOODACRE, Arundel Road, Fontwell, Arundel, West Sussex BN18 0QP
Email wacrebb@aol.com
Website www.woodacre.co.uk

Map Ref 1
Nearest Road A27, A29

Woodacre offers hospitality in a traditional family house with guest accommodation in a separate cottage, joined to the main house. The rooms are spacious and clean, each one having TV and tea/coffee making facilities. We are ideally placed for exploring Chichester, Arundel, the South Downs or the seaside. A full English breakfast (or continental if preferred) is served in our conservatory or dining room overlooking our lovely wild garden. 10% discount for 6 nights or more. Everyone is made welcome. Credit cards accepted.

Vicki Richards
Tel: 01243 814301
Fax: 01243 814344

B&B from £45-£70pr, Rooms 1 en-suite double, 2 twin, 1 family, No smoking, Children & pets welcome, Open all year except Christmas & New Year.

FOX HOLE FARM, Kane Hythe Road, Battle, East Sussex TN33 9QU

Map Ref 2
Nearest Road B2096

Fox Hole Farm is a beautiful and secluded 18th century woodcutters cottage nestling in over 40 acres of its own rolling lush East Sussex land. The farmhouse retains many of its original features and is heavily beamed with a large Inglenook fireplace featuring a woodburning stove. It has been carefully converted to offer three traditionally furnished and well appointed double rooms, all with en-suite bathrooms, TV and tea making facilities. Outside a large country garden containing many species of flower, shrubs, trees and natural pond.

Paul & Pauline Collins
Tel: 01424 772053
Fax: 01424 772053

B&B from £27pp, Rooms 3 en-suite double, No smoking, Children over 10, Pets restricted, Open all year except Christmas.

LITTLE HEMINGFOLD HOTEL, Telham, Battle, East Sussex TN33 0TT

Map Ref 2
Nearest Road A2100, A259

Part 17th century farmhouse, set in 40 acres farm and woodland with two acre trout lake and grass tennis court. Renowned cuisine in relaxed informal atmosphere. Some courtyard rooms with log burning stoves. Quiet pets welcome. Credit cards accepted.

Mr & Mrs Slater
Tel: 01424 774338
Fax: 01424 775351

B&B from £44-£47.50pp, Dinner available from £24.50, Rooms 8 double, 2 twin, 2 family, all en-suite, Restricted smoking, Children over 7, Pets welcome, Open March to end of December.

TIMBERS EDGE, Longhouse Lane, off Spronketts Lane, Warninglid, Bolney, West Sussex RH17 5TE
Email Email: gearlam@aol.com

Map Ref 3
Nearest Road A23, A272

Timbers Edge is a beautiful Sussex country house set in large formal gardens and surrounded by woodlands, creating a quiet peaceful atmosphere. We have two attractive bedrooms with television and beverage making facilities. We are conveniently situated within easy reach of the following: Nymans and Leonardslee Garden (10 mins), Hickstead Show Jumping Ground (10 mins), Ardingly (South of England Showground) (15/20 mins), Brighton (20 mins) and Gatwick Airport (20 mins). The nearest main roads are the A23 and A272.

Geoffrey & Sally Earlam
Tel: 01444 461456
Fax: 01444 461813

B&B from £30-£40pp, Rooms 1 double, 1 twin en-suite, No smoking, children or pets, Open all year except Christmas & New Year.

JUDINS, Heathfield Road, Burwash Weald, East Sussex TN19 7LA
Email sandrajolly@tiscali.co.uk

Map Ref 4
Nearest Road M25, A21, A265

Judins, a delightful 300 year old country house situated in 1066 countryside with outstanding views across the Rolter Valley and you are welcome to stroll or relax in the beautiful gardens. Direct walks to Batemans, former home of Rudyarl Kipling. Breakfast is served in the beamed dining room. TV, alarm/radio, hair dryer, hostess tray. Secure car park. Our home is your home for that peaceful break. Credit cards accepted.

Sandra Jolly
Tel: 01435 882455
Fax: 01435 883775

B&B from £35-£40pp, Dinner £25, Rooms 3 en-suite double, Restricted smoking, Children welcome, No pets, Open all year.

HATPINS, Bosham Lane, Old Bosham, Chichester, Sussex PO18 8HG
Email mary@hatpins.co.uk
Website www.hatpins.co.uk

Map Ref 5
Nearest Road A259

Mary Waller, a former designer of hats and wedding dresses, has combined her talents with a natural flair for decorating to transform her home into delightful bed and breakfast accommodation. Enhancing the decor is the warmth of Mary's hospitality. Bosham is an appealing coastal town and Old Bosham brims with charm and it is fun to wander down to the waterfront and explore the tiny lanes. Also nearby are Portsmouth and the cathedral city of Chichester with its lovely harbour. A few miles inland is Downland Museum - a collection of very old cottages and buildings. Honeymoon couples welcome. ETC 5 Diamonds Silver Award.

Full page photo opposite

Mrs Mary Waller
Tel: 01243 572644
Fax: 01243 572644

B&B from £30-£50pp, Rooms 5 with en-suite/private bathroom, No smoking, Children welcome, No pets, Open all year.

OCKENDEN MANOR, Ockenden Lane, Cuckfield, West Sussex RH17 5LD
Email ockenden@hshotels.co.uk
Website www.hshotels.co.uk

Map Ref 6
Nearest Road A23, A272

This peaceful Elizabeth manor house set in 9 acres of grounds is a peaceful haven, just an hour from London and 20 minutes from Gatwick. In the heart of the Tudor village of Cuckfield, Ockenden is ideally situated for touring the Gardens and Houses of Sussex and Kent or visiting the coastal resort of Brighton. Afterwards enjoy a drink in the panelled bar or in the drawing room. Artists will love sitting on the conservatory terrace to capture the magnificent views. Credit cards accepted.

Adam Smith
Tel: 01444 416111
Fax: 01444 415549

B&B from £160-£300pr, Dinner £38, Rooms 1 single, 21 double, 4 twin, 4 family, all en-suite, Restricted smoking, Children welcome, No pets, Open all year.

SOUTH COTTAGE, 2 The Drove, Ditchling, East Sussex BN6 8TR
Email sonia.stock@amserve.net

Map Ref 7
Nearest Road A23, A27, B2116

Traditional country cottage with pretty garden down private lane and surrounded by fields yet only minutes from the historic village of Ditchling and its three pubs. The cottage is warm and comfortable with tea making facilities and television in each room and has far-reaching views across fields to Ditchling Beacon and the South Downs. It is convenient for Gatwick, Newhaven, Brighton and Glyndebourne and is only a mile from the South Downs Way for walkers, cyclists and riders (stabling and grazing available nearby).

Mrs Sonia Stock
Tel: 01273 846636
Fax: 01273 85338

B&B from £25pp, Rooms 2 single, 1 double, No smoking, Children welcome, Well behaved pets welcome, Open all year except Christmas & New Year.

DUCKYLS, Sharpthorne, near East Grinstead, Sussex RH19 4LP
Email HMTDUCKYLS@aol.com

Map Ref 8
Nearest Road A22, B2028

Full page photo opposite

Duckyls is a large stone built family home situated between East Grinstead and West Hoathly. Wakehurst Place, Hever Castle and Nymans Garden are within easy reach. The Ardingly show ground is nearby, Glyndebourne is 45 minutes by car and Gatwick airport (20 minutes), with excellent rail service to London. TV in rooms.

Lady Taylor
Tel/Fax: 01342 811038

B&B from £35-£45pp, Rooms 3 double, most en-suite, No smoking or pets, Children welcome, Open April to September.

FILSHAM FARM HOUSE, 111 Harley Shute, St Leonards-on-Sea, Hastings, Sussex TN38 8BY
Email filshamfarmhouse@talk21.com
Website www.filshamfarmhouse.co.uk
Map Ref 9
Nearest Road A21, A259

An historic 17th century listed Sussex farmhouse situated in the heart of 1066 country on the outskirts of Hastings. It is within easy reach of the town centre, the sea and the beautiful Sussex countryside with its many historic castles, country houses and other places of interest. The present house was completed in 1684 and still retains many of its original features including old beams, staircases, sloping floors, low doorways and a large inglenook fireplace. The house is furnished in a traditional manner and antique pieces to provide visitors with a high standards of comfort while maintaining a strong sense of the past. Credit cards accepted.

Barbara Yorke
Tel: 01424 433109
Fax: 01424 461061

B&B from £25-£30pp, Rooms 3 double, 1 twin, 1 family, most en-suite, Children over 8, Pets welcome, Open all year.

CLAYTON WICKHAM FARMHOUSE, Belmont Lane, Hurstpierpoint, West Sussex BN6 9EP
Email susie@cwfbandb.fsnet.co.uk
Website www.cwfbandb.co.uk
Map Ref 10
Nearest Road A23, A273, B2116

A warm welcome awaits you in the beautifully restored 14th century farmhouse with masses of beam and huge inglenook in the drawing room. Set in three acres of splendid gardens with tennis court and lovely views. Enviably quiet and secluded, yet conveniently situated for transport facilities and places of interest. Rooms, including one four poster en-suite, are generously equipped. The genial hosts serve truly delicious food with a very wide choice for breakfast. An excellent candlelit dinner, or simpler meal, is available on prior request.

Mike & Susie Skinner
Tel: 01273 845698
Fax: 01273 841970

B&B from £35-£42.50pp, Dinner by prior arrangement, Rooms 1 single, 3 double en-suite, 2 twin 1 en-suite, 1 family, Children & pets welcome, Open all year.

Full page photo opposite

WOODMANS GREEN FARM, Linch, near Liphook, Sussex GU30 7NF
Email peterandmary@woodmansgreen.fsnet.co.uk
Map Ref 13
Nearest Road A272, A3

This lovely old Sussex farmhouse is situated in glorious countryside mid-way between Midhurst and Liphook in a small hamlet. The area is wonderful walking countryside. The sea near Chichester is an easy drive away also Goodwood races and polo at Midhurst. There is an attractive garden and swimming pool heated in summer. One large double room en-suite and one granary room with shower and complete privacy. Also family and twin rooms sharing a bathroom. Meals by arrangement in evenings.

Peter & Mary Spreckley
Tel: 01428 741250

B&B from £22.50-£30pp, Dinner by prior arrangement £8-£12, Rooms 1 single, 1 double, 1 twin, 1 family, most en-suite, No smoking, Children welcome, Open March to November.

AMBERFOLD, Heyshott, Midhurst, West Sussex GU29 0DA

Map Ref 12
Nearest Road A286

Amberfold, situated in the scenic hamlet of Heyshott, represents English countryside at its best. Miles of unspoiled woodland walks start on your doorstep. An ideal hideaway for nature lovers, yet only five minutes drive from historic Midhurst and close to local attractions of Chichester, Goodwood and coast. Accommodation comprises two self-contained annexe, with access all day. Double bedroom, shower room, toilet, central heating and television. In addition, electric kettle, cafetiere, toaster. A fridge, lavishly replenished daily with selection of food, is provided for self-service continental breakfast.

Alex & Annabelle Costaras
Tel: 01730 812385
Fax: 01730 812842

B&B from £27.50pp, Rooms 2 double en-suite, No smoking or pets, Open all year.

REDFORD COTTAGE, Redford, Midhurst, West Sussex GU29 0QF

Map Ref 11
Nearest Road A272, A286

A warm welcome in attractive country house dating back to the 16th century in an area of outstanding natural beauty. Comfortable rooms include a self-contained garden suite with own beamed sitting room and studio annex all with en-suite facilities. Convenient to Midhurst, Petworth, Goodwood, Chichester and South Downs. Excellent walks and National Trust Properties within easy reach. An ideal retreat for a peaceful stay.

Caroline Angela
Tel: 01428 741242

B&B from £37.50pp, Rooms 3 double/twins, all en-suite, Open all year except Christmas & New Year.

RIVER PARK FARM, Lodsworth, Petworth, West Sussex GU28 9DS
Email info@riverparkfarm.co.uk
Website www.riverparkfarm.co.uk

Map Ref 14
Nearest Road A286, A272, A283, A3

River Park Farm is a lovely 17th century tile hung West Sussex farmhouse set on the edge of the South Downs. The Moss family have been welcoming guests to their home for bed and breakfast accommodation for thirty years, and many guests return to the house regularly. The house lies at the end of a mile long private drive on the site of a former Monastery, the legacy of which is a beautiful four and a half acre fishing lake lying adjacent to the grounds.

Ms Moss
Tel: 01798 860799

B&B from £22.50-£24.50pp, Rooms 1 double with private bathroom, 1 en-suite family, No smoking or pets, Children welcome, Open all year except Christmas & New Year.

LITTLE ORCHARD HOUSE, West Street, Rye, Sussex TN31 7ES
Website www.littleorchardhouse.com

Map Ref 15
Nearest Road A259, A268

Little Orchard House is centrally situated in peaceful surroundings. Rebuilt in 1745, the house has been lovingly renovated over the years and retains it original fascinating character. Both bedrooms are en-suite with a 4 poster. There are personal antiques, paintings, books and bears throughout the house. There is a peaceful book room and a sitting room with an open fire. The generous breakfast provides as much as can be eaten at a time to suit you. Large walled garden available for guests' use. ETC 5 Diamonds. Credit cards accepted, VISA and Mastercard

Sara Brinkhurst
Tel: 01797 223831

B&B from £32pp, Rooms 2 double, No smoking, Children over 12, Open all year.

WHITE LION FARM COTTAGES, Shortgate, Lewes, Sussex

Map Ref 16

Situated in the hamlet of Shortgate are two converted stables of a 16th century coaching inn. Attractively decorated, fully equipped, TV, microwave, cooker, washing machine and fridge. Own patio. Set in 8½ acres with 2 lakes. Rural location. Convenient for coastal resorts, South Downs, Glyndebourne, Ashdown Forest, East Sussex National Golf Club and many other places of interest. ETB 3 Stars.

2 cottages, sleeps 4, 4, Price per week £160 low season, £285 high season, No smoking, Children welcome, No pets, Available all year.

Contact: Ivor & Diana Green, White Lion Farm, Shortgate, Lewes, Sussex BN8 6JP
Tel/Fax: 01825 840288

"Can't you just see the lords and ladies and knights?" asked Belle
"Well" said Bertie "actually, no I can't"
BELLE & BERTIE IN WALES

WARWICKSHIRE & WEST MIDLANDS

Although many visitors flock to Warwickshire to visit Stratford-upon-Avon, birthplace of William Shakespeare and England's most popular tourist attraction outside London, there is a lot more to explore within this pleasant Midland area. Picturesque villages, attractive waterways and stately homes abound, while dramatic castles such as Warwick and Kenilworth provide a fascinating insight into the long and sometimes turbulent history of the region.

Situated within the West Midlands, Coventry was a major centre for the wool industry in medieval times and, although many of its historic buildings have disappeared, there are still a few medieval cottages to be found here, as well as some fine Georgian townhouses. Enthusiasts of more modern architecture will also enjoy St Michael's Cathedral – designed by Sir Basil Spence and built between 1955 and 1962. This stunning structure is built beside the ruins of its medieval counterpart – razed to the ground during the Second World War – and is celebrated for its particularly fine stained glass and soaring western glass wall.

Journeying south, the pleasant town of Kenilworth is certainly worth a look, and in particular its impressive red sandstone castle. Originating back to the 12th century, Kenilworth Castle was once a stronghold of great Lords and Kings and enjoyed major restoration and enlargement in both the 14th and 16th centuries. In 1563 Queen Elizabeth I gifted the castle to Robert Dudley, Earl of Leicester and it was here that he entertained her with 'Princely Pleasures' during her famous 19 day visit. The castle was deliberately ruined just under a century later during the Civil War.

The ancient town of Warwick, situated upon the River Avon, boasts some fine medieval buildings – many of which were rebuilt in the handsome style of the late 17th and early 18th century after the Great Fire of 1694. The town's main claim to fame, Warwick Castle, fortunately escaped damage, however, and is recognised today as one of the most dramatic and complete medieval castles in England. Now owned by Madame Tassaud's, it rewards the visitor with an atmospheric and fascinating day out.

Situated to the north of the Cotswolds, Stratford-upon-Avon is, of course, birthplace of that most celebrated Elizabethan playwright William Shakespeare. An absolute magnet for summer tourists, it is a fascinating town to visit, especially the five buildings associated with Shakespeare and now looked after by the Shakespeare Birthplace Trust. Situated in and around the town, these beautifully preserved Tudor homes include Shakespeare's Birthplace, Nash's House, Hall's Croft, Anne Hathaway's Cottage and Mary Arden's House.

Many other fine period homes are to be found around Stratford – Ragley Hall, Coughton Court and Upton House to name but a few. One in particular, however, Charlecote Park, enjoys a quirky Shakespearian connection that tends to go down well with enthusiasts of The Old Bard. It was said to be in the grounds of this fine 16th century manor that owner Sir Thomas Lucy apprehended William Shakespeare for poaching. Shakespeare was reputed to base the character of Justice Shallow in the 'Merry Wives of Windsor' on Sir Thomas as a result of the event.

WARWICKSHIRE & WEST MIDLANDS

Mrs Linda Grindal, Park Farm House
Tel: 024 76 612628
Map Ref 1 *see page 254*

Christine Jenkin, Garden Cottage
Tel: 01926 338477
Map Ref 3 *see page 254*

Mrs Charlotte Field, Ashby House
Tel: 01608 684286
Map Ref 4 *see page 254*

Paul & Dreen Tozer, Victoria Spa Lodge
Tel: 01789 267985
Map Ref 5 *see page 256*

Angie Wright, Alderminster Farm B&B
Tel: 01789 450774
Map Ref 6 *see page 256*

John & Julia Downie, Holly Tree Cottage
Tel: 01789 204461
Map Ref 7 *see page 256*

Mrs Lyon, Winton House
Tel: 01789 720500
Map Ref 8 *see page 257*

Margaret & Ted Mander, Pear Tree Cottage
Tel: 01789 205889
Map Ref 9 *see page 257*

Mrs Elizabeth Draisey, Forth House
Tel: 01926 401512
Map Ref 10 *see page 257*

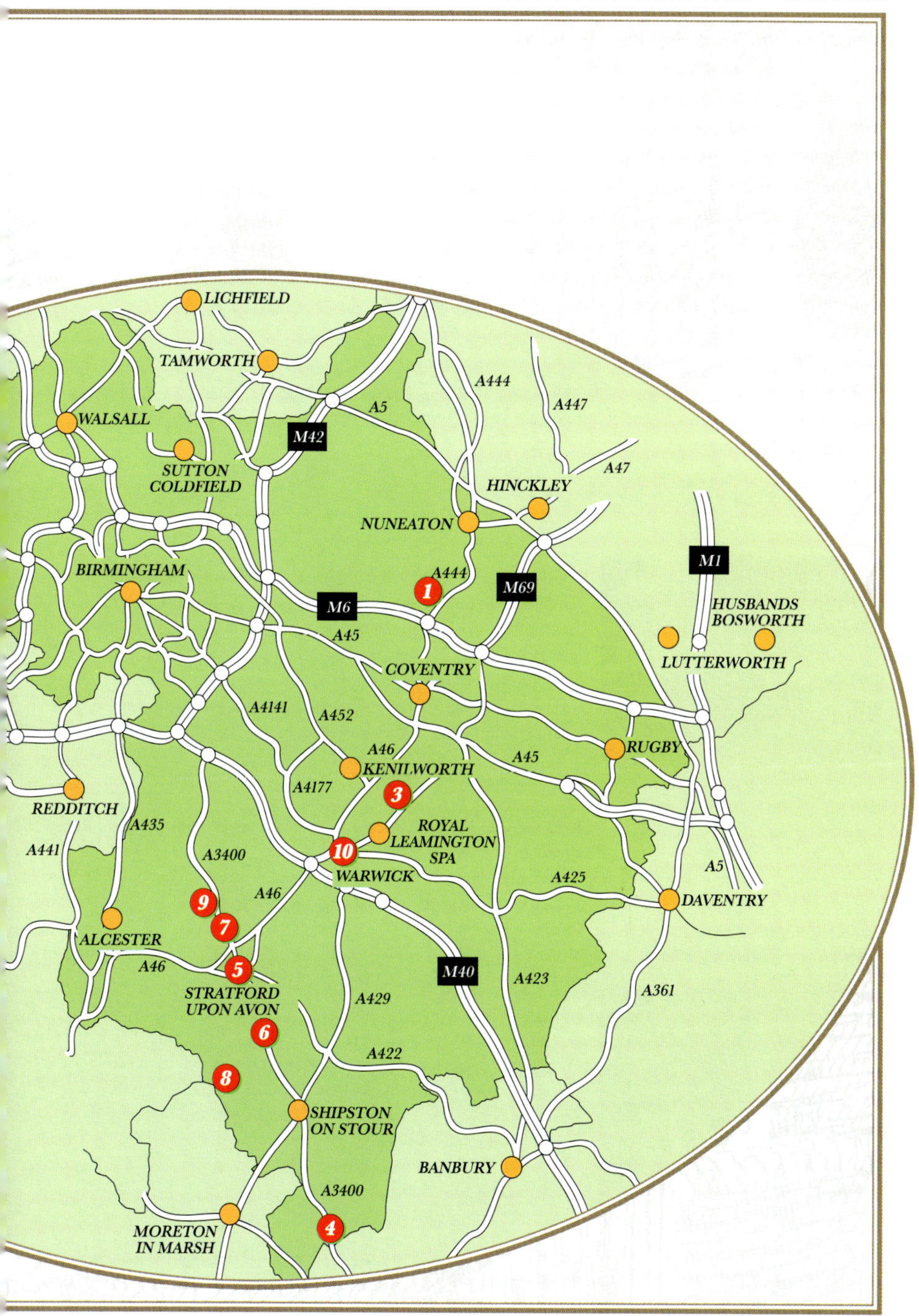
LICHFIELD
TAMWORTH
WALSALL
SUTTON COLDFIELD
M42
A5
A444
A447
A47
HINCKLEY
NUNEATON
M1
M69
BIRMINGHAM
A444
1
M6
HUSBANDS BOSWORTH
A45
LUTTERWORTH
COVENTRY
A4141
A452
RUGBY
A46
A45
KENILWORTH
A4177
3
REDDITCH
ROYAL LEAMINGTON SPA
A435
10
A441
A3400
WARWICK
A5
A46
A425
9
DAVENTRY
7
ALCESTER
A46
5
M40
A423
STRATFORD UPON AVON
A361
A429
6
A422
8
SHIPSTON ON STOUR
BANBURY
A3400
MORETON IN MARSH
4

PARK FARM HOUSE, Spring Road, Barnacle, near Shilton, Coventry, Warwickshire CV7 9LG

Map Ref 1
Nearest Road M6, M69

A Grade II Listed building, originally moated, Park Farm House is quiet, comfortable and elegant, five minutes from M6/M69 motorway with easy access to NEC, Birmingham, NEC at Stoneleigh and Coventry, Warwick, Rugby and Straford-upon-Avon. We have three beautifully appointed en-suite bedrooms, and a private sitting room. Dinners, business lunches, small conferences are available for our guests, by prior arrangement. For friendly attentive service, warm hospitality and delicious food, look no further.

Mrs Linda Grindal
Tel: 024 76 612628
Fax: 024 76 616010

B&B from £35-£46pp, Dinner £19, Rooms 1 double, 1 twin, 1 family, all en-suite, No smoking or pets, Children over 12, Open all year.

GARDEN COTTAGE, 52 Kenilworth Road, Royal Leamington Spa, Warwickshire CV32 6JW
Email christine@gardencottage.fsworld.co.uk

Map Ref 3
Nearest Road A452, M40, A46

A warm welcome awaits you in this charming and quiet coach house which is on the A452, five minutes from the town centre. Garden Cottage is ideally located for Stratford-upon-Avon, Warwick, Kenilworth, Royal Agricultural Centre, Warwick University, Birmingham NEC and airport. The accommodation comprises one spacious twin room with an adjoining conservatory and private bathroom and one double with large en-suite shower room. Television, coffee/tea making facilities. Off road parking. Garden.

Christine Jenkin
Tel/Fax: 01926 338477

B&B from £23-£30pp, Rooms 1 double, 1 twin, both en-suite, Restricted smoking, Children welcome, Open all year.

ASHBY HOUSE, Clarks Lane, Long Compton, Shipston-on-Stour, Warwickshire CV36 5LB
Email epfield@fieldashby.demon.co.uk
Website www.ashbyhouse.co.uk

Map Ref 4
Nearest Road A3400

If you want jacuzzis, sky TV, vending machines and tiny rooms don't come here! We provide spacious rooms, peace and quiet (but a pub in the village) and the many attractions of Oxford, Stratford, Warwick and the Cotswold villages. Why not try one of Charlottes dinners which can be provided by arrangement. Bring your own wine and celebrate!

Full page photo opposite

Mrs Charlotte Field
Tel: 01608 684286

B&B from £19-£23pp, Dinner £12, Rooms 1 double, 1 twin, 1 family, all private bathroom, No smoking or pets, Children over 10, Open all year.

VICTORIA SPA LODGE, Bishopton Lane, Stratford-upon-Avon, CV37 9QY
Email ptozer@victoriaspalodge.demon.co.uk
Website www.stratford-upon-avon.co.uk/victoriaspa.htm

Map Ref 5
Nearest Road A46, A3400

An attractive Victorian building, originally, a Spa opened in 1837. Queen Victoria graciously gave it her name and her coat of arms is built into the gables. Situated in a country setting overlooking Stratford canal. Pleasant walks along the canal tow path to Stratford and other villages. Bruce Bairnsfather (creator of 'Old Bill' during the Great War) lived here as also did Sir Barry Jackson founder of the Birmingham Repertory Theatre. Comfortable bedrooms are equipped with hostess tray, TV, hair dryer and radio/alarm. Ample parking, full fire certificate. Completely non smoking. RAC, ETC and AA 4 Diamonds and Silver Award. Warm Welcome and Sparkling Diamond Award. RAC Best Small Hotel Award for midland region.

Paul & Dreen Tozer
Tel: 01789 267985
Fax: 01789 204728

B&B from £65pr, Rooms 1 twin, 3 double, 3 family, all en-suite, No smoking, Children welcome, No pets, Open all year.

ALDERMINSTER FARM B&B, Alderminster, Stratford-upon-Avon, Warwickshire CV37 8BP
Email angie_wright5@hotmail.com

Map Ref 6
Nearest Road A3400, M40

Alderminster Farm is a Georgian three storey house. It enjoys a very rural location, being set in fields by the River Stour. Stratford upon Avon and its Royal Shakespeare Theatre is three miles away, also nearby are Warwick Castle. The Cotswolds and Hidcote Gardens. Our spacious guest room, decorated in cream and peach overlooks the fields to the front of the house and can be booked as a twin, double or family room. It is en-suite with TV and tea making facilities. Good pubs nearby.

Angie Wright
Tel: 01789 450774
Fax: 01789 450623

B&B from £55-£65pr, Rooms 1 double/twin/family en-suite, Restricted smoking, Children welcome, Pets by prior arrangement, Open all year except Christmas.

HOLLY TREE COTTAGE, Birmingham Road, Pathlow, Stratford-upon-Avon, Warwickshire CV37 0ES
Email john@hollytree-cottage.co.uk
Website www.hollytree-cottage.co.uk

Map Ref 7
Nearest Road A3400, M40 jct 15

Period cottage dating back to 17th century with beams, antiques, tasteful furnishings, fresh flowers and friendly atmosphere. Collection of porcelain and paintings. Picturesque gardens with views over open countryside. Situated 3 miles north of Stratford-upon-Avon toward Henly-in-Arden on A3400. Ideal for theatre, touring Shakespeare country, Cotswolds, visiting Warwick Castle, Blenheim Palace and the abundance of National Trust properties all within easy reach. Well situated for National Exhibition Centre. Television, tea/coffee in all rooms. Speciality breakfast includes full English, continental or vegetarian. Pubs and restaurants nearby.

John & Julia Downie
Tel/Fax: 01789 204461

B&B from £25-£38pp, Rooms 1 double, 1 twin, 1 family, all en-suite, No smoking, Children & pets welcome, Open all year.

WINTON HOUSE, The Green, Upper Quinton, near Stratford-upon-Avon, Warwickshire CV37 8SX
Email gail@wintonhouse.com
Website www.wintonhouse.com

Map Ref 8
Nearest Road B4632, M40 jct 15

Historic Victorian farmhouse, situated in an area of natural beauty, 6 miles from Stratford and the Cotswolds. 4 poster antique beds with hand made quilts and en-suite bathrooms. Heartbeat award winning breakfasts with organic fruit from our orchard. Log fires. Cycles for hire. The Greenway part of the National Sustran route nearby. Village pub. A lovely spot for walking and touring.

Mrs Lyon
Tel: 01789 720500
Mobile: 07831 485483

B&B from £32.50pp, Rooms 1 twin, 2 double, 1 family, 2 en-suite, 1 private bathroom, No smoking or pets, Children welcome, Open all year.

PEAR TREE COTTAGE, Church Road, Wilmcote, Stratford-upon-Avon, Warwickshire CV37 9UX
Email mander@peartreecot.co.uk
Website www.peartreecot.co.uk

Map Ref 9
Nearest Road A3400

The stone and half timbered house of great character and period charm is quietly situated in its country garden overlooking Mary Arden's house. Three and a half miles from Stratford and seven miles from Warwick. All rooms have individual luxury furnishings and private facilities. There is plenty of parking and pubs to eat at within walking distance. Close to major attractions yet away from the bustle of towns. We offer a cosy and welcoming B&B base for long or short stays, when touring or visiting the NEC.

Margaret & Ted Mander
Tel: 01789 205889
Fax: 01789 262862

B&B from £26pp, Rooms 1 twin, 3 double, 1 family, all en-suite, No smoking or pets, Children over 3, Open all year except Christmas & New Year.

FORTH HOUSE, 44 High Street, Warwick CV34 4AX
Email info@forthhouseuk.co.uk
Website www.forthhouseuk.co.uk

Map Ref 10
Nearest Road M40 jct 15

Our rambling Georgian family home within the old town walls of Warwick provides two peaceful guest suites hidden away at the back. One family sized ground floor suite opens onto the garden whilst other overlooks it. Both en-suite with private sitting rooms and dining rooms. TV, fridges, hot and cold drink facilities. Ideally situated for holidays or business. Stratford, Oxford, Birmingham and Cotswold villages within easy reach. Breakfasts, full English or continental at times agreed with our guests. J15 of M40 two miles away.

Mrs Elizabeth Draisey
Tel: 01926 401512
Fax: 01926 490809

B&B from £30pp, Rooms 1 double/twin, 1 family, both en-suite, No smoking, Children welcome, Open all year.

Wiltshire

An absolutely fascinating county for history-lovers, Wiltshire is home to the spellbinding Stone Age monuments of Stonehenge and Avesbury, and the beautiful town of Salisbury with its fine Middle Ages architecture and wonderful cathedral. Even the rolling chalk downs of the county, scattered with hill figures dating as far back as prehistoric times, demonstrate the impact of past civilisations upon this intriguing south-west landscape.

To the south of the county, the standing stones of Stonehenge – begun around 3,000 BC and built and rebuilt over a period of 1,500 years – represent one of the most celebrated Stone Age sites in the world. Although the sun-influence alignment of the Stones is significant, the actual purpose of the site remains an intriguing mystery still much debated by historians today.

Not far from Stonehenge, stone encircled Avebury is thought to stand at the centre of a complex prehistoric ceremonial site and this pretty village certainly warrants a visit for its atmosphere alone. England's finest burial mound – West Kennet Long Barrow – dating from 3,500 BC and dramatically guarded by huge sarsens and the mysterious Silbury Hill can also be found nearby.

Main town of the county and also situated in the south, Salisbury has formed a busy marketing hub for over 600 years and makes a fine base for discovering Wiltshire. It also boasts one of England's finest and most-visited cathedrals. Finished in 1258, Salisbury Cathedral is built to the shape of a double cross in Early English Gothic style and features the tallest spire in Britain and perhaps the most beautiful walled close. The cathedral houses many historical treasures including an ancient clock mechanism dating from 1386 and thought to be one of the oldest pieces of working machinery in the world. Markets are still a way of life in Salisbury and the Market Square has seen on-going use since around 1361. It is dominated by the 18th century Guildhall, although much older buildings can be found opposite the hall, on Fish Row and at Poultry Cross.

On an altogether grander scale, Wilton House is situated just three miles west of Salisbury and is regarded as one of England's finest country mansions. Home to the present 17th Earl of Pembroke, the house was rebuilt after a fire in Palladian style by Inigo Jones and John Webb, with further alterations made by James Wyatt from 1801. Highlights of the house include magnificent 17th century state apartments, including the Single and Double Cube Rooms, and a particularly fine art collection.

Although spectacular, Wilton is by no means Wiltshire's only significant stately home. Continuing to the far western border of the county, the fine country house and quite outstanding gardens of Stourhead, near Stourton, are certainly worth a detour; while close to the elevated town of Warminster, Longleat enjoys a stunning situation and a reputation as one of the finest examples of Elizabethan architecture. Equally impressive are Longleat's lakeside grounds, designed by famous architect Lancelot Capability Brown and including a host of attractions including a safari park and the world's longest hedge maze.

Capability Brown also left his distinctively brilliant mark on two significant houses to the north of the county. The first, Corsham House near Chippenham – an Elizabethan home extended to house one of the finest collections of paintings and statuary in England; and also Bowood House, home to the Marquis of Lansdowne and situated near the village of Colne. Bowood Gardens feature a Doric temple, a fine aboretum and prolific Rhododendrons – while the charming Georgian house boasts a Diocletian wing designed by Robert Adam and containing a splendid sculpture gallery in which some of the famous Lansdowne Marbles are displayed.

WILTSHIRE

Richard & Gloria Steed, The Cottage
Tel: 01380 850255
Map Ref 1 *see page 263*

Anna Moore, Church House
Tel: 01249 782562
Map Ref 2 *see page 263*

Gill Stafford, Pickwick Lodge Farm
Tel: 01249 712207
Map Ref 3 *see page 263*

Mrs Carol Pope, Hatt Farm
Tel: 01225 742989
Map Ref 4 *see page 264*

Jenny Daniel, Heatherly Cottage
Tel: 01249 701402
Map Ref 5 *see page 264*

Mrs Kate Jones, Church Farm
Tel: 01249 715180
Map Ref 6 *see page 264*

Mrs Edna Edwards, Stonehill Farm
Tel: 01666 823310
Map Ref 7 *see page 267*

Sarah Campbell, Enford House
Tel: 01980 670414
Map Ref 8 *see page 267*

Diana Gifford Mead, The Mill House
Tel: 01722 790331
Map Ref 9 *see page 267*

Rosie & Ian Robertson, Wyndham Cottage
Tel: 01722 716343
Map Ref 10 *see page 268*

Mrs Mary Tucker, 1 Riverside Close
Tel: 01722 320287
Map Ref 11 *see page 268*

John Lanham, Newton Farmhouse
Tel: 01794 884416
Map Ref 12 *see page 268*

Mrs Pat Hoddinott, Ashen Copse Farm
Tel: 01367 240175
Map Ref 13 *see page 269*

Jill Awdry, Spiers Piece Farm
Tel: 01380 870266
Map Ref 14 *see page 269*

Allan & Sue Edwards,
The Manor House
Tel: 01380 831210
Map Ref 15 *see page 269*

CIRENCESTER
LECHLADE
TETBURY
CRICKLADE
A36
13 FARINGDON
A429
7
A4040
Oxon
A420
SWINDON
WANTAGE
MALMESBURY
M4
A3102
A361
A345
Berkshire
6 CHIPPENHAM
CALNE
AVEBURY
MARLBOROUGH
5
A350
A4
A4
1
A361
HUNGERFORD
NEWBURY
DEVIZES
A346
PEWSEY
A338
14
TROWBRIDGE
A360
UPAVON
A338
A350
15
8
WESTBURY
A345
ANDOVER
WARMINSTER
A303
A36
AMESBURY
Hampshire
A338
9
A303
10
WILTON
11
SALISBURY
A30
12
A36
A338
A354

THE COTTAGE, Westbrook, Bromham, Chippenham, Wiltshire SN15 2EE
Email RJSteed@cottage16.freeserve.co.uk

Map Ref 1
Nearest Road A342, A3102

This delightful cottage is reputed to have been a Coaching Inn dating back to 1450. There are 3 charming ground floor bedrooms, all with shower, TV and tea/coffee making facilities, in a beautiful converted barn. Breakfast is served in the old beamed dining room. A lovely garden and paddock surround the property. An ideal centre for visiting Bath, Bristol, Devizes, Avebury, Stonehenge, and Lacock. There is also a self-catering cottage which sleeps 3.

Richard & Gloria Steed
Tel: 01380 850255

B&B from £25-£30pp, Rooms 1 double, 2 twin, all en-suite, Children welcome, No pets, Open all year.

CHURCH HOUSE, Grittleton, near Chippenham, Wiltshire SN14 6AP
Email moore@flydoc.fsbusiness.co.uk

Map Ref 2
Nearest Road M4, J17

Church House began as a Georgian Rectory and is now "home from home" to many returning guests who enjoy our garden, copper beeches, heated covered pool, croquet and sheep! Three and a half miles from the M4 (exit 17) we are the "gateway to the West" offering the delights of historic and prehistoric Wiltshire and of our near neighbours Bath and Malmesbury. Grittleton boasts a good church, pub and cricket club, with horse-riding, golf and tennis within easy reach. All guest rooms have television, tea/coffee making facilities. There is a large drawing room. Dinner is by arrangement - 4 courses plus half a bottle of wine per head and coffee inclusive. There is ample off-road parking.

Anna Moore
Tel: 01249 782562
Fax: 01249 782546

B&B from £35pp, Dinner by arrangement £22.50, Rooms 2 twin, 1 double, 1 family, Restricted smoking, Children under 2 and over 12, No pets, Open all year.

Full page photo opposite

PICKWICK LODGE FARM, Guyers Lane, Corsham, Wiltshire SN13 0PS
Email b&b@pickwickfarm.freeserve.co.uk
Website www.pickwickfarm.co.uk

Map Ref 3
Nearest Road A4, M4 Jct 17

Enjoy a stay in our beautiful home set in wonderful countryside where you can relax in our lovely garden or take a short stroll or longer walk and see pheasants and sometimes a deer. Yet only 15 minutes from Bath. Ideally situated to visit Lacock, Castle Combe, Avebury, Stonehenge and many National Trust properties. Explore idyllic villages, have lunch or supper at a quaint pub or restaurant. 3 well appointed tastefully furnished bedrooms, refreshment trays with home made biscuit. Start the day with hearty breakfast using local produce.

Gill Stafford
Tel: 01249 712207
Fax: 01249 701904

B&B from £25-£30pp, Rooms 1 double, 1 twin, 1 family, all en-suite, No smoking or pets, Children over 8, Open all year except Christmas & New Year.

HATT FARM, Old Jockey, Box, Corsham, Wiltshire SN13 8DJ
Email hattfarm@netlineuk.net

Map Ref 4
Nearest Road A365, B3109

Close to Bath and within the Cotswolds our beautiful farmhouse, set in 250 peaceful acres, offers breathtaking views, wonderful walks, scrumptious breakfasts and every comfort. In summer enjoy sitting in the garden and in winter we offer the warmth of a log fire. Hatt Farm is bordered by Kingsdown Golf Club and is an ideal base for visiting the historic towns and quaint villages of the area. We are less than 2 hours drive from Wales, the coast, the Midlands and London/Heathrow.

Mrs Carol Pope
Tel: 01225 742989
Fax: 01225 742779

B&B from £22.50-£25pp, Rooms 1 double, 1 twin, 1 family, all en-suite, No smoking or pets, Children welcome, Open all year except Christmas & New Year.

HEATHERLY COTTAGE, Ladbrook Lane, Gastard, near Corsham, Wiltshire SN13 9PE
Email ladbrook1@aol.com
Website www.smoothhound.co.uk/hotels/heather3.html

Map Ref 5
Nearest Road A4, B3353

Delightful 17th century cottage in a quiet country lane with two acres and beautiful views across open countryside. Ample off road parking and guests have a separate wing of the house with their own entrance and staircase. All rooms are en-suite, the larger double has a kingsize bed. All are equipped with colour television, clock/radio, tea/coffee tray and hairdryer. Close to Bath, Lacock, Castle Combe, Avebury, Stonehenge and many National Trust properties. Restaurants nearby for good food, one is a 10 minute walk.

Jenny Daniel
Tel: 01249 701402
Fax: 01249 701412

B&B from £24-£26pp, Rooms 2 double, 1 twin, 1 family, No smoking or pets, Children over 10, Open all year except Christmas & New Year.

CHURCH FARM, Hartham, Corsham, Wiltshire SN13 0PU
Email kmjbandb@aol.com
Website www.churchfarm.cjb.net

Map Ref 6
Nearest Road A4, M4 jct 17

Farmhouse on working farm situated in glorious parkland. En-suite accommodation in farmhouse and new barn adjacent. All rooms either single/double/twin or family. Colour TV, tea/coffee trays, central heating, lovely views and own access. 2 ground floor rooms with patio's and 1 first floor with wonderful views over Hartham Valley. High chair and travel cot available. Plenty of parking. Close to Bath, Castle Combe, Lacock Biddestone and lots of National Trust properties. Good road/rail links. Local produce used where possible. 4 Diamonds ETC/AA. Brochure available.

Mrs Kate Jones
Tel: 01249 715180
Fax: 01249 715572

B&B from £22.50-£30pp, Rooms 4 en-suite single, double, twin or family, No smoking, Pets at owners discretion, Children over 6 months, Open all year except Christmas & New Year.

Full page photo opposite

STONEHILL FARM, Charlton, Malmesbury, Wiltshire SN16 9DY
Email johnedna@stonehillfarm.fsnet.co.uk
Website www.smoothhound.co.uk/hotels/stonehill.html

Map Ref 7
Nearest Road M4, B4040

Stonehill has been our home since 1970, we love it and enjoy sharing it with you. It is on a family run dairy farm in lush rolling countryside on the Wiltshire/Gloucestershire border, ideal for 1 night or several days. Oxford, Bath, Stratford upon Avon, Stonehenge and the delightful Cotswold hills and villages are within easy reach by car. We have 3 rooms (1 en-suite), all with hospitality trays and TVs, and offer full English breakfast using local produce and homemade preserves.

Mrs Edna Edwards
Tel/Fax: 01666 823310

B&B from £22.50-£35pp, Rooms 2 double (1 en-suite), 1 twin, Children & pets welcome, Open all year.

ENFORD HOUSE, Enford, Pewsey, Wiltshire SN9 6DJ

Map Ref 8
Nearest Road A345

Stonehenge is only five miles away and Enford is surrounded by prehistoric remains of many kinds. The 18th century house and its garden are enclosed by thatch-topped walls. Antiques furnish the panelled sitting-room. Bedrooms are simple, fresh and conventionally furnished. Recommended by the Tourist Board for the last 10 years. Very good local pub which serves excellent meals. Readers comments: Everything quite delightful. Very comfortable. Pleasant and relaxed time. Enjoy the expanse of Salisbury Plain.

Sarah Campbell
Tel: 01980 670414

B&B from £18pp, Rooms 2 twin, 1 double, Restricted smoking, Children welcome, Well behaved pets, Open all year except Christmas & New Year.

THE MILL HOUSE, Berwick St James, near Salisbury, Wiltshire SP3 4TS

Map Ref 9
Nearest Road A36, A303

Stonehenge three miles. Diana welcomes you to the Mill House set in acres of Nature Reserve. An island paradise with the River Till running through the working mill and beautiful garden. Diana's old fashioned roses long to see you as do the lovely walks. Built by the miller in 1785, the bedrooms with all facilities and television, command magnificent views. Fishing or swimming in the mill pool. Golf and riding nearby. Attention to healthy and organic food. Sample superb cuisine at "The Boot" Berwick St James.

Diana Gifford Mead
Tel/Fax: 01722 790331

B&B from £25-£35pp, Rooms 2 single, 4 double, 1 twin, 1 family, most en-suite, Children over 5, No pets, Open all year.

Full page photo opposite

WYNDHAM COTTAGE, St Mary's Road, Dinton, Salisbury, Wiltshire SP3 6HH
Email IRbrtsn1@aol.com

Map Ref 10
Nearest Road B3089, A303, A36

A charming 18th century thatched stone cottage, lovingly restored and set in magnificent National Trust countryside, on edge of picturesque village. Delightful walks with marvellous views of the surrounding area. The cottage garden opens to the public under the National Garden scheme. Excellent pubs nearby. Ideally situated for several days sightseeing at some wonderful historic places, cities and gardens. Stonehenge, Avebury, Salisbury, Bath, Wells, Wilton House, Stourhead, Longleat and many more. Tea/coffee facilities and colour TV.

Rosie & Ian Robertson
Tel: 01722 716343

B&B from £27pp, Rooms 2 en-suite double, No smoking or pets, Open April to October.

---

1 RIVERSIDE CLOSE, Laverstock, Salisbury, Wiltshire SP1 1QW
Email marytucker@fdn.co.uk

Map Ref 11
Nearest Road A30

Charming, well appointed home, in a quiet area 1½ miles from Salisbury Cathedral. Tastefully furnished suites enjoying their own en-suite bath or shower room, TV and drink making facilities. Salisbury is the centre of an area steeped in antiquity, rich in natural beauty, with many places of outstanding historical interest. Your hosts take endless care to ensure the well being of their guests and are happy to plan itineraries for them

Mrs Mary Tucker
Tel/Fax: 01722 320287

B&B from £25pp, Dinner from £12 with 48 hours notice, Rooms 1 double, 1 family, No smoking, Open all year.

NEWTON FARMHOUSE, Southampton Road, Whiteparish, Salisbury, Wiltshire SP5 2QL
Email enquiries@newtonfarmhouse.co.uk
Website www.newtonfarmhouse.co.uk

Map Ref 12
Nearest Road A36

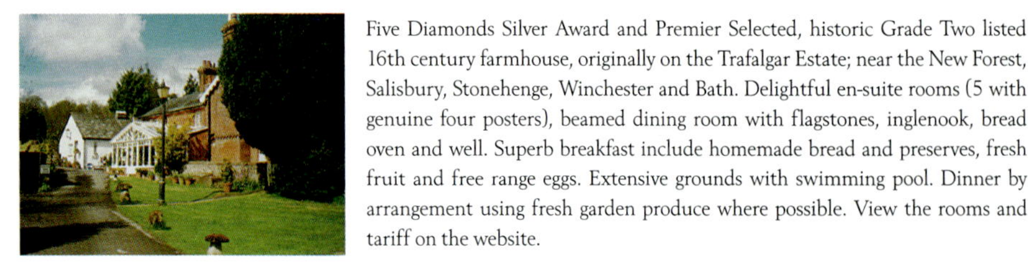

Five Diamonds Silver Award and Premier Selected, historic Grade Two listed 16th century farmhouse, originally on the Trafalgar Estate; near the New Forest, Salisbury, Stonehenge, Winchester and Bath. Delightful en-suite rooms (5 with genuine four posters), beamed dining room with flagstones, inglenook, bread oven and well. Superb breakfast include homemade bread and preserves, fresh fruit and free range eggs. Extensive grounds with swimming pool. Dinner by arrangement using fresh garden produce where possible. View the rooms and tariff on the website.

John Lanham
Tel: 01794 884416

B&B from £25-£35pp, Dinner by prior arrangement £25, Rooms 3 double, 2 twin, 3 family, all en-suite, No smoking or pets, Children welcome, Open all year.

ASHEN COPSE FARM, Coleshill, Highworth, Swindon, Wiltshire SN6 7PU
Email pat@hodd.demon.co.uk
Website www.hodd.demon.co.uk

Map Ref 13
Nearest Road B4019, A420, A361

Our 17th century stone and brick National Trust farmhouse is set in beautiful peaceful countryside, free from road noise. Spacious, comfortable bedrooms and guest lounge with lovely views. British bacon and free range eggs. Scenic way-marked footpaths radiate from the farmhouse. Good pubs/restaurants nearby. Ideal touring base for Cotswolds, Oxford, Swindon, Avebury, Bath and Stratford. Hidden away from B4019, half a mile from Coleshill village (Faringdon side). No smoking in the house, please.

Mrs Pat Hoddinott
Tel: 01367 240175

B&B from £25-£35pp, Rooms 1 single, 1 twin, 1 en-suite family, No smoking or pets, Children welcome, Open all year except Christmas & New Year.

SPIERS PIECE FARM, Steeple Ashton, Trowbridge, Wiltshire BA14 6HG
Email spierspiece@hotmail.com

Map Ref 14
Nearest Road A350

For a great break, or just visiting, our home from home comfortable B&B could be just what you need. Try us and see for yourselves. It's only our home, but we love it, and hope you will also. Our Georgian farmhouse lies in the heart of Wiltshire, on the edge of Salisbury Plain. Fantastic views, spacious garden, peace and tranquility. At affordable prices from £19pppn. Bath, Stonehenge, Stourhead, Longleat and many tourist attractions within easy reach. Our farm is family run.

Jill Awdry
Tel/Fax: 01380 870266

B&B from £19-£21pp, Rooms 2 double, 1 twin, Children welcome, Pets by prior arrangement, Open February to November.

THE MANOR HOUSE, Lower Road, Edington, near Westbury, Wiltshire BA13 4QW
Email allan@cerronovo.com

Map Ref 15
Nearest Road B3098

Sue and Allan welcome you to their comfortable, Victorian country house. The large bedrooms are well furnished and overlook well maintained and colourful gardens with views of Salisbury Plain. The elegant drawing room leads out through French windows to the terrace and lawns. The village is dominated by the magnificent 14th century Priory church - home every August to a famous music festival. There are many lovely walks and much to see in the area. We serve a delicious breakfast with fresh home produced eggs.

Allan & Sue Edwards
Tel: 01380 831210
Fax: 01380 831455

B&B from £25-£30pp, Rooms 1 single, 1 en-suite double, 1 en-suite twin, Children over 8, Pets welcome, Open all year except Christmas & New Year.

YORKSHIRE

Heralded as one of the most picturesque counties in Britain – and also the largest - Yorkshire covers an impressive 1000 square miles of northern England. From Durham and the Cumbrian borders in the north to the Derbyshire and Nottingham borders in the south, this vast county is punctuated by historic cities, industrial towns and pretty villages – as well as four national parks celebrating and protecting some of the finest scenery in the country.

Resplendent in the north lies the ancient city of York, famed for its medieval tangle of streets, fortified 13th century city walls and England's largest Gothic cathedral, York Minster. Visitors flock to York by the million each year and, although the city offers many splendid features, there is also much to be discovered outwith its ancient walls.

North York Moors National Park can be found to the north-east of the county and features panoramic views across the dales leading to dramatic North Sea cliffs. The flowering heather is a sight to behold on the moors between July and September, and a ring of towns and villages surrounding the park exemplify the history and traditions of the area. Helmsley is one such town, built around a central market place and a particularly good base for visitors wishing to enjoy the history of the area.

As well as ancient Helmsley Castle, dating back as far the 12th century, and the superb ruins of the Cistercians Rievaulx Abbey and Rievaulx Terrace and Temples, look out for delightful Nunnington Hall, a particularly elegant 17th century manor house, and Duncombe Park – a grand, neo-classical country home set amid 35 acres of landscaped gardens and 400 acres of parkland.

To the north west of the county lies the Yorkshire Dales National Park, representing a vast chunk of beautiful, open countryside dominated by exposed limestone hills that give way to sheltered dales – some broad and undulating, others rugged and demanding. Many come here for the walking, although the area does boast other attractions – including some beautiful towns. Richmond, with its cobbled streets, sloping market square and precariously perched castle is possibly one of England's best kept secrets; Kirkby Stephen has some fine Georgian-style houses along its attractive High Street and the charming spa town of Harrogate features grand Victorian terraces – and an unmistakable hint of affluence.

If family history strikes a chord, don't miss nearby Ripley Castle – home to the Ingilby family for a staggering twenty six generations. The stunning grounds feature extensive Victorian Walled Gardens and in Spring the National Hyacinth Collection is a feast for the senses not to be missed.

Not far from Harrogate and four miles south east of Ripon, Newby Hall is another gardening enthusiasts dream – standing amid 25 acres of glorious herbaceous borders, flowering shrubs and yew hedges sweeping graciously down to the River Ure. The 17th century house, built in the style of Sir Christopher Wren, contains many treasures housed within a splendidly domed Sculpture Gallery and Tapestry Room created by Robert Adam.

Also renowned for its Adam architecture and stunning interiors is the much celebrated Harewood House, equidistant from either Harrogate or Leeds. Designed in 1759 by John Carr, Harewood is home to many fine artefacts, including the opulent Chippendale State Bed – now restored to its former glory and previously unseen for 150 years. Harewood's 1000 acres of parkland were landscaped by Capability Brown and feature lakeside walks and a magnificent Rhododendron collection.

West Yorkshire, and particularly the village of Haworth, was home to the famous Bronte family and the Georgian Parsonage where the literary family lived – and indeed many of them died – is an extremely popular tourist attraction. If you've braved the crowds and crave a little tranquillity, nearby East Riddlesden Hall on the outskirts of the village of Keighley makes for a pleasant retreat. This beautiful 17th century merchant's house features fine ceilings, beautiful furniture and some exquisite embroideries; while the gardens are sure to delight and with their mixture of orchards, herbs and reviving lavender.

YORKSHIRE

Phillip Gill & Anton Van Der Horst, Shallowdale House
Tel: 01439 788325
Map Ref 1 *see page 275*

Laura & Charlie Greenwood, Rudstone Walk
Tel: 01430 422230
Map Ref 2 *see page 275*

Daphne & John Tanner-Smith, Alderside
Tel: 01347 822132
Map Ref 3 *see page 275*

Dr & Mrs Bloom, Manor House Farm
Tel: 01642 722384
Map Ref 4 *see page 276*

Jennifer Mackay, Franklin View
Tel: 01423 541388
Map Ref 5 *see page 276*

Mrs Sue Smith, Laskill Grange
Tel: 01439 798268
Map Ref 6 *see page 276*

May & Ted Fussey, Forest Farm Guest House
Tel: 01484 842687
Map Ref 7 *see page 278*

Julie Richardson, Burr Bank
Tel: 01751 417777
Map Ref 8 *see page 278*

Susan Parks, Nuns Cottage
Tel: 01748 822809
Map Ref 9 *see page 278*

Sue Ormston, Lane Head Farm
Tel: 01833 627378
Map Ref 10 *see page 279*

Maggie Johnson, Mallard Grange
Tel: 01765 620242
Map Ref 11 *see page 279*

Alison & Paul Richardson, Orchard House
Tel: 01751 432904
Map Ref 12 *see page 279*

Bill Pitts & Rosie Blanksby, Holmwood House Hotel Tel: 01904 626183
Map Ref 13 *see page 281*

Kim & Ann Sluter-Robbins, Arnot House
Tel: 01904 641966
Map Ref 13 *see page 281*

Adrian & Ann Bradley, Barbican House
Tel: 01904 627617
Map Ref 13 *see page 281*

Kristine Livingstone, St Georges Hotel
Tel: 01904 625056
Map Ref 13 *see page*

Tony Finn, The Worsley Arms Hotel
Tel: 01653 628234
Map Ref 14 *see page*

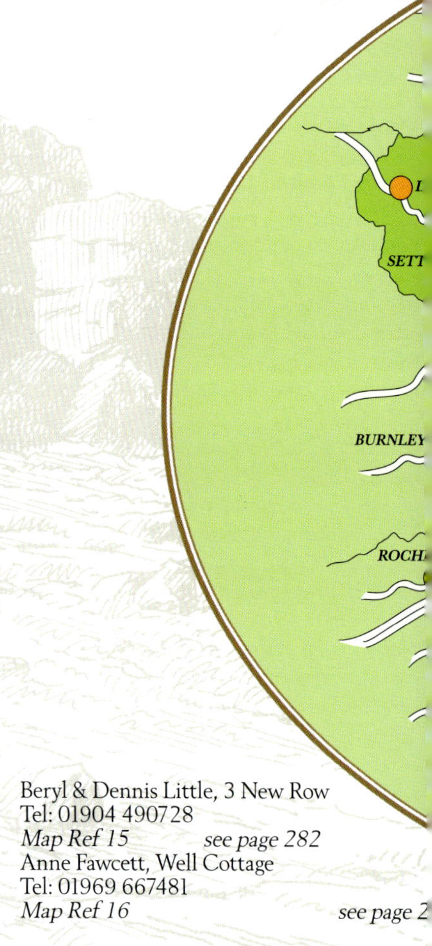

Beryl & Dennis Little, 3 New Row
Tel: 01904 490728
Map Ref 15 *see page 282*

Anne Fawcett, Well Cottage
Tel: 01969 667481
Map Ref 16 *see page 2*

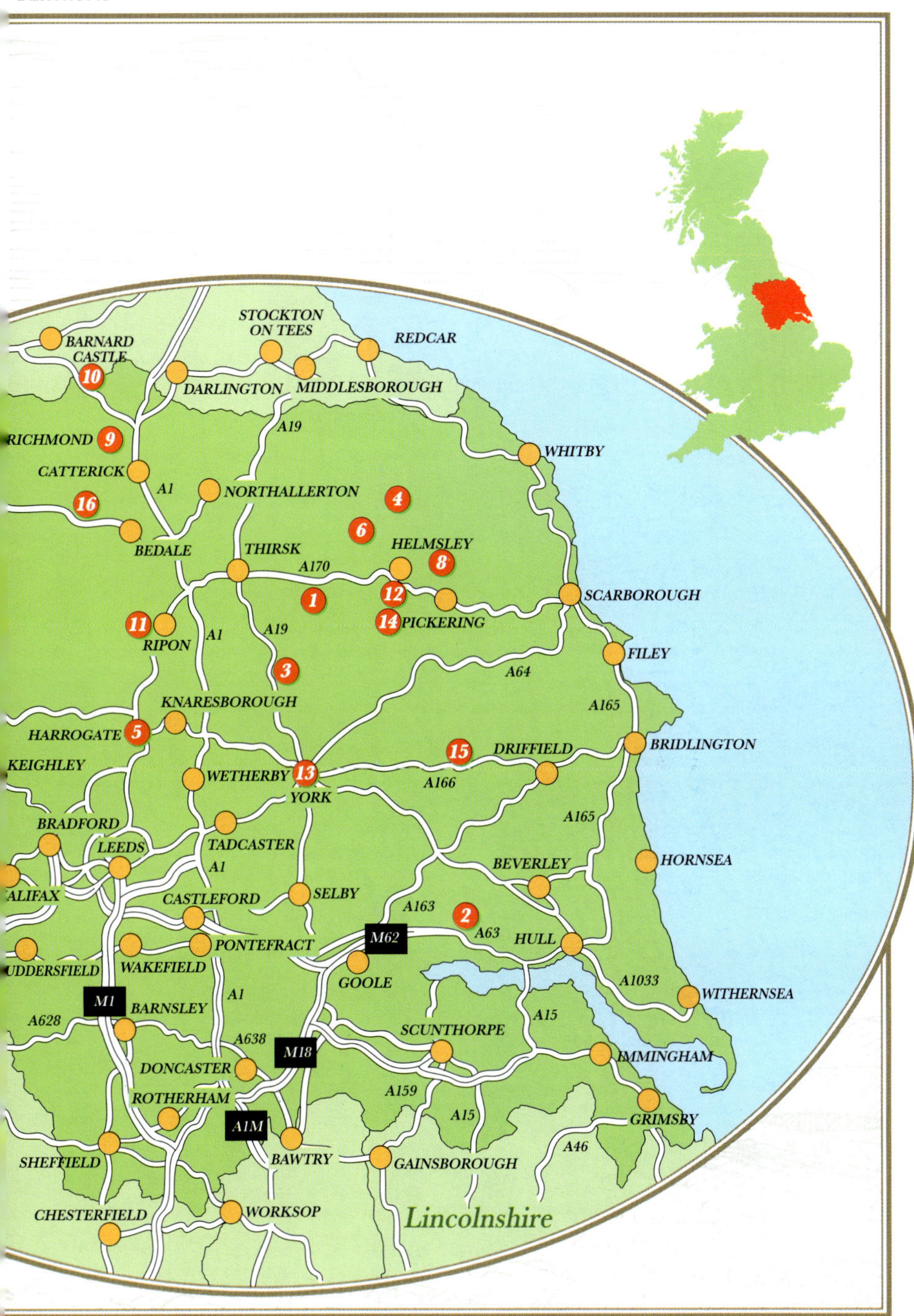
STOCKTON ON TEES
REDCAR
BARNARD CASTLE
10
DARLINGTON
MIDDLESBOROUGH
A19
RICHMOND 9
WHITBY
CATTERICK
A1
NORTHALLERTON
4
16
6
BEDALE
THIRSK
HELMSLEY
8
A170
1
12
SCARBOROUGH
11
14 PICKERING
RIPON
A1
A19
FILEY
3
A64
KNARESBOROUGH
A165
HARROGATE 5
15
DRIFFIELD
BRIDLINGTON
KEIGHLEY
WETHERBY
13
A166
YORK
A165
BRADFORD
LEEDS
TADCASTER
HORNSEA
A1
BEVERLEY
ALIFAX
CASTLEFORD
SELBY
A163
2
M62
A63
HULL
PONTEFRACT
UDDERSFIELD
WAKEFIELD
GOOLE
A1033
M1
A1
WITHERNSEA
BARNSLEY
A628
A15
SCUNTHORPE
A638
M18
IMMINGHAM
DONCASTER
A159
ROTHERHAM
A15
A1M
GRIMSBY
A46
SHEFFIELD
BAWTRY
GAINSBOROUGH
CHESTERFIELD
WORKSOP
Lincolnshire

SHALLOWDALE HOUSE, West End, Ampleforth, near Helmsley, North Yorkshire YO62 4DY
Email stay@shallowdalehouse.demon.co.uk
Website www.shallowdalehouse.demon.co.uk
Map Ref 1
Nearest Road A170, B1363

Shallowdale House captivates guests from the moment they arrive with its wonderful views and spacious light filled rooms. Anton and Phillip have built up a reputation for cosseting hospitality and excellent freshly prepared food. There are two king size/twin en-suite rooms and a double with private bathroom: all are furnished thoughtfully with style. A sheltered hillside garden extends to over two acres and you are surrounded by beautiful countryside with the North York Moors National Park to the north and York 20 miles south. Credit cards accepted.

Phillip Gill & Anton Van Der Horst
Tel: 01439 788325
Fax: 01439 788885

B&B from £35-£42pp, Dinner £24.50, Rooms 2 double, 1 twin, all en-suite, No smoking or pets, Children over 12, Open all year except Christmas & New Year.

RUDSTONE WALK, South Cave, near Beverley, East Yorkshire HU15 2AH
Email office@rudstone-walk.co.uk
Website www.rudstone-walk.co.uk
Map Ref 2
Nearest Road A1034, B1230

A unique country house set in its own acres on the edge of the unspoilt Yorkshire Wolds, with magnificent views over the Vale of York and Humber Estuary. Luxurious en-suite bed & breakfast accommodation is provided in a courtyard garden development surrounding the 400 year old Farmhouse, where delicious home-cooked meals are served. If you prefer, self-catering accommodation is available, sleeping 1-6 people. An ideal location for exploring the historic towns of York and Beverley and the surrounding countryside and the heritage coastline, all within easy reach of us.

Laura & Charlie Greenwood
Tel: 01430 422230
Fax: 01430 424552

B&B from £29.50pp shared, Dinner from £18.50, Rooms 6 twin, 7 double, 1 family, all en-suite, Restricted smoking & pets, Children welcome, Open all year.

ALDERSIDE, Thirsk Road, Easingwold, Yorkshire YO61 3HJ
Email john.TSmith@tinyonline.co.uk
Map Ref 3
Nearest Road A19

Alderside is a comfortable Edwardian family home quietly situated in its own large gardens, yet only a ten minute walk into Easingwolds Georgian market place and within easy reach of historic York, the moors and the coast. The two double bedrooms are individually furnished and have either en-suite or private bathrooms, colour television, radios and tea/coffee making facilities. There is an additional room for accompanying relatives or friends. Excellent breakfasts. Freshly prepared and homemade preserves. Good eating places nearby. Private parking.

Full page photo opposite

Daphne & John Tanner-Smith
Tel/Fax: 01347 822132

B&B from £22.50pp, Rooms 2 double, 1 en-suite, 1 private bathroom, 1 twin, No smoking or pets, Children over 12, Open April to December.

MANOR HOUSE FARM, Ingleby Greenhow, near Great Ayton, North Yorkshire TS9 6RB
Email mbloom@globalnet.co.uk

Map Ref 4
Nearest Road A172, B1257

Delightful farmhouse (part 1760) built of Yorkshire stone, set in 164 acres of park and woodlands at the foot of the Cleveland hills in the North York Moors National Park. Environment is tranquil and secluded. Ideal for nature lovers, relaxing, touring and walking. Accommodation is attractive with exposed beams and interior stonework. Atmosphere is warm and welcoming. Guests have separate entrance, lounge and dining room. Fine evening dinners, special diets if required, excellent wines. ETC 4 Diamonds Guest Accommodation. Brochure. Debit and credit cards accepted.

Dr & Mrs Bloom
Tel: 01642 722384

DB&B from £45-£50pp Rooms 1 double, 2 twin, all en-suite, No smoking, Children over 12, Open January to November.

FRANKLIN VIEW, 19 Grove Road, Harrogate, North Yorkshire HG1 5EW
Email jennifer@franklinview.com
Website www.franklinview.com

Map Ref 5
Nearest Road A1, A61

Franklin View is a very comfortable Edwardian home. It has been carefully restored preserving all original features including the Gothic windows situated on a tree lined avenue in the heart of Harrogate. A great reception awaits you in a relaxed informal atmosphere. All of the en-suite rooms have an individual character and are tastefully furnished and decorated in keeping with the style of the house. Breakfasts served in our elegant dining room overlooking the walled garden. Totally smoke-free environment. Private lit car park. Credit cards accepted.

Jennifer Mackay
Tel: 01423 541388
Fax: 01423 547872

B&B from £25-£29pp, Rooms 2 double, 1 twin, No children or pets, Open all year except Christmas & New Year.

LASKILL GRANGE, Hawnby, near Helmsley, Yorkshire YO62 5NB
Website www.laskillfarm.co.uk

Map Ref 6

A delightful country house. Emphasis is placed on comfort, food, value for money. Beautiful one acre walled garden with lake, duck, peacock, swans and visiting otter. We offer complete relaxation in our lovely en-suite rooms. Attention to detail. Lots to do and see or simply enjoy peace and tranquility. A walkers paradise in the North Yorkshire Moors. Recommended on BBC "Holiday" programme, Which magazine in top 20 best establishment in the country. York 40 minutes, Stately homes, museums, gardens, excellent eating places locally.

Mrs Sue Smith
Tel: 01439 798268
Fax: 01439 798498

B&B from £28.50-£30pp, Rooms 1 single, 3 double, 2 twin, all en-suite, No smoking or pets, Open all year except Christmas & New Year.

Full page photo opposite

FOREST FARM GUEST HOUSE, Mount Road, Marsden, Huddesfield, West Yorkshire HD7 6NN

Map Ref 7
Nearest Road A62

In the heart of 'Last of the Summer Wine' country Forest Farm is situated on the edge of the village of Marsden 1,000ft above sea level overlooking the golf course and moorland. It is over 200 years old, a former weavers cottage constructed in stone. It has been restored keeping many aspects of it's original character. Forest Farm offers evening meals, B&B, packed lunches. TV room. Car parking. We can boast spring water, free range eggs: special diets available with prior arrangement. Come as a guest and leave as a friend! All major credit cards accepted.

May & Ted Fussey
Tel/Fax: 01484 842687

B&B from £18pp, Dinner from £7, Rooms 1 twin, 1 double, 1 family, Restricted smoking & pets, Children welcome, Open all year except Christmas & Boxing Day.

BURR BANK, Cropton, Pickering, North Yorkshire YO18 8HL
Email bandb@burrbank.com
Website www.burrbank.com

Map Ref 8
Nearest Road A170

Five Diamond with Gold Award. Winner Guest Accommodation of the Year 2000 for Yorkshire. Comfortable, warm ground floor en-suite rooms, personal attention with home cooking. Easy access to York, the Coast, the Dales, the Moors, the Wolds and the Forest Park. Lots to do and see 52 weeks of the year. Direct footpath access to Cropton Forest with a 2 acre garden and 80 acres of fields and woodland. On the edge of a moorland village with fabulous views. Come and be cosseted.

Julie Richardson
Tel: 01751 417777
Fax: 01751 417789

B&B £29pp, Dinner £18, Rooms 1 double, 1 twin, both en-suite, No smoking or pets, Children over 12, Open all year.

NUNS COTTAGE, 5 Hurgill Road, Richmond, North Yorkshire DL10 4AR
Email alan.parks@btinternet.com
Website www.richmond.org.uk/business/nunscottage

Map Ref 9
Nearest Road A6108

18th century listed building, set behind high stone walls with secluded gardens. The house is furnished in period decor with antique furniture throughout, open fire, beams and old world charm. Guests have their own sitting room and gardens. Large guest bedrooms, all with private bathrooms; pine beds, TV's, videos, refreshment tray, sherry, fruit, towelling robes etc. Wide choice of breakfasts and dinner is available. The house is only five minutes walk from Richmond Market place and the Georgian theatre. Ample car parking is available.

Susan Parks
Tel: 01748 822809

B&B from £25pp, Dinner £15, Rooms 2 double, 1 twin, all private bathrooms, No smoking or pets, Children over 12, Open all year except Christmas Day.

LANE HEAD FARM, Hutton Magna, Richmond, North Yorkshire DL11 7HF
Email j.orm@farmersweekly.net
Website www.britnett/laneheadfarm

Map Ref 10
Nearest Road A66

Stunning panoramic views over beautiful Teesdale from our old farmhouse. A warm welcome awaits you in our attractive creeper clad house. A cosy sitting room, facilities for hot drinks/making picnics. Log fires in winter and central heating. Drying room for walkers clothes. Excellent location for walking/touring Dales and Moors. Many places of interest locally, pubs with excellent food in close proximity. Colour TV, ample off road parking. We straddle Yorkshire/Durham border, great location to see both counties.

Sue Ormston
Tel: 01833 627378
Fax: 01833 627150

B&B from £20-£25pp, Rooms 1 en-suite double, 2 twin, Restricted smoking, Children & dogs welcome, Open all year.

MALLARD GRANGE, Aldfield, near Fountains Abbey, Ripon, North Yorkshire HG4 3BE
Email Mallard.Grange@btinternet.com

Map Ref 11
Nearest Road B6265

Rambling 16th century farmhouse, full or character and charm in glorious countryside near Fountains Abbey. Offering superb quality and comfort, spacious rooms furnished with care and some lovely antique pieces. En-suite bedrooms have large comfortable beds, warm towels, colour TV, hairdryer and refreshment tray. Delicious breakfasts using fresh local produce and homemade preserves. Pretty walled garden tended by enthusiastic amateur. Safe parking. Excellent evening meals locally. Ideally based for Dales, Harrogate, York, historic houses and gardens all within easy reach. VISA, Mastercard, Delta accepted.

Maggie Johnson
Tel/Fax: 01765 620242
Mobile: 07720 295918

B&B from £27.50-£32pp, Rooms 2 double, 2 twin, all en-suite, No smoking or pets, Children over 12, Open all year except Christmas & New Year.

ORCHARD HOUSE, Marton, near Sinnington, Yorkshire YO62 6RD
Email orchard.house1@btinternet.com

Map Ref 12
Nearest Road A170

Built in 1784, situated four miles west of Pickering and set in a two acre garden bordering the river Seven, Orchard House offers peace and comfort, wonderful food and wine, log fires, low beams and high standards. Marton is an excellent base for exploring the North York Moors and coast with many historic houses and sites in the area. Castle Howard (Brideshead) is just eight miles away while York or Whitby are easily reached within 40 minutes. Heartbeat country, steam trains; a Yorkshire experience. Brochure available. ETB Highly Commended.

Alison & Paul Richardson
Tel: 01751 432904

B&B from £24pp, Dinner from £13.50, Rooms 1 twin, 2 double, all en-suite, No smoking, Open all year.

HOLMWOOD HOUSE HOTEL, 114 Holgate Road, York, Yorkshire YO24 4BB

Map Ref 13

Holmwood House Hotel was built as two private houses in the 19th century, backing onto one of the prettiest squares in York. The 2 listed buildings have been lovingly restored to retain the ambience of a private home and provide peaceful elegant rooms where the pressures of the day disappear. Bedrooms have their own en-suite facilities with shower, bath or even spa-bath, plus the usual TV, coffee/tea making facilities, direct dial telephone, etc. There is a car park to the rear and we are only 7-8 minutes walk from the City Walls with railway station and city centre 15 minutes walk away.

Bill Pitts & Rosie Blanksby
Tel: 01904 626183
Fax: 01904 670899

B&B from £35-£52.50pp, Rooms 3 twin, 8 double, 1 triple, 2 family suites, all en-suite, No smoking, Children over 8, No pets, Open all year.

ARNOT HOUSE, 17 Grosvenor Terrace, York, Yorkshire YO30 7AG
Email kim.robbins@virgin.net
Website www.arnothouseyork.co.uk

Map Ref 13
Nearest Road A19

Built in the 1880's, Arnot House stands over looking Bootham Park, five minutes walk from York Minster. The four guest bedrooms are furnished with antiques and paintings, brass or wooden beds, colour TV, alarm clock radio, hair dryer and hospitality tray. There is guest car park. Breakfast includes cereals, fruit juices, fresh fruit salad, English or vegetarian breakfast or even scrambled eggs with smoked salmon! Arnot House is totally non smoking. Runner up - Best Bed & Breakfast in Yorkshire, 1999. 4 Diamonds, Silver Award.

Full page photo opposite

Kim & Ann Sluter-Robbins
Tel/Fax: 01904 641966

B&B from £27.50-£30pp, Rooms 1 twin, 3 double, all en-suite, No smoking, children or pets, Open all year.

BARBICAN HOUSE, 20 Barbican Road, York, North Yorkshire YO10 5AA
Email info@barbicanhouse.com
Website www.barbicanhouse.com

Map Ref 13
Nearest Road A19, A1079

Barbican House overlooks the famous medieval city walls and is a 10 minute stroll to all city centre attractions. You can leave your car in our floodlit car park. All rooms are en-suite and non smoking. We have been awarded Four Diamonds from the English Tourist Board. A full English breakfast is served in our attractive dining room. Vegetarian or alternative breakfast menu is available. We always serve a fresh fruit platter, yoghurts and muffins. All rooms have colour TV and hospitality tray. Credit cards accepted.

Adrian & Ann Bradley
Tel: 01904 627617
Fax: 01904 647140

B&B from £29-£32pp, Rooms 5 double, 1 twin, all en-suite, No smoking or pets, Children over 12, Open February to December.

ST GEORGES HOTEL, 6 St Georges Place, York, Yorkshire YO24 1DR
Email sixstgeorg@aol.com
Website members.aol.com/sixstgeorg/
Map Ref 13
Nearest Road A1036, A64

A ten bedroomed family run guest house in a quiet select area of York. All en-suite accommodation includes four posters, family and double with one bedroom being on the ground floor. Situated opposite Yorks beautiful racecourse, it is only a ten minutes walk to the historic city walls, restaurants, shops and places of interest. Regular bus service and excellent park and ride system. Excellent access from all routes and well places for outings to Scarborough, Whitby and Bronte Country, Castle Howard and Herriot Country. Credit cards accepted.

Kristine Livingstone
Tel: 01904 625056
Fax: 01904 625009

B&B from £25-£30pp, Rooms 5 double, 3 twin, 2 family, all en-suite, Children & pets welcome, Open all year.

THE WORSLEY ARMS HOTEL, Hovingham, York, North Yorkshire YO62 4LA
Email worsleyarms@aol.com
Website www.worsleyarms.com
Map Ref 14
Nearest Road B1257, A64

Situated in the picturesque village of Hovingham opposite Hovingham Hall - birthplace of the Duchess of Kent, The Worsley Arms offers 19 comfortable bedrooms including a antique four poster bedroom, open log fires, gardens, an award winning two red rosette restaurant, bar/bistro and open lounges for morning coffee and afternoon tea. Located halfway between Helmsley and Malton, Castle Howard is two miles down the road and York is only 20 minutes away. The Worsley Arms also offers meeting rooms and has a civil wedding licence. Special rates available for midweek breaks. Credit cards accepted.

Tony Finn
Tel: 01653 628234
Fax: 01653 628130

B&B from £40pp, Dinner £10, Rooms 2 single, 8 double, 7 twin, 2 family, all en-suite, Children & pet welcome, Open all year.

---

3 NEW ROW, Fimber, East Riding of Yorkshire
Email little2@tinyworld.co.uk
Website www.yorkshireholidaycottage.com
Map Ref 15

High in the Yorkshire Wolds, 3 New Row, Fimber offers comfortable self-catering accommodation for up to 6 people. There is one double bedroom, one room with bunk beds and one sofa bed in lounge. Fully equipped kitchen/large garden/barbecue. Makes an ideal base for walking holidays, the Wolds Way being accessible at Fridaythorpe or Thixendale. Convenient for visits to York or the coast, or just somewhere to chill out "away from it all". Nearest shop, garage and restaurant at Fridaythorpe, two miles away.

1 cottage, sleeps up to 6, No smoking, Children welcome, No pets, Available all May to mid September

Contact: Beryl & Dennis Little, 11 Oaklands, Strensall, York, Yorkshire YO32 5YD
Tel: 01904 490728

WELL COTTAGE, West Burton, Leyburn, North Yorkshire
Email milehousefarm@hotmail.com
Website www.wensleydale.uk.com

Map Ref 16

Really delightful 17th century stone cottage overlooking the village green with extensive views to the fells in charming peaceful village. Beamed ceilings, exposed stone work, open fire and Laura Ashley prints. Two bedrooms, bathroom with separate shower, oil fired central heating. Washing machine/tumble drier, microwave, dishwasher, payphones, barbecue area, colour TV/video, double glazed windows, antique furniture, warm and cosy. Pretty walled garden, large garage and free trout fishing on farm.

1 cottage, sleeps 4, Price on application, Restricted smoking, Children & pets welcome. Available all year

Contact: Anne Fawcett, Mile House Farm, Hawes, Wensleydale, North Yorkshire DL8 3PT
Tel: 01969 667481
Fax: 01969 667425

"Bertie! Don't start getting ideas! The Morgan's quite fast enough!" laughed Belle
BELLE & BERTIE IN WALES

SCOTLAND

Roughly half the size of England, Scotland occupies the most northerly area of Britain and boasts a rich historic past, an intensely independent national identity and some of the most dramatic scenery in the world. Divided into three distinct areas, it is a country of hugely contrasting landscape and ever-changing weather that has long captured the imagination of poets, painters and visitors from around the world.

To the south lie the Borders, an area bound up in much historic marauding over the centuries as the Scots resisted English imperialism during their wars of independence. Indeed in earlier years, so disgusted was the Roman Emperor Hadrian by this 'inhospitable land of mists, bogs, warring peoples and midges' that he built his famous wall to keep the northern tribes out. Fortunately these days, the Borders region represents peaceful agricultural land, rolling hills and stunningly beautiful valleys without so much as a claymore in sight.

As the name suggests, the Central Lowlands are to be found to the middle of the country and it is here that the majority of Scotland's population can be found. Historically an industrial area, most of the indigenous industries such as mining, steel and ship-building have long since vanished, although the visitor can still revel in the vibrancy of

Glasgow, the history of Stirling and the breathtaking splendour of Edinburgh – rightfully celebrated as one of the most beautiful cities in the world.

Making up the third and most northerly area of Scotland, and covering two-thirds of the country's land mass, are the Highlands and Islands. An extraordinary combination of lochs and glens, towering mountain ranges (Ben Nevis near Fortwilliam is Britain's highest peak), dramatic seascapes and desolate moorland, it is here that the unique Scottish light plays on the soft hues of the countryside to create a beauty and a drama seldom witnessed elsewhere in Britain.

Just as Scotland abounds in historic battle sites, romantic islands, and dramatic scenery, so many breathtaking castles, glorious gardens and grand country homes are also be found punctuating the landscape.

A particularly vast example of a fine Lowland castle is that of Floors near Kelso – home to the Duke and Duchess of Roxburghe and said to be the largest inhabited castle in Scotland. Designed by William Adam, this truly majestic building was started in 1721 and later adorned with a multitude of spires and domes in the mid 19th century. Another celebrated example of the work of William Adam is Culzean Castle near Maybole – dramatically perched on a cliff high above the Firth of Clyde it is fondly referred to as 'the castle in the air' and set within Scotland's first, and quite magnificent, country park. Childhood home to the Queen Mother and birthplace of Princess Margaret, Glamis Castle by Forfar is certainly worth a visit for those who enjoy royal connections; and for the sheer romance of the place, don't miss Dunvegan Castle on the Isle of Skye. With parts dating back to 1200 AD, this is the oldest home in Scotland continuously inhabited by the same family and an enduring legacy of the Clan spirit.

Presently owned by the Murray family, Scone Palace near Perth is perhaps one of Scotland's most historic sites; once home to the Stone of Destiny and the crowning place of Scottish kings such as Macbeth and Robert the Bruce. Extensively rebuilt in the early 19th century, the Palace today features fine furniture and porcelain collections and the grounds delight with the unique Murray Star Maze. Nearby in the Kingdom of Fife, Falkland Palace also enjoys historic renown as country retreat to the eight Stuart monarchs, including the legendary Mary Queen of Scots. A splendid example of Renaissance architecture, the grounds also feature an enchanting Chapel Royal as well as – somewhat unexpectedly – the oldest Royal Tennis Court in the world.

Particularly beautiful and historically important, Drummond Castle Gardens in Perthshire are perhaps the finest of many gardens to be found around Scotland. Reached by way of a stunning beech-lined avenue, Drummond's formal gardens are thought to be among the most impressive in Europe and include an Italianate parterre and a fascinating John Milne sundial. In a more northerly direction, horticultural enthusiasts should also pay homage to the stunning and surprising gardens of Inverewe in Wester Ross. Described as a 'mecca for gardeners', Inverewe lies on a more northerly latitude than Moscow yet, thanks to its sheltered lochside location and the all-important North Atlantic drift, boasts scented Chinese rhododendrons, exotic lilies and the tallest Australian Gum in Britain.

SCOTLAND

David & Stella Cash, Meall Mo Chridhe
Tel: 01972 510238 *Map Ref 1* *see page 288*
Tony & Beryl Harrison, Balmory Hall
Tel: 01700 500 669 *Map Ref 3* *see page 288*
Stewart MacDonald, Kirkton House
Tel: 01389 841 951 *Map Ref 4* *see page 288*
Grace Brown, Lomondview Country House
Tel: 01301 702477 *Map Ref 2* *see page 289*
Mrs M.MacPherson, Invercairn Bed & Breakfast
Tel: 01631 770301 *Map Ref 5* *see page 289*
George & Anne Hay, Low Coylton House
Tel: 01292 570615 *Map Ref 6* *see page 290*
Mrs Vera Dunlop, Glengennet Farm
Tel: 01465 861220 *Map Ref 7* *see page 290*
Jonathan Cardale, The Eisenhower Apartment
Tel: 01655 884455 *Map Ref 8* *see page 290*
Mary Whitsell, Hartfell House
Tel: 01683 220153 *Map Ref 9* *see page 292*
Mrs Ramsay, The Studio
Tel: 01620 895150 *Map Ref 10* *see page 292*
Mrs Joanna Furness, Cuddy's Hall Holiday Cottage
Tel: 016977 48160 *Map Ref 30* *see page 292*
Mr & Mrs Broom-Smith, Auchenskeoch Lodge
Tel: 01387 780277 Map Ref 11 see page 293
Margaret Davies, Balcary Mews
Tel: 01556 640276 *Map Ref 31* *see page 293*
Alan & Angela Vidler, Rowan Guest House
Tel: 0131 667 2463 *Map Ref 12* *see page 295*
Rhoda Mitchell, Hopetoun
Tel: 0131 667 7691 *Map Ref 12* *see page 295*
Nan & Eden Stark, Ben Cruachan
Tel: 0131 5563709 *Map Ref 12* *see page 295*
Mrs Niven, International Guest House
Tel: 0131 667 2511 *Map Ref 12* *see page 296*
Susan Virtue, The Town House
Tel: 0131 2291985 *Map Ref 12* *see page 296*
Susan Virtue, The Town House Apartments
Tel: 0131 2291985 *Map Ref 12* *see page 298*

Mrs Elizabeth Linn, Newmills Cottage
Tel: 0131 449 4300 *Map Ref 12* *see page 296*
David & Joyce Playfair, Abbey Mains
Tel: 01620 823286 *Map Ref 13* *see page 298*
Mary Millar, Westfield Mansion House
Tel: 01334 655699 *Map Ref 22* *see page 298*
Struan Hall
Tel: 013398 87241 *Map Ref 15* *see page 299*
Feith Mhor Lodge
Tel: 01479 841621 *Map Ref 16* *see page 299*
Melville & Johan McDonald, West Manse B&B
Tel: 01542 841189 *Map Ref 17* *see page 299*
Alexandra Henderson, Ashburn House
Tel: 01397 706000 *Map Ref 18* *see page 300*
Mrs Jackie Macleod, Rustic View
Tel: 01397 704709 *Map Ref 18* *see page 300*
Mr R L Withers, Craigard House
Tel: 01809 501258 *Map Ref 19* *see page 300*
Mrs Margaret Cairns, Invergloy House
Tel: 01397 712681 *Map Ref 20* *see page 301*
Mrs Newham, Dunvegan Castle Cottages
Tel: 01470 521206 *Map Ref 26* *see page 301*
Mr & Mrs Streeton, 1, 2 & 3 Bracadale Cottages
Tel: 01470 572231 *Map Ref 27* *see page 301*
Mr Knatchbull, New Kelso Lodge
Tel: 01233 503636 *Map Ref 28* *see page 302*
Frances MacKenzie, Attadale Holiday Cottages
Tel: 01520 722862 *Map Ref 28* *see page 302*
Mr Millar, Loch Tay Lodges
Tel: 01887 830209 *Map Ref 29* *see page 302*
Janet Anderson, East Lochhead Country House
Tel: 01505 842610 *Map Ref 21* *see page 304*
Dorothy Mailer, Ashgrove House
Tel: 01786 472640 *Map Ref 23* *see page 304*
Mrs Val Willis, The Barns of Shannochill
Tel: 01877 382878 *Map Ref 24* *see page 304*
Mrs Jill Inglis, Thornton
Tel: 01506 844693 *Map Ref 25* *see page 305*

THURSO
JOHN O'GROATS
DURNESS
WICK
A836
A897
SCOURIE
A838
ALTNA HARRA
A9
A837
HELMSDALE
LEDMORE
BONAR BRIDGE
DORNOCH
ULLAPOOL
TAIN
A835
GAIRLOCH
DINGWALL
ELGIN
BANFF
FRASERBURGH
A832
NAIRN
A98
A96
PETERHEAD
ACHNASHEEN
DUFFTOWN
A947
INVERNESS
HUNTLY
A890
ISLE OF SKYE
KYLE OF LOCHALSH
GRANTOWN ON SPEY
RHYNIE
DRUMNADROCHIT
A939
A87
AVIEMORE
ABERDEEN
A93
INVERGARRY
BALLATER
STONEHAVEN
BRAEMAR
MALLAIG
A830
A9
FORT WILLIAM
A93
MONTROSE
BLAIR ATHOLL
CORRAN
FORFAR
A82
PITLOCHRY
A827
ARBROATH
DUNDEE
ISLE OF MULL
PERTH
A85
CRIANLARICH
ST. ANDREWS
OBAN
A9
INVERARY
CALLENDER
KIRKCALDY
A816
A82
STIRLING
NORTH BERWICK
LOCHGILPHEAD
DUNFERMLINE
DUMBARTON
CUMBERNAULD
DUNBAR
FALKIRK
EDINBURGH
GLASGOW
BERWICK UPON TWEED
A68
ISLE OF JURA
GREENOCK
ISLE OF ISLAY
PAISLEY
EAST KILBRIDE
LANARK
GALASHIELS
PEEBLES
PORT ELLEN
KILMARNOCK
ARDROSSEN
JEDBURGH
ABINGTON
A70
HAWICK
AYR
CUMNOCK
OTTERBURN
ISLE OF ARRAN
A76
MOFFAT
A7
A77
THORNHILL
M74
GIRVAN
A713
LOCKERBIE
England
A75
NEW GALLOWAY
DUMFRIES
A69
NEWTON STEWART
STRANRAER
CARLISLE
GATEHOUSE OF FLEET
A596

MEALL MO CHRIDHE, Kilchoan, Acharacle, Argyll PH36 4LH
Email meallmo@lineone.net

Map Ref 1
Nearest Road B8007

Meall Mo Chridhe (pronounced: Mel Mo Cree) is a fine shoreline Grade B listed Georgian former Manse. Standing within its own 45 acres, it enjoys spectacular views over Kilchoan and the Sound of Mull. Stella creates a set five course dinner menu daily, making good use of seasonal local produce including seafood, game, home grown vegetables, salads, and fruit from the kitchen garden. Ingredients are 'organic' whenever possible. Meall Mo Chridhe plans to reopen during the 2003 season after a comprehensive but sympathetic restoration.

David & Stella Cash
Tel/Fax: 01972 510238

B&B from £40-£75pp, Dinner £33, Rooms 2 double, 1 twin, all en-suite, No smoking or pets, Children welcome, Open all year except Christmas & New Year.

BALMORY HALL, Ascog, Isle of Bute PA20 9LL
Email mail@balmoryhall.com
Website www.balmoryhall.com

Map Ref 3

Standing in a 10 acre wildlife haven of woodland and gardens, Balmory Hall, a grade A listed property with a distinctive neo-classical style, is one of the finest examples of Victorian architecture on the island. Within this splendid country home, sympathetically restored to preserve the elegance of opulent bygone times, individual self-catering or serviced apartments, and spacious en-suite bedrooms are available. The gate lodge stands alone and is ideal for guests seeking complete seclusion. Credit cards accepted.

Tony & Beryl Harrison
Tel/Fax: 01700 500 669

B&B from £40-£70pp, Rooms 2 double, 1 twin, all en-suite, No smoking, Children over 12, Pets by arrangement, Open all year.

KIRKTON HOUSE, Darleith Road, Cardross, Arygll & Bute G82 5EZ
Email gpts@kirktonhouse.co.uk
Website www.kirktonhouse.co.uk

Map Ref 4
Nearest Road A814, A82, M8

Converted 19/20th century farmstead hotel, near Loch Lomond, Glasgow and west highlands routes. In tranquil setting above Cardross village with panoramic views of River Clyde. Ample private parking. All rooms en-suite with all usual hotel facilities including telephone. Wine and Dine to "taste" of Scotland, home cooked dinners served at oil lamp lit individual tables per party. Extensive choice menu varied daily. Public rooms have exposed stone walls and rustic fireplaces. Large garden, stabling and paddock. Excellence local walks and gardens. Recommended in "Good Hotel Guide". Credit cards accepted.

Stewart MacDonald
Tel: 01389 841 951
Fax: 01389 841 868

B&B from £30-£39.50pp, Dinner £17.50, Rooms 2 twin, 4 family, all en-suite, Restricted smoking, Children & pets welcome, Open February to November.

LOMONDVIEW COUNTRY HOUSE, Tarbet, Loch Lomond, Argyll G83 7DG
Email lomondviewhouse@aol.com
Website www.lomondview.co.uk

Map Ref 2
Nearest Road A82

A warm friendly Scottish welcome is assured at our home overlooking the bonnie banks of Loch Lomond. Magnificent scenery and picturesque Loch views from your en-suite room. A must for a romantic breaks. Relaxing strolls, energetic hill walks and Loch cruises minutes away. Ideal touring base. Enjoy your breakfast at your own table while watching the cruise boats sail by. Complimentary sherry in the guests lounge. Credit cards accepted.

Grace Brown
Tel/Fax: 01301 702477

B&B from £27.50-£35pp, Rooms 2 double, 1 twin, No smoking, children or pets, Open all year.

INVERCAIRN BED & BREAKFAST, Musdale Road, Kilmore, By, Oban, Argyll PA34 4XX
Email invercairn.kilmore@virgin.net
Website www.invercairn.com

Map Ref 5
Nearest Road A816

Kilmore lies 3 miles south of Oban on the A816 ,Invercairn is situated 1 mile from the main road amid magnificent highland scenery. Invercairn was designed to provide excellent accommodation for six guests with all three en-suite bedrooms having superb views. Awarded 4 Stars by the STB. Oban is an attractive port and busy local centre. It offers good restaurants and entertainment with a variety of tourist excursions including daily sailing's to Mull and Iona. Perfect base for capturing 'the spirit of Scotland'. A warm 'Scottish welcome'.

Mrs Margaret MacPherson
Tel/Fax: 01631 770301

B&B from £24-£26pp, Rooms 2 double, 1 twin, all en-suite, No smoking or pets, Children over 14, Open Easter to end of September.

Please mention

A GREAT PLACE TO STAY

when enquiring about accommodation

LOW COYLTON HOUSE, Manse Road, Coylton, Ayrshire KA6 6LE
Email xyi22@btopenworld

Map Ref 6
Nearest Road A70

Spacious, very comfortable and quiet country house (Old Manse 1820) set in attractive garden with apple parking. TV and tea/coffee facilities in bedrooms. Golfers paradise courses nearby including Ayr, Troon, Turnberry. Ayr 5 miles safe sandy beaches. Hill walking. Culzean Castle (National Trust). Prestwick Airport 10 miles. Glasgow 35 miles. Edinburgh 70 miles. Robert Burns Cottage. Good inexpensive eating places nearby.

George & Anne Hay
Tel/Fax: 01292 570615

B&B from £25-£30pp, Rooms 1 double, 1 twin, both en-suite, Children & pets welcome, Open all year except Christmas & New Year.

GLENGENNET FARM, Barr, Girvan, Ayrshire KA26 9TY
Email vsd@glengennet.fsnet.co.uk
Website www.glengennet.co.uk

Map Ref 7
Nearest Road A77

Victorian shooting lodge on hill farm. Lovely views over Stinchar Valley and neighbouring Galloway forest park. En-suite bedrooms with tea trays, TV, lounge. Near conservation village with hotel for evening meals. Good base for Glentrool, Culzean Castle, Burns country and Ayrshire coast. Golf, walking and cycling trails all within easy reach.

Mrs Vera Dunlop
Tel/Fax: 01465 861220

B&B from £21-£25pp, Rooms 1 double, 1 twin, both en-suite, No smoking or pets, Children welcome, Open April to October.

THE EISENHOWER APARTMENT, Culzean Castle, Maybole, Ayrshire KA19 8LE
Email culzean@nts.org.uk
Website www.culzeancastle.net

Map Ref 8
Nearest Road A719, A77

In the very top of the Castle, Eisenhower's holiday home now provides country house style accommodation in six double bedrooms. With access by lift, the apartment is completely self-contained and separate from the rest of the Castle. The Eisenhower Suite has twin beds, bathroom and dressing room; the Ailsa Suite has a splendid four-poster bed and private bathroom: the Kennedy, Gault and Cairncross Suites are twin-bedded rooms each with private bathroom. The Adam Suite has a double bed and private bathroom. The comfortable round drawing room and elegant dining room both have superb sea views. Credit cards accepted.

Full page photo opposite

Jonathan Cardale
Tel: 01655 884455
Fax: 01655 884503

B&B from £140-£250pp, Dinner £50, Rooms 2 double, 4 twin, all but one en-suite, No smoking or pets, Children welcome, Open all year.

HARTFELL HOUSE, Hartfell Crescent, Moffat, Scotland DG10 9AL
Email enquiries@hartfellhouse.co.uk
Website www.hartfellhouse.co.uk

Map Ref 9
Nearest Road M74, A701

An elegant Victorian manor in a quiet semi-rural setting overlooking the Moffat Hills. Our family run guest house offers American 'Southern hospitality' with comfortable, well-appointed rooms and a warm welcome. Ideal as a stopover or for touring the areas that inspired Burns, Buchan and Sir Walter Scott. Beautiful scenery, gardens, castles, stately homes, Hadrian's Wall, hill walking and a Tibetan monastery. Edinburgh, Glasgow or Carlisle one and a half hours away or just stay with us and enjoy the friendliness of the town of Moffat.

Mary Whitsell
Tel: 01683 220153

B&B from £24-£34pp, Dinner by arrangement £13.50, Rooms 1 single, 3 double, 1 twin, 2 family, all en-suite, No smoking, Children & pets welcome, Open all year except Christmas & New Year.

THE STUDIO, Grange Road, North Berwick, East Lothian EH39 4QT
Email johnvramsay@compuserve.com
Website www.b-and-b-scotland.co.uk/studio.htm

Map Ref 10
Nearest Road A198, A1

Refurbished and extended historic building, tastefully decorated and furnished. Situated within a walled garden. Guests enjoy a high degree of privacy in rural surroundings, yet convenient for town and railway station. All rooms have private patios with garden furniture. Parking. Regret no smoking. STB 5 Star Bed and Breakfast.

Mrs Ramsay
Tel: 01620 895150
Fax: 01620 895120

B&B from £30-£40pp, Rooms 2 double, 1 twin, all en-suite, No smoking, children or pets, Open all year.

CUDDY'S HALL HOLIDAY COTTAGE, Bailey, Newcastleton, Roxburghshire
Email joannafurness@btopenworld.com
Website www.cuddys-hall.co.uk

Map Ref 30

Cumbrian/Scottish borders. Traditional family cottage, well maintained and equipped throughout. Set amidst beautiful forest and winding streams (part of Kielder Forest Park) abundant with wildlife. Superb forest walks/cycle routes, start right at the door. Private garden, patio and barbecue/lockable shed for cycles, fishing tackle etc. On the 'Reivers Cycle Route'. Bed linen, duvets, towels, electricity, central heating and a welcome food pack inclusive. Good base to explore - Hadrians Wall, the Lakes and Scotland. Pony trekking, fishing and golf nearby. Short breaks available.

1 cottage, sleeps up to 5, Price per week £200 to £300 (at peak times), No smoking, Children welcome over 7, No pets, Available all year.

Contact: Mrs Joanna Furness, No. 2 Cuddy's Hall, Bailey, Newcastleton, Roxburghshire TD9 0TP
Tel/Fax: 016977 48160

AUCHENSKEOCH LODGE, By Dalbeattie, Kirkcudbrightshire DG5 4PG
Email brmsmth@aol.com
Website www.auchenskeochlodge.com

Map Ref 11
Nearest Road B793

Former Victorian shooting lodge in a peaceful, rural setting, 5 miles from Dalbeattie and 3 miles from the coast. 20 acre grounds including croquet lawn, woodlands and productive vegetable garden. House of charm and character traditionally furnished throughout. 3 spacious well equipped bedrooms each with en-suite bathroom, panelled billiard room with full sized table. Candlelit dinners, house party style. Good wine list. Credit cards accepted.

Christopher & Mary Broom-Smith
Tel/Fax: 01387 780277

B&B from £31-£34pp, Dinner £18, Rooms 2 double, 1 twin, all en-suite, Children over 12, Pets welcome, Open Easter to end of October.

BALCARY MEWS, Balcary Bay, Auchencairn, Castle Douglas, Scotland DG7 1QZ
Website www.geocities.com/BalcaryMews/

Map Ref 31
Nearest Road A711

Balcary Mews is set in an elevated position on the shores of Balcary Bay. 4 Stars STB. AA 4 Diamonds. It commands magnificent uninterrupted views across the bay with the Galloway Hills and coastline beyond, and Hestan Island to the fore. It is extremely comfortable and beautifully furnished throughout. All rooms have sea views. We have a large guest sitting room with panoramic frontage. Ample private parking. Friendly personal service. Smuggling connections! Superb Scottish breakfast using local produce. Perfect base for touring Galloway. Walking, birdwatching, fishing, golf, horseriding, or just relaxing in peace and tranquility.

Margaret Davies
Tel: 01556 640276

B&B from £28pp, Autumn/winter breaks 3 nights B&B £130 per couple, Rooms 1 double, 1 twin, 1 family, all en-suite, No smoking, Children welcome, No pets, Open all year.

"Criccieth Castle - what a setting!" said Bertie "Apparently there was a trebouchet, a giant catapult here in Edward's time - I wish they'd build a replica"

BELLE & BERTIE IN WALES

HOPETOUN
15
AA

ROWAN GUEST HOUSE, 13 Glenorchy Terrace, Edinburgh, Scotland EH9 2DQ
Email angela@rowan-house.co.uk
Website www.rowan-house.co.uk

Map Ref 12
Nearest Road A701, A702, A7

Rowan Guest House is an elegant 19th century Victorian home in a quiet leafy conservation area. It has free parking and is only a ten minutes bus ride to the centre. The Castle, Royal Mile, Holyrood Palace, University Theatres, restaurants and other amenities are easily reached. The bedrooms are charmingly decorated and have television, tea/coffee and biscuits. A hearty Scottish breakfast is served, including porridge and freshly baked scones. Alan and Angela will make every effort to ensure visitors have an enjoyable stay. Credit cards accepted.

Alan & Angela Vidler
Tel/Fax: 0131 667 2463

B&B from £24-£35pp, Rooms 3 single, 3 double, 2 twin, 1 family, most en-suite, No smoking, Children & pets welcome, Open all year.

HOPETOUN, 15 Mayfield Road, Edinburgh, Lothian EH9 2NG
Email hopetoun@aol.com
Website www.hopetoun.com

Map Ref 12
Nearest Road A720, A1, A7, A68

Hopetoun is a small friendly B&B close to Edinburgh University, 2 KM south of Princes Street and with an excellent bus service into town. A 25 minute walk through a park takes you to the Royal Mile and Castle. Hopetoun is completely non-smoking with two large guest bedrooms, both with private toilet and shower. Both rooms have TV, central heating and tea/coffee making facilities. Parking is available and a good choice of breakfast is provided. The owner prides herself on providing personal attention to all guests. Credit cards accepted.

Rhoda Mitchell
Tel: 0131 667 7691
Fax: 0131 466 1691

B&B from £20-£45pp, Rooms 1 double, 1 family, both en-suite, No smoking or pets, Children over 5, Open all year except Christmas.

Full page photo opposite

BEN CRUACHAN, 17 McDonald Road, Edinburgh, Lothian EH7 4LX
Website www.bencruachan.com

Map Ref 12
Nearest Road A1

A most friendly welcome awaits you at our centrally located high standard accommodation within walking distance of the Castle the Royal Mile, Holyrood Palace and Princes Street one of Britain's most picturesque shopping venues. Many varied restaurants within 5 minute walk. Our en-suite rooms are tastefully decorated, have TV, central heating and tea/coffee making facilities. Excellent breakfast served. Unrestricted street parking. Non smoking. STB 3 Star Commended.

Nan & Eden Stark
Tel: 0131 5563709

B&B from £26pp, Rooms 1 twin, 1 double, 1 family, all en-suite, No smoking or pets, Children over 10, Open April to November.

INTERNATIONAL GUEST HOUSE, 37 Mayfield Gardens, Edinburgh, Lothian EH9 2BX
Email intergh@easynet.co.uk
Website www.accommodation-edinburgh.com
Map Ref 12

Attractive stone built Victorian house situated one and a half miles south of Princes Street on the main A701. Private parking. Luxury bedrooms with en-suite facilities, colour television, telephone and tea/coffee makers. Magnificent views across the extinct volcano of Arthur's Seat. Full Scottish breakfast served on the finest bone china. International has received many accolades for its quality and level of hospitality. A 19th century setting with 21st century facilities. 'In Britain' magazine has rated the International as their 'find' in all Edinburgh. Ground floor room for guests with limited disability. STB 4 Stars. AA 4 Diamonds.

Mrs Niven
Tel: 0131 667 2511
Fax: 0131 667 1112

B&B from £25.50pp, Rooms 3 single, 1 twin, 2 double, 3 family, all en-suite, Restricted smoking, Children welcome, No pets, Open all year.

THE TOWN HOUSE, 65 Gilmore Place, Edinburgh, Scotland EH3 9NU
Email susan@thetownhouse.com
Website www.thetownhouse.com
Map Ref 12
Nearest Road A1, A102

The Town House is an attractive, privately owned Victorian house, located in the city centre. Theatres and restaurants are only a few minutes walk away. The Town House has been fully restored and tastefully decorated. Retaining many original architectural features. The bedrooms are individually furnished and decorated, all have en-suite bath or shower and toilet, central heating, radio alarm, colour television, hair dryer and tea/coffee tray. Varied menu including traditional Scottish porridge, kippers and fish cakes. Parking is situated at the rear of the house.

Full page photo opposite

Susan Virtue
Tel: 0131 2291985

B&B from £30-£40pp, Rooms 1 single, 2 double, 1 twin, 1 family, all en-suite, No smoking or pets, Children over 10, Open all year except Christmas.

NEWMILLS COTTAGE, 472 Lanark Road West, Balerno, Edinburgh, Scotland EH14 5AE
Email info@newmillscottage.co.uk
Website www.newmillscottage.co.uk
Map Ref 12
Nearest Road A70

Delightful house built by the owners in 1992 in lovely grounds with ample private parking. 3 guests rooms are available on first floor offering privacy to visitors. One room has a full shower room en-suite, the other 2 rooms share a private bathroom with shower over bath, particularly suitable for 4 people travelling together. All 3 are extremely spacious with sitting area. Edinburgh city centre, Heriot Watt University and the airport are nearby. An excellent bus service is available. Credit cards accepted.

Mrs Elizabeth Linn
Tel/Fax: 0131 449 4300

B&B from £25-£35pp, Rooms 3 twin, 1 en-suite, 1 private bathroom, No smoking or pets, Children welcome, Open all year except Christmas & New Year.

The Town House
LES ROUTIERS
65

ABBEY MAINS, Haddington, Scotland EH41 3SB
Email joyce.abbeymains@farmersweekly.net

Map Ref 13
Nearest Road A1

Abbey Mains is situated in the beautiful farmland of East Lothian. The large stone farmhouse has superb views of the Lammermuir hills, and is only 35 minutes from central Edinburgh and 2 miles from the historic town of Haddington. Within the county there are many excellent golf courses. The beaches are only a 10 minutes drive away. Other attractions in the area are a bird sanctuary, sea bird centre, Museum of Flight and the Glenkinchie Distillery.

David & Joyce Playfair
Tel: 01620 823286
Fax: 01620 826348

B&B from £40pp, Dinner £20, Rooms 2 double, 1 family, all en-suite, No smoking, Children welcome, Pets by arrangement, Open all year.

THE TOWN HOUSE APARTMENT, Edinburgh
Email susan@thetownhouse.com
Website www.thetownhouse.com

Map Ref 12

Exceptional, newly built 2 bedroom flat. Lounge and hall with beautiful wooden floor, fitted kitchen, dishwasher, microwave, fan oven, hob and washer/dryer. Master bedroom with kingsize bed and shower en-suite. The second bedroom has twin beds. Both bedrooms have fitted illuminated wardrobes and lovely French Toiles De Jouy curtains. Private covered parking, landscaped gardens. Close to shops, cinemas, theatres, swimming pool and all historic attractions and restaurants. STB 5 Stars. Website available.

1 apartment, sleeps 4, 2 nights minimum stay £90-£140per night, No smoking or pets, Children over 10, Available all year.

Contact: Mrs Susan Virtue, 65 Gilmore Place, Edinburgh EH3 9NU
Tel: 0131 229 1985

WESTFIELD MANSION HOUSE, Westfield Road, Cupar St Andrews, Fife KY15 5AR
Email westfieldhouse@standrews4.freeserve.co.uk
Website www.standrews4.freeserve.co.uk

Map Ref 22

A warm friendly welcome and deluxe facilities await you at this handsome listed Georgian mansion - one of only a few STB 5 Stars B&B throughout Scotland. Elegantly furnished with special amenities such as bathrobes in every room. Old world charm, with all modern facilities, home made marmalade and superb Scottish breakfast. Central for Edinburgh, Dundee, Perth and the beautiful Perthshire highlands. 10 minutes from St. Andrews and accessible to a myriad of wonderful golfing experiences including Carnoustie and Muirfield. Elegant but not pretentious, we look forward to your visit.

Mary Millar
Tel: 01334 655699
Fax: 01334 650075

B&B from £40-£70pp, Rooms 1 double, 2 twin, all en-suite, No smoking or pets, Children over 12, Open all year.

STRUAN HALL, Ballater Road, Aboyne, Aberdeenshire AB34 5HY
Email struanhall@zetnet.co.uk
Website www.struanhall.co.uk

Map Ref 15
Nearest Road A93

Struan Hall is quietly situated in 2 acres of woodland garden, half a mile from the centre of the village of Aboyne. We offer quality bed and breakfast accommodation for a maximum of six persons in various combinations of twin, double or single rooms. All bedrooms have en-suite facilities, except for the single, which has a private bathroom. Your hosts Phyllis and Michael, have 18 years experience as accommodation providers and, throughout this period, have consistently achieved the highest Scottish Tourist Board Quality Grading. Credit cards accepted.

Tel/Fax: 013398 87241

B&B from £27.50-£30pp, Rooms 1 single, 1 double, 2 twin, all en-suite/private bathroom, No smoking or pets, Children over 7, Open January to end of October.

FEITH MHOR LODGE, Carr-bridge, near Aviemore, Inverness-shire PH23 3AP
Email feith.mhor@btinternet.com
Website www.feithmhor.co.uk

Map Ref 16

Feith Mhor offers Bed & Breakfast throughout the year and provides an ideal base for exploring the Highlands, visiting it's attractions or a walking holiday. Well appointed comfortable bedrooms with en-suite facilities, private shower or bathrooms, television and tea and coffee making facilities. Breakfast normally includes 'Kathleeen's porridge', home-made cakes, preserves made from our own home-grown fruit. Local farm yard eggs and venison sausages off our own hill. Dogs are welcome. Spacious drawing room with a log fire during the winter months.

Tel: 01479 841621

B&B from £20pp, Rooms 3 twin, 2 double, 1 single, all en-suite, Dogs welcome, friendly hospitality, Open all year.

WEST MANSE B&B, West Manse, Deskford, Buckie, Banffshire AB56 5YJ
Email WestManseDeskfrd@aol.com
Website www.westmanse.co.uk

Map Ref 17
Nearest Road B9018, A98

Situated in a quiet corner of rural Banffshire, yet within reach of the rocky Moray coastline with its quaint unspoilt harbours and villages. This quality B&B provides a high standard of welcome and service, 4 Stars Commended by the Scottish Tourist Board and a member of Scotland's Best B&Bs. Located half way between Inverness and Aberdeen, ideal for golf, walking, fishing and cycling. near the distilleries of the malt whisky trail and close to numerous Scottish castles. Bedrooms with scenic views. Private off road parking.

Melville & Johan McDonald
Tel: 01542 841189
Fax: 01542 840544

B&B from £27-£33pp, Dinner £17-£20, Rooms 1 double, 1 twin, No smoking or pets, Children over 14, Open all year except Christmas & New Year.

ASHBURN HOUSE, 2 Ashburn Lane, Fort William, Scotland PH33 6RQ
Email ashburn.house@tinyworld.co.uk
Website www.highland5star.co.uk

Map Ref 18
Nearest Road A82

Overlooking Loch Linnhe. Ashburne is a most relaxing B&B. The Highland owners pay every attention to detail but do not impose on your privacy, even separate tables in the Victorian Corniced breakfast room. The house has achieved all the highest accolades, AA, ETC 5 Diamonds. All rooms are en-suite, central heating, TV. Free off road parking. Full fire certificate. An excellent centre to tour the magical Highlands and Skye. Discount for week booking. Colour brochure. Credit cards accepted.

Alexandra Henderson
Tel: 01397 706000
Fax: 01397 702024

B&B from £30-£40pp, Rooms 3 single, 4 double, all en-suite, No smoking or pets, Children welcome, Open all year except Christmas & New Year.

RUSTIC VIEW, Lochyside, Fort William, Inverness-shire PH33 7NX

Map Ref 18
Nearest Road A82

Rustic View is quietly situated within its own extensive grounds. All rooms are en-suite. Breakfast is served in the conservatory, looking to Ben Nevis and surrounding hills. Varied breakfast menu. Large private parking area. Excellent base for touring the Highlands. A short distance from town centre. A warm Highland welcome awaits you.

Mrs Jackie Macleod
Tel/Fax: 01397 704709

B&B from £20-£25pp, Rooms 2 double, 1 twin, all en-suite, No smoking, children or pets, Open April to October.

CRAIGARD HOUSE, Invergarry, Inverness-shire PH35 4HG
Email bob@craigard.saltire.org
Website www.craigard.saltire.org

Map Ref 19
Nearest Road A87, A82

Set in the breathtaking splendour of the Highlands, Craigard, a large country house on the western outskirts of the village of Invergarry is the perfect base for a relaxing and varied holiday. Each of the well furnished bedrooms has tea/coffee making facilities. Guests can enjoy a quiet drink in the relaxed atmosphere of the residents' lounge and on cooler evenings pull up to a roaring log fire. TV in all bedrooms. The magnificent scenery surrounding Craigard makes it an ideal point for touring.

Mr R L Withers
Tel: 01809 501258

B&B from £20pp, Dinner £15, Rooms 2 double en-suite, 1 single en-suite, 3 double and 1 twin with wash hand basin, Non smoking, Children over 12, No pets, Open all year.

INVERGLOY HOUSE, Spean Bridge, Inverness-shire PH34 4DY
Email cairns@invergloy-house.co.uk
Website www.invergloy-house.co.uk

Map Ref 20
Nearest Road A82

Invergloy House, a 130 year old converted coach house/stables is set in 50 acres of wooded grounds in Great Glen. Guests have own sitting room with magnificent view over Loch Lochy and mountains. Three bedrooms, one double-bedded, two twin bedded, all en-suite, are tastefully and traditionally furnished. Peacefully located 5 miles north of Spean Bridge on road to Inverness and Isle of Skye. Private shingle beach reached by footpath. Good eating places nearby for evening meals. "Non-smokers" only.

Mrs Margaret Cairns
Tel/Fax: 01397 712681

B&B from £25pp, Rooms 1 double, 2 twin, all en-suite, No smoking, Children over 8, Open all year except Christmas & New Year.

DUNVEGAN CASTLE SELF CATERING COTTAGES, Dunvegan, Isle of Skye
Email info@dunvegancastle.com
Website www.dunvegancastle.com

Map Ref 26

Three self catering cottages, comfortably appointed and each of individual character and charm. On the estate of Dunvegan. Romantic and historic Dunvegan offers the ideal base for exploring Skye and outer Isles. We welcome you to spend some time with us on the enchanted Isle and reconnect with some simple old fashioned values.

3 cottages, sleeps 6, Price per week £170 low season, £490 high season, Children & pets welcome, Available all year.

Contact: Mrs Melanie Newham, MacLeod Estates, Dunvegan House, Dunvegan, Isle of Skye IV55 8WF
Tel: 01470 521 206
Fax: 01470 521 205

1,2 & 3 BRACADALE COTTAGES, Struan, Isle of Skye
Email astreeton@aol.com
Website www.isleofskyecottage.com

Map Ref 27

Each cottage is equipped with microwave, washer-drier, TV, video, payphone and electric heating complemented by a open fire, coal supplied, all linen and towels supplied. Cot by arrangement. Each cottage has three bedrooms, one double, and one single. This location has fantastic views and abundant wildlife can be seen from the doorstep. Good central location to tour the best of Skye and the mainland.

3 cottages, sleeps 5, Price per week £185 low season, £335 high season, Children welcome, No pets, Available all year.

Contact: Mr & Mrs Streeton, The Sycamores, 2 Balgown, Struan, Isle of Skye IV56 8FA
Tel: 01470 572231

SELF CATERING

NEW KELSO LODGE, Strathcarron, Ross-shire
Email b@knatchbull.com

Map Ref 28

The property is part of a period house blending older style interior with modern conveniences. Garden and tennis court are shared with adjoining house. Lochcarron village with shopping and restaurants is 3 miles away. 20 miles from Isle of Skye. 65 miles from Inverness Airport. 2 double, 2 twin-bedded, 2 bathrooms, telephone, dishwasher, fridge, freezer, hob (stove top), washing machine, clothes dryer, oven and TV. Situated in beautiful western highlands, close to sea.

1 cottage, sleeps 8, Price per week £265 low season, £450 high season, Children & pets welcome, Available all year.

Contact: Mr M J Knatchbull, Kelso Hotels Ltd, Newhouse, Mersham, Ashford, Kent TN25 6NQ
Tel: 01233 503636
Fax: 01233 502244

ATTADALE HOLIDAY COTTAGES, by Strathcarron, Ross-shire
Email cottages@attadale.com
Website www.attadale.com

Map Ref 28

A mile from the sea on a private road, four well equipped and attractively furnished cottages. Beyond lies a 32,000 acre estate. A wilderness ideal for wildlife, birds, loch fishing and hill walking. Well placed for exploring Skye and the west coast. No television but deer can be seen from the windows. Launderette at main house. Excellent restaurant 1mile. STB 4 Star.

4 cottages, sleeps 4-8, Price per week from £255 to £445, Children & pets welcome, Available March - November.

Contact: Frances MacKenzie, Attadale Holiday Cottages, Strathcarron, Ross-shire IV54 8YX
Tel/Fax: 01520 722862

LOCH TAY LODGES, Aberfeldy, Perthshire
Email remondy@btinternet.com
Website www.lochtaylodges.co.uk

Map Ref 29

Escape the rat race. Enjoy highland village tranquillity beside Loch Tay. Breath taking scenery. Superb wildlife, boating, golf at Kenmore and Taymouth. Fishing, hill-walking and touring. Water sports centre, half a mile, also riding nearby. Open all year. Children and pets welcome. STB 4 Star. Log fires and drying room facilities available.

6 cottages, sleeps 2-8, Price per week £185 low season, £485 high season, Children & pets welcome, Available all year.

Contact: Mr Duncan Millar, Loch Tay Lodges, Aberfeldy, Perthshire PH15 2HR
Tel: 01887 830209
Fax: 01887 830802

---

left, **East Lochhead Country House,** *Lochwinnoch - please see page 304 for details*

Full page photo on page 303

EAST LOCHHEAD COUNTRY HOUSE & COTTAGES, Largs Road, Lochwinnoch, Renfrewshire PA12 4DX
Email eastlochhead@aol.com
Website www.eastlochhead.co.uk
Map Ref 21
Nearest Road A760, M8

Warm welcome awaits you at award winning East Lochead. 120 year old farmhouse with spectacular views set in two acres of gardens. Janet Anderson's Taste of Scotland breakfast a speciality. Five self-catering cottages also available. Only 15 minutes from Glasgow Airport. Ideal centre for exploring Clyde Coast, Arran, Bute, Loch Lomond and Trossachs. Cultural, shopping and social attractions of Glasgow only 25 minutes. Winner STB Thistle Award, finalist Taste of Scotland Beds B&B, STB B&B of the year 2001/2. Gold Green Tourism Business Award. Credit cards accepted.

Janet Anderson
Tel/Fax: 01505 842610

B&B from £30-£35pp, Dinner £20, Rooms 1 double, 1 twin, 1 family, all en-suite, No smoking, Children & pets welcome, Open all year.

ASHGROVE HOUSE, 2 Park Avenue, Stirling, Scotland FK8 2LX
Email ashgrovehouse@strayduck.com
Website www.ashgrove-house.com
Map Ref 23
Nearest Road M80

A warm welcome awaits you at this elegantly restored Victorian town house which is a fine example of a James Allan Mansion. Two minutes walking distance of Stirling Castle. An ideal base for touring Scotland. The house is non smoking and we do not accept children under 15 years of age. Stirlings only Five Start B&B. Four poster bed available. House resides in a lovely residential area with golf courses nearby.

Dorothy Mailer
Tel/Fax: 01786 472640

B&B from £60-£70pr, Rooms 2 double, 1 twin, all en-suite, No smoking or pets, Children over 15, Open April to Mid October.

THE BARNS OF SHANNOCHILL, By Aberfoyle, The Trossachs, Stirlingshire FK8 3UZ
Email shannochill@aol.com
Website thebarnsofshannochill.co.uk
Map Ref 24
Nearest Road A81

Peacefully situated in the Trossachs. A barn conversion sleeping 4 people. Superb views for 180°. Own entrance, sitting area, en-suite shower room. Excellent Aga cooked breakfasts with local produce. Dinners made by arrangement. Separate dining kitchen for self-catering. Ideal base for touring, Edinburgh, Glasgow and Perth an hours drive and Stirling and Loch Lomond half an hours. We overlook the Lake of Menteith; surrounded in history with an abundance of outdoor activities to enjoy. Personal attention and a warm welcome awaits you. Credit cards accepted.

Mrs Val Willis
Tel: 01877 382878
Fax: 01877 382964

B&B from £30-£35pp, Dinner £15.20, Rooms 1 double/twin, 1 family, all en-suite, No smoking, Children & pets welcome, Open all year.

THORNTON, Edinburgh Road, Linlithgow, West Lothian EH49 6AA
Email inglisthornton@aol.com
Website www.thornton-scotland.com

Map Ref 25
Nearest Road M8, M9, A904

Linger longer in Linlithgow, there is so much to see and do nearby. Thornton, a delightful family-run Victorian home surrounded by peaceful gardens, is only a few minutes walk along the scenic canal to the town centre. Visit Linlithgow Palace (birth place of Mary Queen of Scots), Hopetoun House, Blackness Castle, the House of the Binns, Cairnpapple's Archaeological site, or the amazing new boat lifting wheel at Falkirk. Take the train to Edinburgh, Glasgow, Stirling. Enjoy our comfortable rooms and award-winning breakfasts. Popular so book early. Credit cards accepted.

Mrs Jill Inglis
Tel: 01506 844693
Fax: 01506 844876

B&B from £25-£30pp, Rooms 1 double, 1 twin, both en-suite, No smoking, Children over 12, No dogs except guide dogs, Open February to end of November.

"Five! Do you think St Cybi would mind you skimming stones on his stream?" asked Belle "He and his Holy Well both seem a bit doubtful" said Bertie "but its a nice story."

BELLE & BERTIE IN WALES

WALES

Surrounded by sea on three sides, the beautiful and proud country of Wales meets England on its eastern border and has, by its very proximity, experienced a historically turbulent relationship with its more dominating neighbour over the centuries. Indeed, Wales' many magnificent medieval castles - Caernarfon, Conwy, Beaumaris and Harlech to name but a few – were actually built by English kings to maintain their authority and ward off the Welsh nationalists of the day. Nowadays, the Welsh are still proud to be classed as a people apart and have retained their own distinctive accent and indigenous Celtic culture. The Welsh language is also still very much alive, as is the Welsh independent spirit, as proved in the 1997 elections when the country said yes to a Welsh Assembly.

It is, however, the beautiful scenery of Wales that draws the visitor to this charming and diverse corner of western Britain, with the most stunning countryside now under the protection of three very different National Parks. The Brecon Beacons National Park covers the rolling hills and valleys to the south; Pembrokeshire Coast National Park remains Britain's only coastal park to the south-west and features some of the most dramatic seascapes in the country; while to the north, Snowdonia National Park is dominated by impressive mountains, including mighty

Snowdonia – at 1113m the highest peak in England and Wales.
As well as the busy cities of Cardiff and Swansea to the south east, rolling moorland, rustic villages and bleak mining towns form the intrinsic character of Wales – and, although mining is no longer the lifeblood of the country, the windswept valleys where so many collieries once operated should certainly not be overlooked by the visitor if the true spirit of Wales is to be appreciated.
Representing the entirely opposite end of the economic spectrum, an abundance of charming stately homes also exist in Wales, built by aristocrats over the centuries who appreciated the green countryside and fine vistas – and none has a more beguiling tale to tell than Aberglasney House in the southern county of Carmarthenshire. The house itself, built by Bishop Rudd of St David's around 1600, was turned into a private palace by his son and magnificent Jacobean features were added to the garden from around 1614. From these splendid, opulent years the house fell into a state of decay over the centuries and by the time it came into the hands of The Restoration Trust it was in such a derelict state that it was considered almost beyond repair. It wasn't until the undergrowth was cleared and the archaeologists called in that the historic importance of the garden was recognised and the fascinating restoration project got underway. Stunning features now again exposed include the Jacobean Cloister Garden, the Pool Garden and the parapet walkway – thought to date back to the days of Elizabeth I and the only remaining example in the country.
Another of South Wales' fine houses includes Tredegar House near Newport, the lavish ancestral home of the Morgan family extensively rebuilt in the 17th century. Situated in 90 acres of parkland with exquisite formal gardens, the interior of the house balances the splendour of its setting to perfection, offering 30 rooms to browse both above and below stairs, including some quite breathtaking State Rooms.
North Wales also boasts some fine stately highlights and none come more breathtaking by situation than Plas Newydd in Anglesey. Enjoying unrestricted views over the Menai Strait and Snowdonia, this elegant 18th century home features delightful gardens and a long association with Rex Whistler, whose largest painting is housed here.
Situated between the Menai Strait and Snowdonia, nearby Penrhyn Castle also provides a fascinating and dramatic stop for the visitor. Fairytale-like by design, it was built in neo-Norman style by Thomas Hopper between 1820 and 1845 for the wealthy Pennant family – who had amassed their fortune from the sugar trade and Welsh slate. Highlights of this fantasy castle include fine paintings, intricate carvings and – somewhat fittingly – an amazing Welsh slate bed made for Queen Victoria and weighing in at just over a ton.

WALES

Mrs Jane Bown, Drws-y-Coed
Tel: 01248 470473
Map Ref 1 see page 311
Peter Andrews, Llanerch Vineyard
Tel: 01443 225877
Map Ref 2 see page 311
Peter Andrews, The Stables Cottages
Tel: 01443 225877
Map Ref 2 see page 311
Charlotte & Gerard Dent, Plas Alltyferin
Tel: 01267 290662
Map Ref 3 see page 313
Mr & Mrs Whittingham, Fron Heulog Country House
Tel: 01690 710736
Map Ref 4 see page 313
Christopher Nichols, Hafod Country House
Tel: 01492 640029
Map Ref 5 see page 313
Mrs I Henderson, The Old Barn
Tel: 01824 704047
Map Ref 6 see page 314
Marion & Jim Billingham, Preswylfa
Tel: 01654 767239
Map Ref 7 see page 315
Richard & Beryl, Melin Meloch
Tel: 01678 520101
Map Ref 8 see page 315
Mrs L H Hind, Abercelyn Country House
Tel: 01678 521109
Map Ref 8 see page 315
Mr & Mrs Jones, Frondderw Guest House
Tel: 01678 520301
Map Ref 8 see page 316
Sue Ashe, Cae Du
Tel: 01766 830847
Map Ref 10 see page 316
Mrs Jane Llewelyn Pierce, Ty-Mawr Farm
Tel: 01248 670147
Map Ref 11 see page 316
Sue Williamson, Min Y Gaer
Tel: 01766 522151
Map Ref 12
see page 317
Mr & Mrs Salter,
Noddfa Guest House
Tel: 01766 780043
Map Ref 13 see page 317
Mrs Gray- Parry, Bryn Bras Castle
Tel: 01286 870210
Map Ref 22 see page 317
The Wenallt
Tel: 01873 830694
Map Ref 14 see page 318
Mrs Sue Armitage, Ty'r Ywen Farm
Tel: 01495 785200
Map Ref 15 see page 318
Danielle Sheahan, The West Usk Lighthouse
Tel: 01633 810126
Map Ref 16 see page 318
Lee & Mherly Ravenscroft, Wychwood House
Tel: 01834 844387
Map Ref 17 see page 319
Mr & Mrs Dale,
Beacons Guest House & Restaurant
Tel: 01874 623339
Map Ref 18 see page 320
Mary Cole, Dolycoed
Tel: 01874 658666
Map Ref 19 see page 320
John Underwood, Cwmllechwedd Fawr
Tel: 01597 840267
Map Ref 20 see page 320
Mrs Anderson, Old Vicarage Cottage
Tel: 01874 658639
Map Ref 19 see page 321
Amanda Davies, Crossways House
Tel: 01446 773171
Map Ref 21 see page 321

LIVERPOOL
AMLWCH
BIRKEN
LLANDUDNO
ABERGELE
LLANGEFNI
CONWAY
HOLYHEAD
A55
BANGOR
DENBIGH
A5
CAERNARFON
BETWS-Y-COED
RUTHIN
A49
A487
A5
CORWEN
WREXHAM
NEFYN
PORTHMADOG
FESTINIOG
LLANGOLLEN
BALA
PWLLHELI
HARLECH
A496
A494
OSWESTRY
A5
BARMOUTH
DOLGELLAU
SHREWSBURY
A483
MALLWYD
A458
WELSHPOOL
MACHYNLLETH
A470
NEWTOWN
LLANIDLOES
A49
ABERYSTWYTH
A44
LLANGUIRIG
A483
LUDLOW
A44
RHAYADER
LLANDRINDOD WELLS
ABERAERON
A487
A4112
LEOMINSTER
TREGARON
BUILTH WELLS
A487
A438
CARDIGAN
LAMPETER
LLANWRTYD-WELLS
HAY -ON- WYE
HEREFORD
LLANDOVER
FISHGUARD
A484
BRECON
A485
A49
A465
A40
A478
A40
A479
LLANDEILO
A470
HAVERFORD WEST
CARMARTHEN
A40
A483
A4067
MERTHYR TYDFIL
EBBW VALE
ABERGAVENNY
A48
MONMOUTH
A477
MILFORD HAVEN
PONTYPOOL
CHEPSTOW
A4058
A472
PEMBROKE
LLANELLI
NEATH
CWMBRAN
SWANSEA
PONTYPRIDD
NEWPORT
M4
BRIDGEND
CARDIFF
A48

DRWS-Y-COED, Llannerch-y-Medd, Anglesey LL71 8AD
Email drws.ycoed@virgin.net
Website www.smoothhound.co.uk/hotels/drwsycoed.html

Map Ref 1
Nearest Road A55, A5, A5025, B5111

Drws-y-Coed, a 550 acre working farm, is a wonderful retreat with panoramic views of Snowdonia and countryside. Reputation for first class accommodation, warm hospitality, excellent breakfasts and attention to detail. Relax in the inviting spacious lounge with antiques and log fire. Full central heating. Interesting historic Grade 2 listed farmstead, walks and games room. Centrally located to explore Anglesey yet only 10 minutes to beaches and 25 minutes to Holyhead Port. Guests return year after year. WTB 4 Stars. RAC 4 Diamonds, Warm Welcome and Sparkling Diamond awards. Credit cards accepted.

Mrs Jane Bown
Tel/Fax: 01248 470473

B&B from £25pp, Rooms 1 double, 1 twin, 1 family, all en-suite, No smoking or pets, Children welcome, Open all year except Christmas Day.

LLANERCH VINEYARD, Hensol, Pendoylan, near Cardiff, CF72 8GG
Email enquiries@llanerch-vineyard.co.uk
Website www.llanerch-vineyard.co.uk

Map Ref 2
Nearest Road M4 jct 34

B&B at Llanerch Vineyard is provided in en-suite rooms in the farmhouse or in new deluxe self contained studios. Each of the comfortable bedrooms has tea/coffee making facilities, TV and clock/radio. Additionally self contained studios have been converted from the old winery to provide the ultimate in B&B. Each studio has a superb bathroom, fridge, microwave, telephone and Internet access. Only 15 minutes from Cardiff. Ample car parking. One of Wales' Great Little Places. Recently award Four Stars by the Wales Tourist Board. Credit cards accepted.

Peter Andrews
Tel: 01443 225877
Fax: 01443 225546

B&B from £50per room, Rooms 5 double, 5 twin, all en-suite, No smoking or pets, Children over 8, Open all year.

Full page photo opposite

THE STABLE COTTAGES, Llanerch Vineyard, Hensol, Pendoylan, Vale of Glamorgan
Email enquiries@llanerch-vineyard.co.uk
Website www.llanerch-vineyard.co.uk

Map Ref 2

Converted from 19th Century farm buildings, the Stable Cottages at Llanerch Vineyard offer superb accommodation in an idyllic setting with six acres of vines and a further ten acres of gardens, conservation woodlands and lakes. 15 minutes from Cardiff and convenient for touring all South Wales. Rated 5 Stars by the WTB, the highest accolade for quality, ambience and facilities which include washing machine, dishwasher, microwave, central heating, TV and telephone. Ample car parking.

2 cottages, sleeps 4, Price per week from £280 low season to £570 high season, No smoking or pets, Children welcome, Available all year

Contact: Peter Andrews, Llanerch Vineyard, Hensol, Pendoylan, Vale of Glamorgan CF72 8JU
Tel: 01443 225877
Fax: 01443 225546

PLAS ALLTYFERIN, Pontargothi, Nantgaredig, Carmarthen, Carmarthenshire SA32 7PF
Email dent@alltyferin.fsnet.co.uk

Map Ref 3
Nearest Road A40, M4

A classic Georgian country house lying in the hills above the beautiful Towy valley, overlooking a Norman Hill fort and the River Cothi - famous for salmon and sea trout. 2 en-suite twin bedrooms each with stunning views, for guests who are welcomed as friends of the family. Antique furniture. Log fires. Excellent local pubs and restaurants. Totally peaceful. Ideal touring country for castles, beaches and rural Wales. National Botanic Garden of Wales only five miles.

Charlotte & Gerard Dent
Tel/Fax: 01267 290662

B&B from £25-£30pp, Rooms 1 en-suite twin, 1 twin with private bathroom, Children over 10, Pets welcome, Open all year except Christmas & New Year.

FRON HEULOG COUNTRY HOUSE, Betws-y-Coed, LL24 0BL
Email jean&peter@fronheulog.co.uk
Website www.fronheulog.co.uk

Map Ref 4
Nearest Road A5, A470, B5106

This is an elegant stone-built Victorian house with excellent standards of comfort, food and modern amenities. Your hosts offer you their personal hospitality and local knowledge in a friendly atmosphere. Betws-y-Coed is the place to stay to visit all Snowdonia; at Fron Heulog you will receive the warm welcome for which Wales is famous. Turn off the busy A5 road over picturesque Pont-y-Pair Bridge (B5106), immediately turn left between shop and river. Fron Heulog is up ahead 150 metres from bridge in quiet peaceful wooded riverside scenery with private parking. Truly 'the Country House in the village'.

Full page photo opposite

Jean & Peter Whittingham
Tel: 01690 710736
Fax: 01690 710920

B&B from £22-£30pp, Lower rates for longer stay, Rooms 2 double, 1 twin, all en-suite, No small Children, No smoking, No pets, Open all year.

HAFOD COUNTRY HOUSE, Trefriw, LL27 0RQ
Email hafod@breathemail.net
Website www.hafodhouse.co.uk

Map Ref 5
Nearest Road A55, A5, A470, B5105

The Hafod (the summer dwelling) is a tiny individual hotel for guests who recognise the difference between price and value; style and fashion; quality and the mundane; hospitality and service. Positioned on the edge of one of Snowdonia's prettiest village, the location offers unrivalled access to both, the area's main attractions and lovely countryside, to explore and enjoy. Guests enjoy exceptional food and wine, in a rambling, former farmhouse, with extensive grounds, which combines antiques with a colourful, highly individual sense of style. Credit cards accepted. Welsh Tourist Board 4 Stars.

Christopher Nichols
Tel: 01492 640029
Fax: 01492 641352

B&B from £30-£46pp, Dinner £23.50, Rooms 4 double, 2 twin, all en-suite, Children over 11, Pets by prior arrangement, Open February to December.

THE OLD BARN, Esgairlygain, Llangynhafal, Ruthin, Denbighshire LL15 1RT

Map Ref 6
Nearest Road A494

Escape the crowds and enjoy the peace and tranquility. Converted stone barn set within an area of outstanding natural beauty. Sleep in the haylofts and breakfast where the cows used to be milked. Comfortable accommodation, keeping original beams and low sloping ceilings. Direct access to Clwydian Hills, Offa's Dyke and mountain bike tracks. Central for Llangollen, Chester, Snowdonia, castles and coast with a wealth of National Trust properties within the area. Refreshments on arrival and a warm welcome assured.

Mrs I Henderson
Tel/Fax: 01824 704047

B&B from £21-£25pp, Rooms 1 double, 1 twin, 1 family, all en-suite, No smoking, Children & pets welcome, Open March to end of December.

"Harlech, out last castle" said Belle "You're going to have a great collection of photos, Bertie. We'll have to get a special album."

BELLE & BERTIE IN WALES

PRESWYLFA, Aberdovey, Gwynedd LL35 0LE
Email info@preswylfa.co.uk
Map Ref 7

Three Star country house. Preswylfa is an attractive Edwardian family home with breathtaking sea views, secluded in a large mature garden. Only 3 minutes walk from the beach and village. The en-suite luxury bedrooms have central heating, king sized beds, TV and tea/coffee making facilities. The period lounge has a grand piano and leads into a large sunny dining-room, with double doors into the garden. Ample car parking. Evening meals by arrangements. Friendly, unpretentious and relaxing. Telephone for brochure

Marion & Jim Billingham
Tel: 01654 767239
Fax: 01654 767983

B&B from £25pp, Dinner from £16, Rooms 1 twin, 2 double, all en-suite, No smoking, children or Pets, Open January to December.

MELIN MELOCH, Bala, Gwynedd LL23 7DP
Email theoldmill@mac.com
Map Ref 8
Nearest Road B4401, A494

This picturesque former watermill close to Bala stands in 2 acres of beautiful water scaped gardens, a delight for garden lovers. Pretty en-suite rooms some with own front doors in Granary and Millers Cottage, TV and hot drinks tray. The spectacular galleried interior of the mill is furnished with antiques and paintings. Breakfast is served in a friendly relaxed atmosphere. 2 minutes drive to Bala lake and town, excellent for touring. Near to White Water Rafting Centre. Ample easy parking. Peaceful location. Highly Commended, WTB 3 Star. Private fishing on Dee by arrangement with Richard.

Richard & Beryl
Tel: 01678 520101

B&B from £20pp, Rooms 2 single, 2 twin, 2 double, 1 family, most en-suite, No smoking, Children welcome, Pets by arrangement, Open March to November.

ABERCELYN COUNTRY HOUSE, Llanycil, Bala, Gwynedd LL23 7YF
Email info@abercelyn.co.uk
Website www.abercelyn.co.uk
Map Ref 8
Nearest Road A494

An 18th century Grade II listed Georgian, former rectory set in landscaped grounds with a stream running alongside. The bright and spacious bedrooms are all en-suite with tea/coffee making facilities. Log-fires burn on cold evenings and breakfasts include hot home-made bread, preserves and fresh coffee. Close to Bala lake, Abercelyn is ideally located for visiting the unspoilt beauty of North and Mid Wales. In addition there is a self-catering garden cottage, let either on a self-catering or B&B basis. Guided walking service.

Mrs L H Hind
Tel: 01678 521109
Fax: 01678 520848

B&B from £22.50-£35pp, Rooms 1 twin, 1 double, 1 family, all en-suite, No smoking or pets, Children welcome, Open all year except Christmas & New Year.

FRONDDERW GUEST HOUSE, Stryd-y-Fron, Bala, Gwynedd LL23 7YD
Email gpts@thefron.co.uk
Website www.thefron.co.uk

Map Ref 8
Nearest Road A494

Whilst the occasional owl may break the silence. The peace and tranquillity of this magnificent 16th century mansion will captivate you. With spectacular views across to the Berwyn Mountains and the north end of Bala Lane, this is the perfect setting for a relaxed break. An ideal centre for touring north and mid Wales, walking, cycling and local sports. Only five minutes walk from Bala town centre. A warm welcome is assured from Janet and Norman. Colour television in all rooms. Credit cards accepted.

Norman & Janet Jones
Tel: 01678 520301

B&B from £23-£27pp, Rooms 1 single, 2 double, 2 twin, 2 family, most en-suite, No smoking or pets, Open March to November.

CAE DU, Manod, Blaeau Ffestiniog, Gwynedd LL41 4BB
Email caedu@tinyworld.co.uk

Map Ref 10
Nearest Road A470

Picturesque 16th century former farmhouse in a magnificent mountain setting of the Snowdonia National Park. Comfortable en-suite rooms with colour TV, tea/coffee making facilities, home cooking, stunning panoramic views, 2 lounges, private parking and a warm friendly atmosphere makes this an ideal base for exploring the wonders of Snowdonia. The surrounding mountains, woods, moors and coastline include Portmerion, Ffestiniog Steam Railway, Slate Caverns, Mines, Castles, sandy beaches, golf, mountain walks - direct from 'Cae Du' and much much more. "It's our home make it yours".

Sue Ashe
Tel/Fax: 01766 830847

B&B from £24pp, Dinner £12, Room 2 double, 1 twin, all en-suite, No smoking or pets, Children over 12, Open all year except Christmas & New Year.

TY-MAWR FARM, Llanddeiniolen, Caernarfon, Gwynedd LL55 3AD
Email jane@tymawrfarm.freeserve.co.uk
Website www.tymawrfarm.co.uk

Map Ref 11
Nearest Road B4366, A5

17th century, 100 acre working farm. Comfortable, well appointed farmhouse with uninterrupted views of Snowdonia. Centrally situated between Caernarfon and Snowdon. Fully central heated with log fires in 2 lounges. Separate panelled dining room with separate tables. Ideal for touring North Wales and Anglesey. All rooms en-suite with colour TV and beverage tray. Evening meals optional. Snowdon only 4 miles away. Ample parking. Brochure available on request.

Mrs Jane Llewelyn Pierce
Tel/Fax: 01248 670147

B&B from £22-£30pp, Dinner £13.50, Rooms 2 double, 1 twin, all en-suite, Restricted smoking, Children & pets welcome, Open all year.

MIN Y GAER, Porthmadog Road, Criccieth, Gwynedd LL52 0HP
Email info@minygaer.co.uk
Website www.minygaer.co.uk

Map Ref 12
Nearest Road A497, B4411

A family run ten bedroom hotel situated near the beach with delightful views of Criccieth Castle and the scenic Cardigan Bay coast line. All bedrooms are en-suite and have colour television and tea/coffee facilities. The hotel is fully licensed with a cosy bar and separate lounge. A perfect base for exploring Snowdonia and surrounding areas or to stay and enjoy the local unspoilt countryside. Credit cards accepted.

Sue Williamson
Tel: 01766 522151
Fax: 01766 523540

B&B from £24-£26pp, Rooms 1 single, 4 double, 2 twin, 3 family, all en-suite, Children welcome, No pets, Open March to October.

NODDFA GUEST HOUSE, Ffordd Newydd, Harlech, Gwynedd LL46 2UB
Email richard@noddfa.co.uk
Website www.noddfa.co.uk

Map Ref 13
Nearest Road A496

Noddfa overlooks the Royal St David's Golf Course, with splendid views of the Snowdon mountain range and Tremadog Bay. Noddfa means 'refuge' and was protected by Harlech castle in the 18th century. Extensively rebuilt in 1850 it offers comfortable bedrooms with en-suite or private bathrooms. The historic town of Harlech offers restaurants, swimming pool, theatre and spectacular sandy beach. Central for the attractions of Wales. Residential licence, evening meals on request. Jane and Richard Salter invite you to enjoy the hospitality of their home.

Jane & Richard Salter
Tel/Fax: 01766 780043

B&B from £26pp, Rooms 1 single, 5 double, some en-suite, Restricted smoking, Children over 5, No pets, Open all year.

Apartments BRYN BRAS CASTLE, Llanrug, near Caernarfon, Gwynedd
Email holidays@brynbrascastle.co.uk
Website www.brynbrascastle.co.uk

Map Ref 22

Welcome to beautiful Bryn Bras Castle - romantic apartments and elegant tower house within distinctive Romanesque castle, enjoying breathtaking scenery amid gentle Snowdonia foothills. Easy reach mountains, beaches, heritage, local restaurant and inns. Each fully self-contained, individual character, spacious and peaceful. Central heating, hot water and linen inclusive. All highest grade. 32 acre gardens, woodlands and panoramic walks. Enjoy comfort, warmth and privacy in serene surroundings.

7 apartments, sleep 2-4, Price per week £360-£625, Short breaks e.g from £170 for 2 persons for 2 nights, No young children or pets, Available all year.

Contact: Mrs Marita Gray-Parry, Bryn Bras Castle, Llanrug, Caernarfon, Wales LL55 4RE
Tel/Fax: 01286 870210

THE WENALLT, Abergavenny, Monmouthshire

Map Ref 14
Nearest Road A465

This historic 15th century longhouse, Wenallt nestles in the rolling hills of the Brecon Beacons described by some guests as the perfect peace and tranquillity. The small quiet hotel offers comfort, personal service and excellent home cooking. This ideal location for enjoying country walks, breathtaking views or just relax on the spacious lawns, if you happen to be budding artist or photographer then this is the ideal base with its panoramic views. En-suite rooms. Inglenook log fires. Restaurant licensed. RAC 3 Stars.

Tel: 01873 830694

B&B from £19.50pp, Dinner from £13, Rooms 4 single, 1 twin, 5 double, 1 family, all en-suite, Children & pets welcome, Open all year.

TY'R YWEN FARM, Lasgarn Lane, Trevethin, Pontypool, Monmouthshire NP4 8TT
Email susan.armitage@virgin.net
Website freespace.virgin.net/susan.armitage/webpage3.htm

Map Ref 15

Ty'r Ywen Farm is a very isolate 16th century Welsh longhouse high on the Gwent Ridgeway in the Brecon Beacons National Park. It has breathtaking views down the Usk Valley and across the Bristol Channel. Each large double bedroom has a four poster bed, one having it's own Jacuzzi. All rooms have colour TV and tea/coffee making facilities. Our 55 acres being a nature reserve with interesting walks and many beautiful birds. Nearby, some of the largest medieval fortifications in Europe including Caerphilly and Chepstow. Credit cards accepted.

Mrs Sue Armitage
Tel/Fax: 01495 785200

B&B from £20-£30pp, Rooms 3 double, 1 twin, all en-suite, No smoking or children, Pets welcome, Open all year except Christmas & New Year.

THE WEST USK LIGHTHOUSE, St Brides, Wentloog, near Newport, Gwent NP10 8SF
Email lighthousel@tesco.net
Website www.westusklighthouse.co.uk

Map Ref 16
Nearest Road A48, B4239

Super B&B in real lighthouse with en-suite wedged shaped water and 4 poster bedrooms. Internal wishing well and glorious roof garden not to mention 360° lantern room for watching ships go by. Rolls Royce drive and champagne breakfast for that special occasion! Top local restaurant in village and all amenities nearby plus wonderful tourist attractions. Other facilities include flotation tank for deep relaxation, complimentary therapies such as aroma, reflexology, Shiatsu, Indian head massage, heath screening and hypno smoke. Warm friendly relaxed ambience, distinctly different. Credit cards accepted.

Danielle Sheahan
Tel: 01633 810126

B&B from £45, Rooms 2 double, 1 family, all en-suite, No smoking, Children welcome, Pets by prior arrangement, Open all year except Christmas.

WYCHWOOD HOUSE, Penally, Tenby, Pembrokeshire SA70 7PE
Email wychwoodbb@aol.com
Website www.guestaccom.co.uk/601.htm

Map Ref 17
Nearest Road A4139, A478

Wychwood house is a large country house offering sea views from some of the elegant and spacious bedrooms, some with a large sun balcony and four poster bed. Dine by candlelight and enjoy Lee's interesting and freshly cooked 4 course menu of the day. Nearby is an excellent beach which you can walk along to the ancient walled town of Tenby. Boat trips are also available to visit the monastic island of Caldry. Two golf courses nearby. Wychwood is recommended in the 'Which?' consumer guide. Credit cards accepted.

Lee & Mherly Ravenscroft
Tel: 01834 844387
Fax: 01834 844425

B&B from £25-32.50pp, Dinner £21, Rooms 2 double, 1 family, all en-suite, No smoking, Children over 12, Open all year.

"That looks a good castle" said Bertie
"Our version of Harlech" said the children's father "Why don't you join us?"
BELLE & BERTIE IN WALES

BEACONS GUEST HOUSE & RESTAURANT, 16 Bridge Street, Brecon, Powys LD3 8AH
Email beacons@brecon.co.uk
Website www.beacons.brecon.co.uk

Map Ref 18
Nearest Road A470, A40

Recently restored 17th/18th century house retaining many original features such as moulded ceilings, low doors, sloping floors, beams and fireplaces. Choose from a variety of well-appointed standard, en-suite or luxury period rooms. Relax with a drink in the original meat cellar (complete with hooks) or in a comfortable armchair in front of the fire. Enjoy excellent food and fine wines in the candlelit restaurant (5 nights). Please ring Stephen & Melanie Dale for more information. Private car park. WTB 3 Star. AA, RAC 3 Diamonds.

Stephen & Melanie Dale
Tel/Fax: 01874 623339

B&B from £19-£30pp, Dinner from £9.95-£17.85, Rooms 1 single, 3 twin, 4 double, 6 family, most en-suite, Restricted smoking, Children & pets welcome, Open all year.

DOLYCOED, Talyllyn, Brecon, Powys LD3 7SY

Map Ref 19
Nearest Road A40

Dolycoed is a large Edwardian house in a rural setting within the National Park. Two rooms are available for guests. A double with shower and a twin. A private bathroom is for use by guests only. Each room has TV and tea/coffee tray. There is a visitors sitting room and ample off road parking. Brecon is 4 miles away and the lake and village of Llangorse is 2 miles. Talyllyn is a good centre for walking and sight seeing in the park.

Mary Cole
Tel: 01874 658666

B&B from £22pp, Rooms 1 double, 1 twin, No smoking, Children & pets welcome, Open all year except Christmas & New Year.

CWMLLECHWEDD FAWR, Llanbister, Llandrindod Wells, Powys LD1 6UH
Email postmaster@cwmllechwedd.u-net.com
Website www.cwmllechwedd.u-net.com

Map Ref 20
Nearest Road A483, B4356

Organic farm in an area of tranquility. Refurbished early 19th century farmhouse, spacious rooms. Ideal for walking and bird watching. In easy reach of the Cambrian mountains and the border towns of both England and the Welsh marches. A working farm we serve our own or locally grown produce. No licence so bring your own alcohol.

John Underwood
Tel/Fax: 01597 840267

B&B from £25-£30pp, Dinner £15, Rooms 2 en-suite double, No smoking, children or pets, Open all year except Christmas & New Year.

OLD VICARAGE COTTAGE, Llangorse, Brecon, Powys
Email maryanderson@oldvic45.fsnet.co.uk

Map Ref 19

Fully self contained semi detached cottage in lovely quiet location. A short walk from shop and pubs. Facilities include colour TV, video, piano, full central heating and fully equipped kitchen. Children and well behave dogs welcome. Within easy walk of lake. Sailing, fishing, pony trekking and rope climbing can be enjoyed nearby. The cottage is prettily decorated and close carpeted. It is within the Brecon Beacons National Park.

1 cottage, sleeps 4, Price per week £135 low season, £270 high season, Children & well behaved dogs welcome, Available all year.

Contact: Mrs Anderson, The Old Vicarage, Llangorse, Brecon, Powys LD3 7UB
Tel: 01874 658639

CROSSWAYS HOUSE, Cowbridge, Vale of Glamorgan CF7 7LJ
Email enq@crosswayshouse.co.uk
Website www.crosswayshouse.co.uk

Map Ref 21
Nearest Road A48, M4

An historic country manor house with six and a half acres. Situated in the beautiful Vale of Glamorgan, offering bed and breakfast and self catering facilities. All rooms are individually decorated with tea/coffee facilities, TV and clock/radio. A superb "taste of Wales" breakfast is offered. Ideally placed for the coast, castles, mountains and Cardiff with plenty of places to walk and visit. The self catering "Ballroom Flat" is within the house and sleeps 2-4. Cots are available. Tennis court, pool table and gardens at your disposal. Credit cards accepted. Self catering apartments also available.

Amanda Davies
Tel: 01446 773171
Fax: 01446 771707

B&B from £25-£35pp, Rooms 1 double, 1 twin, 1 family, all en-suite/private, No smoking, Children & Pets welcome, Open all year.

BOLD PAGE NUMBERS INDICATE SELF CATERING PROPERTIES, OTHERWISE THEY ARE BED & BREAKFAST

t

uv

wy

THE COUNTIES OF ENGLAND, SCOTLAND & WALES

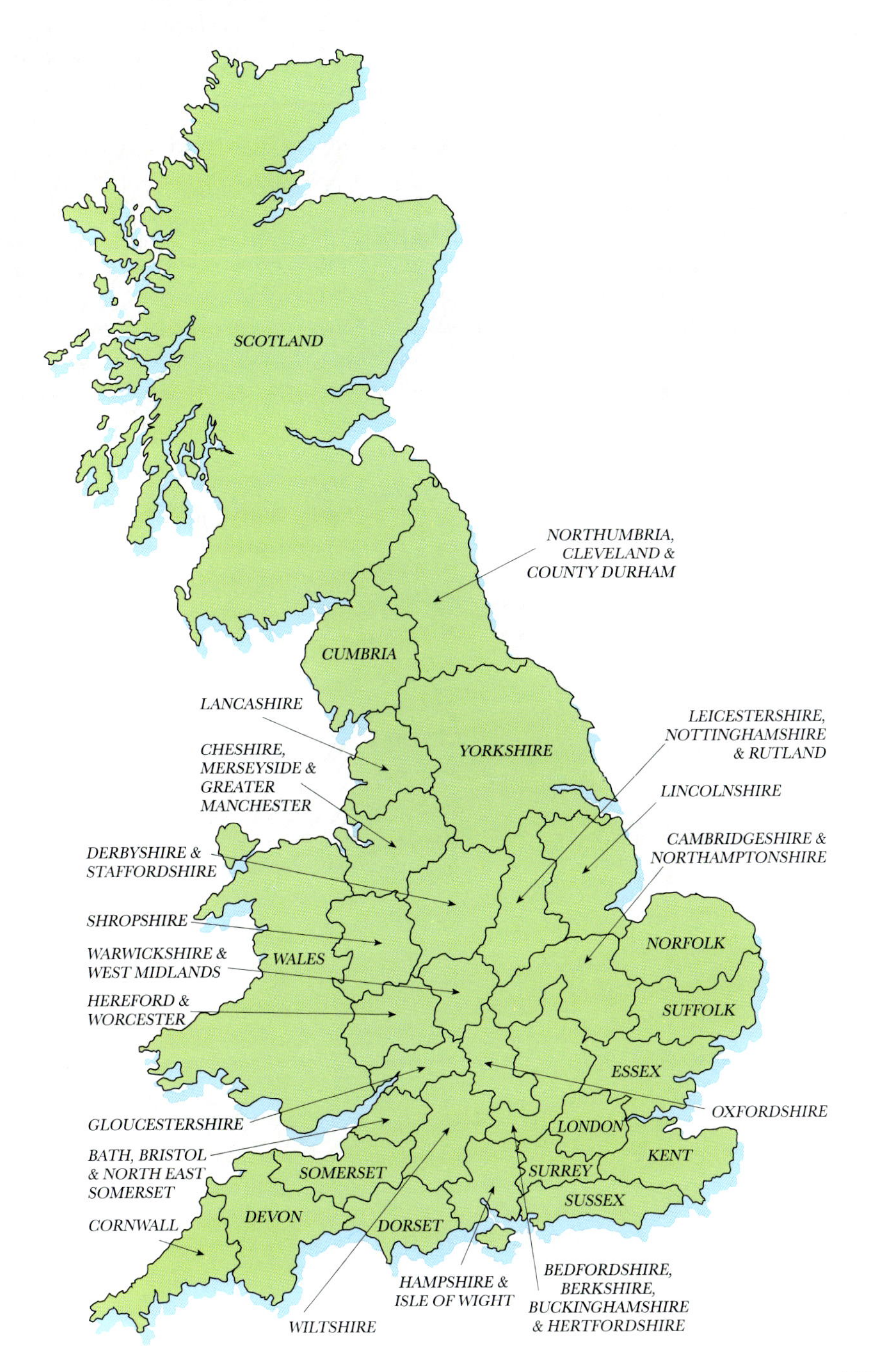

BOLD PAGE NUMBERS INDICATE SELF CATERING PROPERTIES, OTHERWISE THEY ARE BED & BREAKFAST

a

b

"When we're finished I want a photo of the castle and all the builders" said Bertie
"The grand finale of our Welsh castle holiday" smiled Belle
BELLE & BERTIE IN WALES

Published by: Bertrums Ltd, Alaska Building, Ullswater Road, Penrith, Cumbria, CA11 7EH, England
01768 865538